1979

W9-CMI-103

Foster family care :

3 0301 00069662 1

Foster Family Care

Foster Family Care

A HANDBOOK FOR SOCIAL WORKERS, ALLIED PROFESSIONALS, AND CONCERNED CITIZENS

By

CHARLES R. HOREJSI, D.S.W.

Professor, Department of Social Work
University of Montana
Missoula, Montana

CHARLES C THOMAS · PUBLISHER

Springfield · Illinois · U.S.A.

LIBRARY
College of St. Francis
JOLIET, ILL.

Published and Distributed Throughout the World by
CHARLES C THOMAS • PUBLISHER
Bannerstone House
301-327 East Lawrence Avenue, Springfield, Illinois, U.S.A.

This book is protected by copyright. No part of it
may be reproduced in any manner without written
permission from the publisher.

© *1979, by* CHARLES C THOMAS • PUBLISHER
ISBN 0-398-03898-8
Library of Congress Catalog Card Number: 78-26502

*With THOMAS BOOKS careful attention is given to all details of
manufacturing and design. It is the Publisher's desire to present books that
are satisfactory as to their physical qualities and artistic possibilities and
appropriate for their particular use. THOMAS BOOKS will be true to those
laws of quality that assure a good name and good will.*

Library of Congress Cataloging in Publication Data

Horejsi, Charles R.
    Foster family care.

    Bibliography: p. 335
    Includes index.
    1. Foster home care—United States. 2. Social
work with children—United States. I. Title.
HV881.H68   362.7′33′0973   78-26502
ISBN 0-398-03898-8

Printed in the United States of America
C-1

362.733
H812

10-23-79 Publisher $21.99

To my parents,
Longin and Alice Horejsi,
with love and appreciation

87481

Preface

RECENTLY, INFORMED CITIZENS, social workers, and other professionals have become increasingly concerned about our nations' foster care system and what is happening to the 300,000 or more children in foster care, their natural parents, and their foster parents. There are serious problems within the system. Many individuals are calling for reform, but change has been slow because the public is uninformed and because many political and financial barriers impede progress.

Within the field of child welfare, the deinstitutionalization movement began more than thirty years ago. Children's institutions were closed, and the use of foster family care expanded. Later, as the deinstitutionalization movement spread to other areas such as the fields of mental health and developmental disabilities, foster homes were used increasingly in the care of children with serious behavior and health problems. More recently, growing public awareness of child abuse and neglect and mandatory reporting laws have resulted in an increase of referrals to the courts and social welfare agencies. This, too, has resulted in expanded use of foster homes. Although the demand for foster family care has increased, the availability of suitable foster homes has decreased. In addition to this supply and demand problems, child welfare experts have become alarmed over the fact that many children when placed into foster care remain in a state of limbo, without a sense of permanency. Too often, courts and agencies have failed or been unable to make suitable long-term plans for these children, either by arranging for planned long-term foster care, freeing them for adoption or providing those services needed for them to return to their natural homes.

There are no simple answers to the many and complex problems associated with foster care, yet one must hope that an increase in knowledge and awareness will contribute to desired reform and an upgrading of practice. This book has been written with a sense of hope and a belief in the power of knowledge. It is designed to give both the professional and nonprofessional useful information. If citizens, legislators, judges, and human service professionals have a better understanding of foster care, perhaps desirable change will occur.

In particular, this book has been prepared for use by the beginning-level social worker within the field of child welfare. It is the social worker who confronts society's ills on a face-to-face basis. It is the social worker who deals with the human anguish, sorrow, and anger associated with child neglect and abuse. It is the social worker who becomes involved directly with families who no longer can care for their children because of physical or mental illness, poverty, family breakup or other problems. The social worker is in a critical decision-making position as to how such problems and dilemmas are to be approached. These far-reaching decisions affect thousands of children and families. This book has been designed to give the professional social worker information and guidelines that may aid in the formation of sound judgments and decisions related to the use of foster family care. It is hoped that the application of this information will help prevent inappropriate placement of children into foster care and increase the quality of care received by those children who need foster care.

Recently, a great deal of knowledge has been developed. Outstanding research projects on foster care have provided new insights, techniques, and methods for addressing common problems. Unfortunately, many social workers are so overwhelmed with their workload that they do not have time to seek new information. Moreover, recent budget cuts, especially in public agencies, have prevented social workers and decision makers from attending relevant conferences and limited the availability of in-service training and continuing education. Such factors hamper the dissemination of new and useful information. Hopefully, this book will bridge this gap. The author has tried to draw information from many sources and present it in a way that will be understandable to those who have had little experience in foster care. Efforts have been made to write in a simple style and, where possible, avoid the use of professional jargon. The reader has been provided with many citations from professional literature, research reports, and other materials. It is hoped that these references will aid the reader in locating other useful information.

Social work practice in the area of foster family care is exceedingly complex. The practitioner must have an understanding of social work theory, skill in a variety of intervention techniques, a good grasp of human behavior, and a working knowledge of the many public policy and legal issues related to foster care. A single book cannot address all these important areas. Thus, this book is not a substitute for a sound program of social work education and ongoing in-service training and continuing education. It should be a valuable supplement, however, to other types of staff training.

Since a question-answer format has been used, a word of explanation is in order. As one means of ensuring that the content of this book would be relevant to the needs of social workers, the author conducted a survey that elicited questions and concerns about foster care. More than two hundred questions were gathered from social workers and supervisory personnel associated with programs of foster care. Subsequently, additional questions were gathered by personal and telephone interviews. While studying the common concerns and questions about foster care, it became apparent that a question-answer format was attractive to many readers because it permitted relatively short and focused discussions of specific topics. Moreover, it encouraged reading since it allowed the social worker to skim a table of contents and select those topics relevant to his or her immediate concerns.

Some of the two hundred questions could not have been answered in a book twice the size of this one. Furthermore, some questions, especially those that focus on skill, are difficult to answer with the written word. Skills that deal with interpersonal relationships, for example, can be described but seldom can be learned or taught from a book. Knowledge and information can be presented in and learned from a book, but practice skills are best learned within a practicum, tutorial relationship, or workshop setting where modeling, demonstration, and individualized instruction are possible. For these reasons, this book will be most useful as a handbook or desk reference. As such, it does not provide complete information on a topic but will give the reader some basic ideas and direction to sources that provide more detailed information.

The author sought the opinions and advice of many individuals. Some advice was followed; some was not. Thus, the views expressed in this book are those of the author, and he assumes responsibility for the book's shortcomings and limitations.

Work on this handbook was made possible, in part, by a grant from the Denver, Colorado, Region VIII Office of Human Development, United States Department of Health, Education and Welfare (Grant #84-P-96424/8-01). This support is deeply appreciated.

The cooperation of the Social Service Bureau and Staff Development Services of the Montana Department of Social and Rehabilitation Services also is gratefully acknowledged.

A special thanks to Fern Berryman for her tireless and faithful work typing the innumerable drafts that went into the development of this book. Her patience and skill are deeply appreciated. Genie Brier spent many hours reviewing and editing the manuscript. Her efforts are sincerely appreciated.

Many individuals reviewed portions of this book and offered helpful criticisms and suggestions on content and language. Special thanks to Morton Arkava, Betty Bay, Lynne Benz, Elly Bernau, Mary Blake, Gloria Brinkman, Mike Cantrell, Frank Clark, Bill Collins, Dave Cummins, Vera Dersam, Jean Duncan, Russ Francetich, Suzanne Tiddy Larsen, Ron Lewis, Vince Matule, Pat Pomroy, Pat Roesch, Tom Roy, Marlene Salway, Bill Spivey, Jon Vestre, Norma Cutone Vestre, and Al Walters.

Grateful acknowledgment is made to the following individuals, journals, and publishers for permission to use extended quotations from research and project reports and copyrighted materials:

Michael S. Wald for permission to quote from "State Intervention on Behalf of Neglected Children: Standards for Removal of Children from Their Homes, Monitoring the Status of Children in Foster Care and Termination of Parental Rights," from the *Stanford Law Review*, Vol. 28, No. 4, April 1976, copyright 1976, by Michael S. Wald.

Regents of the University of Wisconsin System for permission to use materials contained in *Guidelines for Placement Workers,* copyright 1974, by Martha Aldridge, Patricia Cautley and Diane Lichstein and in *The Selection of Foster Parents: Manual for Homefinders,* 1974, by Patricia W. Cautley and Diane P. Lichstein, copyright 1974.

Ziff-Davis Publishing Company of New York, New York, for permission to quote from "The Myth of the Vulnerable Child," by Arlene Skolnick, published in *Psychology Today* magazine, copyright 1978.

Child Welfare League of America, New York, New York, for permission to reprint *The CWLA Intake Interview Guide* originally printed in Michael Phillips, Barbara Haring, and Ann Shyne, *A Model for Intake Decisions in Child Welfare,* 1972, and quote from *Group Care of Children,* by Morris Mayer, Leon Richman, and Edwin Balcerzak, copyright 1977.

F. E. Peacock Publishers, Inc. of Itasca, Illinois, for permission to quote from *Social Work Practice: Model and Method,* by Allen Pincus and Anne Minahan, copyright 1973.

Midwest Parent-Child Welfare Resource Center of Milwaukee, Wisconsin, for permission to quote from the *Interdisciplinary Glossary on Child Abuse and Neglect: Legal, Medical, Social Work Terms,* 1978.

Lawrence Shulman of the University of British Columbia, Vancouver, British Columbia, Canada, for permission to quote from *A Study of the Helping Process,* copyright 1977.

Human Behavior magazine for permission to quote from "Burned Out," by Christina Maslach, September 1976, copyright 1976.

Janiel Jarrett of the Georgia Department of Human Resources for permission to quote from the *Handbook for Natural Parents,* undated.

The Regents of the University of California, University of California at Berkeley, University Extension Publications, for permission to quote from *Decision Making in Foster Care,* by Theodore Stein and Eileen Gambrill, copyright 1976.

National Association of Social Workers, Inc. of New York, New York, for permission to quote from "Predicting Success for New

Foster Parents," by Patricia Cautley and Martha Aldridge, published in *Social Work*, Vol. 20, No. 1, January 1975, copyright 1975.

State University System of Florida, Tallahassee, Florida, for permission to quote from *The Florida Human Service Task Bank*, Vol. 2, October 1975.

The City of New York, Human Resources Administration, Department of Social Services for permission to quote from *The Parents Handbook*, 1977.

American Public Welfare Association, Washington, D. C. for permission to quote from *Standards for Foster Family Services Systems*, March 1975.

National Foster Parent Association for permission to reprint the "Code of Ethics for Foster Parents," ratified May 3, 1975.

Regional Research Institute for Human Services, Portland State University, for permission to quote from *Permanent Planning for Children: A Handbook for Social Workers*, 1977, by Victor Pike, Susan Downs, Arthur Emlen, Glen Downs, and Denise Case, *Barriers to Planning for Children in Foster Care: A Summary*, 1976, by Arthur Emlen et al. and *Overcoming Barriers to Planning for Children in Foster Care*, 1977, by Arthur Emlen et al.

Minnesota Resource Center for Social Work Education of Minneapolis, Minnesota, for permission to quote from *Support Skills for Direct Service Workers*, by Linda Hall Harris, copyright 1976.

National Association of Attorneys General, Raleigh, North Carolina, for permission to quote from *Legal Issues in Foster Care*, February 1976, prepared by the Committee on the Office of Attorneys General.

St. Paul United Way, St. Paul, Minnesota, for permission to quote from *Casework Notebook*, Alice Overton, Katherine Tinker and associates, copyright 1957.

Macmillan Publishing Company, Inc. of New York, for permission to quote from *Introduction to Social Work Practice*, by Max Siporin, copyright 1975.

Contents

Foster Family Care

CHAPTER 1

An Overview of Foster
Family Care

What Is Child Welfare?

THIS BOOK DISCUSSES one form of substitute child care; foster family care. Because substitute care is only one aspect of the much broader field of child welfare, it seems necessary to provide some information about the child welfare context of foster family services.

Unfortunately, it is not possible to provide a simple definition of child welfare. Kahn (1977) notes that in the United States the term *child welfare* is used in four different ways. It refers to—

1) A field of service
2) A specialized form of social work practice adapted to the needs of service programs for children
3) The overall well being of children or
4) The policies and activities that contribute to the well being of children. In the latter sense the term may overlap that of "family policy" and so be subsumed under social policy. [Pp. 100-101]

In this book, *child welfare* refers to a field of service or a specialized form of social work practice. Within the context of the material presented, the meaning will be apparent to the reader.

As an area or field of service, child welfare services have been described by the U. S. Department of Health, Education and Welfare (1960) as

> those social services that supplement or substitute for parental care and supervision for the purpose of protecting and promoting the welfare of children and youth, preventing neglect, abuse, and exploitation, helping overcome problems that result in dependency, neglect, or delinquency, and, when needed, providing adequate care for children and youth away from their own homes, such care to be given in foster family homes, adoptive homes, child-caring institutions, or other facilities. [P. 3]

3

In describing child welfare as an area of social work practice, Kadushin (1974a) states:

> The term *child welfare* as used here applies to a particular set of social problems which become the responsibility of a group of professionals, the child welfare social workers, who attempt to help in the prevention, amelioration, or improvement of such problematic social situations through the development and provision of particular child welfare services. Our contention is that child welfare services are concerned with a particular set of problems—problems in the social functioning of the parent-child network. [P. 6]

· · ·

> Child welfare services are those services required when parents or children are either incapable or unwilling (or both) of implementing their respective role requirements, or when a serious discrepancy arises between the role expectation of the community and the individual's performance. [P. 12]

A legal definition of child welfare services appears under Title IV, Part B, of the Social Security Act:

> Services which supplement, or substitute for, parental care and supervision for the purpose of (1) preventing or remedying, or assisting in the solution of problems which may result in the neglect, abuse, exploitation, or delinquency of children, (2) protecting and caring for homeless, dependent, or neglected children, (3) protecting and promoting the welfare of children of working mothers, and (4) otherwise protecting and promoting the welfare of children, including the strengthening of their own homes where possible or, where needed, the provision of adequate care of children away from their homes in foster family homes or day-care or other child-care facilities.

What Is Professional Social Work Practice?

Since many sections of this book focus on aspects of social work practice in relation to foster care, the reader who is not a social worker may find a brief description of social work helpful.

It is not easy to explain briefly an activity as varied and complex as social work practice. The fact that there are many specializations, e.g. medical social work, child welfare, community organization and planning, and research and a wide variety of practice settings, e.g. hospitals, community mental health, public social services, day care centers, and alcoholic treatment centers, makes this task even more difficult.

Professional social work in the United States began in the mid 1800s with private associations, commonly known as the Charity Organization Society (COS). COS agencies were common in the large Eastern cities and were created as a reaction and alternative to the public poor-relief programs. Early COS workers—all volunteers—believed that public programs were wasteful, ineffective, and impersonal.

The early COS workers advocated a personalized approach and a systematic assessment of the troubled family and rehabilitation; they operated on the assumption that the cause of problems was to be found within the individual. By the early 1900s, COS workers had learned that the social environment (employment opportunity, crowded housing, inadequate health care, industrial accidents, etc.) also contributed significantly to the problems of individuals and families. Thus, in addition to the case-by-case individualized approach, they began to emphasize social reform and social legislation. This twofold approach is characteristic of modern social work, i.e. concern with broad community and societal problems and also for the social and emotional problems of individuals and families.

As the early COS volunteers gained experience (many were wealthy women), they concluded that they needed formal training. In 1898, a six-week training course was established by the New York COS. By 1904, this educational program was expanded to one year and was offered by New York School of Philanthropy (now the Columbia University School of Social Work). A second major school began in 1901 and was known as the School of Civics and Philanthropy (currently the University of Chicago School of Social Service Administration). The first major textbook, Mary Richmond's *Social Diagnosis*, was published in 1917.

By 1977, there were approximately 215 accredited baccalaureate degree programs in social work and 85 accredited programs offering a master's degree in social work. Doctorates in social work also are offered by some graduate schools of social work. United States programs of social work education are accredited by the

Council on Social Work Education (CSWE). The CSWE developed out of the Association of Training Schools for Professional Social Work, formed in 1919.

In the late 1920s, several professional social work associations had arisen within various fields of practice, e.g. the American Association of Medical Social Workers, American Association of Psychiatric Social Workers, American Association of Group Workers, National Association of School Social Workers, and American Association of Social Workers. In 1955, these specialized organizations merged to form a single professional organization, the National Association of Social Workers.

About one-half of the states have some form of licensing or public regulation of social work practice. Such laws usually set minimum qualifications, require adherence to a code of ethics, and provide for the protection of client confidentiality. Considering the serious issues with which social workers deal, it is not surprising that the public increasingly is concerned with the qualifications and performance of social workers.

Pincus and Minahan (1973) provide an insightful overview of the social work profession. The following excerpts may be helpful to the reader who is unfamiliar with professional social work.

> The social work frame of reference leads the practitioner to focus on three related aspects of social situations: (1) the life tasks people are confronted with and the resources and conditions which would facilitate their coping with these tasks; (2) the interactions between people and their resource systems, as well as the interactions within and among resource systems; and (3) the relationship between the private troubles of people and public issues which bear on them.
>
> In defining what the social worker does to achieve the purposes of social work, the major focus is not on problems of people or problems of resource systems, but on the interactions between people and resource systems and between resource systems. The social worker will perform some functions with people who need help from resource systems and others with people within various resource systems.
>
> Seven major functions of social workers in carrying out the purposes of the profession can be differentiated. The intervention ac-

tivities and tasks performed by social workers are designed to accomplish one or more of the following functions:

1. Help people enhance and more effectively utilize their own problem-solving and coping capacities.
2. Established initial linkages between people and resource systems.
3. Facilitate interaction and modify and build new relationships between people within resource systems.
4. Facilitate interaction and modify and build relationships between people within resource systems.
5. Contribute to the development and modification of social policy.
6. Dispense material resources.
7. Serve as agents of social control.

In practice, a given activity might be performed to achieve several of these functions at the same time. Further, because of the interactional (or transactional) nature of the linkages that exist within, between, and among people and their resource systems, a specific activity or task of the worker that creates a change in the nature of one linkage may set off reciprocal changes in several of the other linkages and thus accomplish other functions. [Pp. 14-15]

Social workers find employment within a wide variety of private and public social service agencies and programs. Areas or fields of practice include day care, child welfare, community mental health, probation, parole, psychiatric hospitals, vocational rehabilitation, medical social services, public assistance, school social work, family services, YMCA or YWCA, prisons, developmental disabilities, and neighborhood and community development. The role or function of the social worker within these settings is related to the purpose and nature of the program, the social worker's level of skill, and the needs of clients. Some common roles are those of counselor, therapist, community organizer, researcher, planner, educator, group leader, advocate, and administrator.

What Is Foster Family Care or Foster Family Service?

According to the Child Welfare League of America (CWLA) *Standards for Foster Family Service* (1975b), foster family care

is the child welfare service that provides substitute family care for a planned period for a child when his own family cannot care for him for a temporary or extended period, and when adoption is either not yet possible or not desirable. [P. 8]

It is important to note that foster family care refers to twenty-four-hour child care within the context of a substitute or surrogate family. Foster family care should be distinguished from other forms of substitute child care, e.g. adoption, residential treatment, or institutional care.

The American Public Welfare Association (APWA) *Standards for Foster Family Services Systems* (1975) defines foster family services as

the child welfare services which provide (1) social work and other services for parents and children and (2) if needed family living in the community for children whose natural family cannot care for them either temporarily or for an extended period of time. Foster family services begin when the question of separating the child from his/her family arises. It ends when the child is stabilized in his/her own or relatives' home, is placed for adoption, is placed in a more appropriate facility or becomes independent. [P. xv]

One obtains an additional and interesting perspective on the complexities of foster family care by reviewing the definition of the term *foster*. According to the dictionary, it means (1) to bring up; rear; nurture; (2) to promote the development or growth of; encourage, cultivate; and (3) to nurse; cherish.

What Are the Historical Roots of Foster Family Care?

The history of child welfare services is fascinating. Slingerland (1919) states, "Under ancient Jewish law and customs, children lacking parental care became members of the household of other relatives if such there were, who reared them for adult life." This apparently was the beginning of foster care. Kadushin (1974a) notes that the early church boarded dependent children with "worthy widows." The need for substitute care in America was apparent from the earliest colonial days. For example, indenture—an early form of foster family care—was used widely during the eighteenth century. Many modern standards and principles in child welfare arose from reactions to past abuses and failures, e.g. almshouses and orphan trains. The reader interested in history should consult the historically oriented texts in social work and social welfare, some of which are classics: Abbott (1938); Axinn and Levin (1974); Cohen (1958); Coll (1969); Lundberg (1947); Pumphrey and Pumphrey (1961); M. Rich (1956); Romanyshyn (1971); Rothman (1971); Wilensky and Lebeaux (1958), and Zietz (1959). A reading of social welfare history is helpful in understanding many current issues and problems. When compared to past practices, modern child welfare is a remarkable development; progress has been made. An understanding of social welfare history also helps one realize that there are no simple answers to complex problems and that many of the present-day new or revolutionary ideas were tried in the past.

What Are the Goals of Foster Family Service?

According to the Child Welfare League of America (1975):

> The ultimate objectives of foster family service should be the promotion of healthy personality development of the child, and amelioration of problems that are personally or socially destructive.
>
> Foster family care is one of society's ways of assuring the well-being of children who would otherwise lack adequate parental care. Society assumes certain responsibilities for rearing and nurture of children when their own parents are unable to do so. It discharges these responsibilities through the services of social agencies and other social institutions. Foster family care should provide, for the child whose own parents cannot do so, experiences and conditions that promote normal maturation (care), prevent further injury to the child (protection), and correct specific problems that interfere with healthy personality development (treatment).
>
> Foster family service should be designed in such a way as to:
> —maintain and enhance parental functioning to the fullest extent. . . .
> —provide the type of care and services best suited to each child's needs and development. . . .
> —minimize and counteract hazards to the child's emotional health inherent in separation from his own family and the conditions leading to it
> —facilitate the child's becoming part of the foster family, school, peer group and larger community
> —make possible continuity of relationship by preventing unnecessary changes
> —protect the child from harmful experiences

—bring about the child's ultimate return to his natural family whenever desirable and feasible, or when indicated develop an alternative plan that provides a child with continuity of care. [Pp. 8-9]

Garrett (1977) provides a concise statement of priorities in foster care.

Foster care services are in fact services for families as well as services for children. All participants in the system subscribe to certain goals by priority in working with families and children:

1. To enable a child's family to maintain him or her at home at an improved level of living;
2. When necessary, to place the child in a suitable foster placement while working to return the child within a reasonable time to an improved family situation. In the majority of situations, the most useful placement is a specially selected foster home of good quality, but some children require the services of a specialized institution or group home;
3. To legally free children who cannot return home for adoption and place them in suitable adoptive homes within a reasonable time;
4. If none of these options is possible within a year, to develop with all parties a written, signed agreement for permanent foster care. [P. 4]

What Types of Substitute Care Are Available for Children Who No Longer Can Remain in Their Own Homes?

Of the children removed from their natural homes, the highest proportion, approximately 75 percent, are placed into foster family homes. Some of these children, however, may spend time in a shelter, emergency home, or an institution prior to placement into a foster family home. The 25 percent not placed into foster family homes are placed in group homes, residential treatment centers, or institutions. Those placed in foster family homes are more likely to be younger and have less serious behavior problems than those placed in other types of substitute care.

In recent years, there has been a trend away from institutional care. This trend is expected to continue. The number of group homes has increased rapidly. Kadushin (1977) defines group homes as "residential facilities providing twenty-four hour care in a group setting for six to twelve children or adolescents." At present, about 5 percent of the children in substitute care are in group homes.

Are There Different Types of Foster Family Homes?

The essential characteristic of a foster family home is that it provides substitute care within a family context. It is possible, however, to identify different types of homes depending on factors, such as the type of financial arrangement involved, the type of youngster served, or the problem situation the home is designed to meet. It should be noted that different states use somewhat different terminology to describe the various types of foster family homes. A uniform terminology does not exist.

Crisis homes, emergency shelters, or receiving homes are kinds of foster family care designed to care for children on short notice and for a limited period, usually a few days. Such homes are critical to effective community programming for the problems of neglect and abuse. Frequently, a child is placed in foster care for a few days pending a court hearing or the further investigation of possible child neglect or abuse. Such homes also are used while a more permanent arrangement for the child is being selected.

Medical foster home is the term sometimes applied to those homes in which care is provided for youngsters having extraordinary medical problems or physical handicaps. Similarly, some foster homes may be designated as capable of caring for children with serious emotional or behavioral problems or for children who are mentally retarded or developmentally disabled.

The terms *free home* and *wage home* are sometimes applied to a form of foster care in which the youngster, usually an adolescent, lives with a family and in return performs light work for the family, e.g. baby-sitting or housecleaning. In these arrangements, the foster home seldom receives a regular foster care payment, but the agency sanctions and supervises the placement. Often, these arrangements are worked out between the adolescent and the foster parents—the child works out his or her own placement. Not infrequently, the free home foster parent and the foster child are related or have known each other prior to the placement.

In some areas, the term *family group home* is applied to those arrangements wherein as many as six or eight children live with a set of foster parents or a foster family. Because the number exceeds the size of a typical family, some professionals are reluctant to classify this form of substitute care as a type of foster family care. Foster family group homes are especially important because they can be used to prevent the separation of siblings from a large family. If a group home becomes too large, it resembles a small institution and loses its family atmosphere. Small group homes are used increasingly for adolescents.

What Are the Principal Reasons Why Children Need Foster Care?

Most children need foster care because one or both parents or the person providing parental care experiences a problem that adversely affects the ability to function as a parent. Although studies indicate that mental or physical illness of the mother is the most common problem precipitating the need for foster care, there usually are multiple and complex reasons behind the need for placement. Kadushin (1974a) states that "Family disruption, marginal economic circumstances, and poor health consistently emerge as factors associated with the need for foster family placements." Sauber and Jenkins (1966) note that "the overall picture of the retrospective year prior to placement shows marginal families without sufficient resources to sustain themselves in the community when additional pressures or problems are added to their pre-existing burdens." It is apparent that a high proportion of foster children come from so-called multiproblem families.

After reviewing several studies of foster care in a large urban area, Ferleger and Cotter (1976) identified characteristics commonly found among the families of children in foster care.

1. One or more of the following have been found to be characteristic of most of the families with children in care: low income, welfare status, low educational levels, single parent, female-headed households, inadequate housing, member of a minority group, limited work history, illegitimacy, migration from birthplace . . .

2. Drug addiction and alcoholism problems were present for a significant number of mothers of children in care. Their children tend to be locked into care at disproportionately high rates. . . .

3. Many mothers of children in care suffer from emotional problems. For example, in one study sample, over half of all mothers were described as depressed. [P. 4]

Research findings reported by Shapiro (1976) indicate that reasons for placement, in order of importance, were (1) unwillingness or inability of parent to continue care (including abandonment of child); (2) neglect or abuse of child; (3) mental illness of parent; (4) unwillingness or inability to assume care, e.g. care of a newborn; (5) child's behavior or personality problems; (6) physical illness; (7) arrest or imprisonment of parent; (8) family conflict; (9) drug addiction; and (10) alcoholism.

How Many Children Are in Foster Family Homes?

It is difficult to answer the question of the number of children in family foster homes accurately because there are state-to-state variations in the definition of foster family care—one of several forms of substitute child care. The collection of accurate data is further complicated by the fact that both public and voluntary agencies provide foster care. Moreover, there are an unknown number of private foster care arrangements that do not involve social agencies and, therefore, are not included in official statistics.

National estimates of the number of children in foster care range between 285,000 and 350,000. An attempt by Kadushin (1974a) to describe the rate of placement indicated that nearly six of every one thousand children are placed in substitute care. Nearly four of every one thousand are placed in foster family care, and this rate of placement is rising. The increase in the use of foster family care parallels a decrease in the use of institutional care. Thus, the deinstitutionalization movement has generated a demand for foster family services. Also contributing to the increasing number of children in foster care is the growing number of homes disrupted by divorce, separation, and desertion. Disruptions leading to the need for foster care are more likely to occur among single-parent families. Kadushin (1977) notes that the rate at which children are placed into foster care varies widely from one jurisdiction to another, e.g. from county to county or state to state. "This leads to the suspicion that the system is responding to many extraneous factors other than the needs and best interests of children" (p. 115).

Is Socioeconomic Status Related to the Rate at Which Children Are Placed into Foster Care?

A disproportionate number of children entering foster care come from lower-socioeconomic-class families and those on public financial assistance, e.g. Aid to Families of Dependent Children (AFDC). According to statistics published by the U. S. Department of Health, Education and Welfare, Social Security Administration (1977), the average cash AFDC payment, per recipient per month, was $75.82. The average AFDC cash payment received by a family was $236.24. Given the fact that most recipients of AFDC continue to be below the poverty line, it is not surprising that their hand-to-mouth existence creates emotional stress, adding to the problems associated with the parenting role.

Is Marital Status Related to the Rate at Which Children Are Placed into Foster Care?

A disproportionate number of children entering foster care come from one-parent families, especially those affected by divorce and desertion. Typically, these families consist of a mother and children.

Are Race and Ethnicity Related to the Rate at Which Children Are Placed into Foster Care?

A disproportionate number of children entering foster care come from minority groups. A case in point is the Native American (Indian). Mindell and Gurwitt (1977) summarize data presented by William Byler, Executive Director of the Association on American Indian Affairs, before the Subcommittee on Indian Affairs of the United States Senate on April 8, 1974. According to Mindell and Gurwitt, "In the state of South Dakota, on a per capita basis, approximately 16 times as many Indian children as white children are living in foster homes. In Montana, the rate is 13 times the national foster home placement rate. In Minnesota, among the Indian children, the rate of foster home placement is five times greater than for non-Indian children" (p. 3).

Owing to the difficulty of establishing a rate of foster care placements, it is possible to question the precision of these figures; it is impossible, however, to question the picture they paint. For a variety of reasons, some of which are discussed, the children of minority families (black, Native American, etc.) are more likely to be placed in foster care than children from nonminority or white families.

Is It Possible to Reduce the Number of Children Placed into Foster Family Care?

The children most likely to be placed into foster care, i.e. the at-risk or vulnerable group, are from one-parent families, families in poverty, families belonging to a racial or ethnic minority, and families in which parents are trying to cope with severe emotional strain and interpersonal conflict. Efforts to reduce the need for foster care therefore must be directed to these families. According to Kadushin (1977), "Available research indicates that more adequate services to children in their own homes, more adequate [financial] assistance grants, and greater availability of some specific services notably protective services, homemaker services, and day care would tend to reduce the number of children needing foster care" (p. 16).

While there is good reason to believe that the rate of placement into foster care can be reduced, it is apparent that foster care, in one form or another, is here to stay. The studies demonstrating that appropriate supportive services to families can prevent and/or shorten placement for children also indicate that in a significant number of cases placement clearly is unavoidable.

If community, county, or state officials want to reduce the number of children going into foster care, they must be willing to commit additional resources to social services and programs of economic assistance. Funds must be spent either in payments for foster care or for those services that prevent the need for foster care. It is more desirable to spend money on the maintenance of an intact family than on foster care once the family has been disrupted.

How Long Do Children Stay in Foster Care?

Kadushin (1977) states that for most of the children the average stay is about one year. A national study indicates that about 25 percent are likely to remain in foster care for more than three years. A study by Fanshel and Grundy (1975) of foster children in New York City found that the average period a child spends in foster care is 5.4 years, and 20 percent of the children in foster care had been in care for 10 or more years.

After reviewing existing research on the subject, staff members at the Regional Research Institute for Human Services (1976) concluded that about one out of four children entering foster care remains for long periods of time. They further estimate that 50 percent of the children in a current foster care case load will remain in care for long periods. These figures underscore the seriousness and long-term implications of all intake decisions. They indicate, for example, that of every four children brought into the foster care system, one is likely to remain in the system until adulthood, and about one-half of the children in a typical foster care case load will experience many years of foster care.

Why Do Some Children Remain in Foster Care Longer Than Others?

A rather uniform research finding is that there is a strong relationship between length of stay and conditions or circumstances that precipitated placement. Physical illness of the parent(s) is associated with shorter stays, while mental or emotional illness and severe family disorganization are associated with longer stays.

What Is the Relationship Between the Length of Stay in Foster Care and the Foster Child's Eventual Return to His or Her Natural Parents?

Research findings are clear on this question. The longer a child stays in foster care, the more likely he or she will remain in foster care. Stated differently, with the passing of each day in foster care, there is a decrease in the likelihood that the child will return to his/her natural parents. Studies by Maas and Engler (1959) and Maas (1969) conclude that the longer a child remains in foster care, the less likely he or she is to be adopted or returned home.

The majority of foster children who leave foster care do so

within the first year of placement. What happens during the first year of placement, therefore, is critical to the outcome. What happens during the first weeks and months of placement is even more critical to outcome. Research data also indicate that, once a child has been in foster care for three years, it is highly unlikely that he or she will leave the foster care system prior to reaching maturity.

What Problems Exist within the Foster Care System?

Foster care is a basic, critical child welfare service. There is no question about the need for this service. There are, however, many problems within the foster care system, and they are of growing concern to social workers, informed citizens, and taxpayers.

A recent United States Department of Health, Education and Welfare study by Vasaly (1976), *Foster Care in Five States*, has taken a careful look at the problems within the foster care system. Drawing upon the results of that study, Garrett (1977) identifies eight major problems.

1. Preventive services are lacking or ineffective, resulting in the placement of many children who should have remained with their own families;
2. Natural parents quickly "get lost" and do not receive the help they need;
3. The average length of placement of children in care on any one day (the cumulative load) is five years;
4. Although it hurts a child to move from home to home, the average was 2.7 moves per child;
5. The average age of foster children was about ten—but specialized foster families for teenagers and children with special needs are in short supply;
6. Medical care and educational services to help the children "catch up" are inadequate;
7. Foster families in most communities subsidize the taxpayer because the reimbursement rate for the child's care is grossly inadequate;
8. Social service agencies are understaffed, in-service training is insufficient, and workloads are so unmanageable that a very small percentage of children return home or are legally freed and placed for adoption. [P. 5]

Lavine (1977) notes related problems.

> There are too many administrative and program barriers standing in the way of a unified delivery system that would embrace social services, mental health, education or special education, medical care, vocational rehabilitation, and other services the children need. . . .
>
> . . . We do not have a placement system that gives reasonable assurance that children are where they ought to be: in either institutional care, foster families, group homes, group residences, or in their own homes with necessary services available to the family and child. . . .
>
> . . . Funding is inadequate and what there is fails to have the impact it would were the funding system less fragmented and were the placement system more directed to the children's needs. [P. 5]

Mnookin (1977) states that there are several problems related to the body of law and legal procedures affecting foster care.

> 1. Existing legal standards are vague, and subjective, and do not define adequately the circumstances that justify removal of children from parental custody. Children are sometimes coercively removed from parental custody or accepted for voluntary placement without the social services agency first making a serious effort to protect the child within his family through less drastic means. While placing a child in foster care is often referred to as a "last resort," available evidence suggests that many communities offer few preventive or protective services for children within the home. The "best interest of the child" standard, used almost universally for the dispositional phase of child neglect proceedings, invites reliance by the judge on personal values. Reported appellate cases (which represent a very small and probably imperfect sample of neglect proceedings) illustrate how a judge's attitude toward child rearing, sexual mores, religion or cleanliness can affect the result of court proceedings. Finally, existing legal standards for removal are inconsistent with the proper allocation of responsibility between the family and the state for they do not make sufficiently clear that the state's role is to enforce minimum social standards, and not to attempt to intervene coercively to serve what a judge or social worker believes to be best for a child.
>
> 2. After children are removed from parental custody, insufficient effort is expended to reunite a child with his natural family by dealing with the problems that initially led to the need for placement. Available evidence suggests that the natural parents of children placed in foster care are largely ignored after the child is removed. Existing legal standards place no obligation on the state to try to

correct the deficiencies that led to removal in the first place.

3. Because of bureaucratic inertia and the avoidance of hard decisions, children who will never be returned to their natural families are allowed to drift in foster care for years—no permanent plans for their care are formulated or implemented. Available data plainly show that very few children placed in foster care are ever adopted, even though for many there is little chance of returning to their natural parents. Moreover, existing evidence suggests that requirements for "annual reviews" of foster care placement do not adequately insure that decisive action is ever taken.

To correct these deficiences, states should adopt policies that will reduce the number of children who must be placed in foster care, and to insure that those children who are placed in foster care will remain in the system as short a time as possible, preferably by returning them home promptly, but if not, then by facilitating adoption or a stable long-term placement. This requires reform of the whole system—greater procedural rights without changing the underlying substantive standards will not be adequate. New legislation addressing a number of interrelated problems at once is essential. [P. 7]

In addition to the problems mentioned by Mnookin—many of which are problems of administration, funding, staffing, and service delivery—experts are concerned increasingly about the type of youngster coming into and remaining in the foster care system. A growing number of youngsters have serious physical, emotional, and behavioral problems. One study indicates that as many as 40 percent of the children in foster care have physical, emotional, or mental handicaps. Many foster parents say that they simply cannot cope with these youngsters or provide the type of help needed.

Given the Many Problems within the Foster Care System, What Are Its Positive Features?

There is much that is good about foster care. Primarily, the foster care system provides substitute homes to children who are no longer able to live with their parents or relatives and who need homes and suitable living arrangements. Moreover, foster family care provides a less restrictive, more normalizing alternative to institutional care. In many cases—but certainly not all—foster family care provides the child with a wholesome environment, one that helps to heal emotional wounds caused by destructive family relationships, abuse, or neglect.

While it is true that there are many problems in foster care, these deficiencies must be viewed within a societal context. Reid (1977) provides such a viewpoint.

> The foster care system has served as a scapegoat for society's ills; its critics charge that the child welfare system does not nurture family life and provide preventive services as it should. Neither, one can argue, does society as a whole. The legacy of hundreds of years of racism, exploitation of women, discrimination along religious, racial and class lines in housing, schooling, and job opportunities cannot be abolished overnight. The country's high unemployment rate, especially among minorities, takes immeasurable toll of the public affected. Families suffer and crumble under the pressure of these external forces, and our job has been picking up the pieces to rebuild families or find new permanent living arrangements for the children.
>
> While our primary emphasis must be on protecting and nurturing the family, we must recognize that in some cases the situation is not salvageable. [P. 7]

The need for foster family service and other types of substitute care reflects the reality that some families, for a variety of reasons, are unable to provide adequate parenting for their children. Short of major and far-reaching social changes that strengthen the families' capacity for parenting, the need for substitute care will continue.

Is Placement into Foster Care Harmful to the Child?

For many children, placement is simply unavoidable. Examples include those children who need foster care because they have been abandoned or left alone by parents who have died or have been hospitalized or imprisoned. Assuming no friends or relatives can care for these children, foster care is the only choice. In cases where placement clearly is unavoidable, one can only ask if one kind of substitute care is more harmful or helpful than another. It is pointless to ask if foster care is more or less harmful than no care at all.

Some children—especially adolescents in unhappy family situations—run away. If returned to their homes, they run away again.

If picked up by the police or referred to a child welfare agency, they may refuse to go home. Some ask to be placed in a foster home. When a child cannot and will not live with his/her parents, the conflicts cannot be resolved, and no one else is available to care for the youngster, foster care may be necessary. In such cases, foster care may keep the child from getting into serious trouble with the law or from street hazards that face runaway youths. In such cases, foster care seems to be a reasonable choice and certainly no more harmful than the alternatives.

Much more serious is the question of harm in those cases where a choice actually exists between leaving a child with his or her parents or placing him/her in foster care. For example, is it better to leave a child with neglecting or abusing parents or to place the child in foster care? If there is reason to believe that a child might be seriously injured or killed if not separated from the parent, few would argue against placement. On the other hand, if the child is not in real physical danger, one can argue that placement may be just as harmful as remaining in an undesirable and chaotic family situation.

There is growing belief among experts that in many cases placement is less desirable than leaving the child in his/her home— even when there are serious deficiencies in the home. Child psychiatrists such as Anna Freud and John Bowlby assert that the separation of parent and child is extremely harmful; moreover, the negative impact occurs even when the child is separated from a neglecting and/or abusing parent. In short, children are attached to their parents, whether good or bad, and separation is harmful. While the generalizations of Freud and Bowlby have been challenged by other experts, few would disagree that separation is painful and that, for some children at least, it has a lasting negative impact.

Those concerned with the harmfulness of placement observe that, in addition to the trauma of separation, the foster child often experiences confusion and uncertainty. At least three sets of adults (natural parents, foster parents, and social workers) are involved in the child's care and supervision. Each may have different expectations of the child, who may receive conflicting

messages. Children, especially young children, may not understand why they were removed from their parents. Some report that
they viewed foster home placement as a punishment for a real
or imagined transgression. As a result of confusing and uncertain
experiences, many foster children suffer problems of identity,
conflicts of loyalty, and anxiety about their future. Many writers
are also concerned about the harm that may occur when a placement disrupts the child's cultural identity and heritage, as when
a Native American or black child is placed in a home with white
foster parents.

After a review of the literature on the effect of foster care on
children, Wald (1976) notes:

> There is substantial evidence that separations cause short-term
> emotional trauma and pain for a child. Most of this evidence comes
> from studies of very young children, however. There are few studies
> of the impact of separation on children over five. . . .
> While the evidence of short-run trauma seems conclusive, at least
> for young children, there are few studies supporting the claims of
> long-run harms from either separation or temporary foster care
> status. Even those studies finding harm do not determine whether
> the harms were caused solely by the breaking of an earlier attach-
> ment, by the breaking of several attachments, or by some combina-
> tion of these or other factors. [Pp. 669-670]

Several of the studies summarized by Kadushin (1974a, pp. 451-
454) indicate that the incidence of criminality, mental illness, and
marital success of individuals who grew up in foster care is similar to that of the general population. Meier (1965) concluded
that children who have experienced foster care usually make
adequate adjustments as young adults. A few studies, however,
suggest that foster children are more likely to experience problems in adulthood.

There is some evidence of long-term negative effects caused by
multiple placements. Each new placement subjects the child to
disruption and added uncertainty. Viewed another way, multiple
placement repeatedly subjects the child to the short-term harmful
effects cited above. While the empirical evidence is thin, there
is reason to believe that the repeated breaking of child-adult attachments is damaging to the child's social and psychological de-

velopment. This is significant when one considers the fact that a high percentage of foster children experience a series of placements.

One of the most significant studies of foster children has been published by Fanshel and Shinn (1978). This is probably the only longitudinal study of foster children. For this reason, the findings are of particular interest. The study followed 624 New York foster children for five years. During this period, the children were repeatedly given psychological assessments. In addition, data were gathered on their school performance and social adjustment. Fanshel and Shinn summarize their findings:

> One of our major interests in studying the children over time was to assess whether continued status in foster care increased the risk of impairment with respect to mental abilities or in the emotional sphere. We do not find that the longer a child spends in foster care, the more likely he is to show signs of deterioration. . . .
>
> In general, we have developed the perspective that continued tenure in foster care is not demonstrably deleterious with respect to IQ change, school performance, or the measures of emotional adjustment we employed. We do not say that the children are in a condition that is always reassuring—but staying in care as opposed to returning home does not seem to compound the difficulties of the children. [Pp. 490-491]

Many of the children in the study had serious social and emotional problems, but the research data did not indicate that the length of stay in foster care, in and of itself, resulted in further deterioration. However, Fanshel and Shinn state:

> We are not completely sure that continued tenure in foster care over extended periods is not in itself harmful to children. On the level at which we were able to measure the adjustment of the children we could find no such negative effect. However, we feel that our measures of adjustment are not without problems, and we are not sure that our procedures have captured the potential feelings of pain and impaired self-image that can be created by impermanent status in foster care. [P. 479]

Some children are placed in foster care not because they are physically abused or neglected but because of emotional neglect or inadequate parental behavior. In such cases, it is argued that the parents are so inconsistent, verbally abusive, or maladjusted that the child is being damaged psychologically and emotionally and that placement in foster care would prevent psychological problems and offer the child greater opportunity for personal development and future happiness. This use of foster care is based on the assumption that the behavior of parents has a strong influence on the child. Increasingly, there is reason to believe that the influence of parents on children has been exaggerated. Skolnick (1978) has stated that

> the image of a troubled adult scarred for life by an early trauma such as the loss of a parent, lack of love, or family tension has passed from the clinical literature to become a cliche of the popular media. The idea that childhood stress must inevitably result in psychological damage is a conclusion that rests on a methodological flaw inherent in the clinical literature: instead of studying development through time, these studies start with adult problems and trace them back to possible causes.
>
> It's true that when researchers investigate the backgrounds of delinquents, mental patients, or psychiatric referrals from military service, they find that a large number come from "broken" or troubled homes, have overpossessive, domineering, or rejecting mothers, or have inadequate or violent fathers. The usual argument is that these circumstances cause maladjusments in the offspring. But most children who experience disorder and early sorrow grow up to be adequate adults. Further, studies sampling "normal" or "superior" people—college students, business executives, professionals, creative artists, and scientists—find such "pathological" conditions in similar or greater portions. Thus, many studies trying to document the effects of early pathological and traumatic conditions have failed to demonstrate more than a weak link between them and later development. [P. 58]

The weak link between the parent's behavior and the child's future adjustment underscores the fact that parent-child relations do not occur in a social vacuum. A wide variety of other factors shape the child's behavior. This is demonstrated by the longitudinal studies of child development.

> The striking differences between retrospective studies that start with adult misfits and look back to childhood conditions, and longitudinal studies that start with children and follow them through time, were shown in a study at the University of California's

Institute of Human Development, under the direction of Jean Mac-farlane. Approximately 200 children were studied intensively from infancy through adolescence, and then were seen again at age 30. The researchers predicted that children from troubled homes would be troubled adults and, conversely, that those who had had happy, successful childhoods, would be happy adults. They were wrong in two-thirds of their predictions. Not only had they overestimated the traumatic effects of stressful family situations, but even more surprisingly, they also had not anticipated that many of those who grew up under the best circumstances would turn out to be unhappy, strained, or immature adults (a pattern that seemed especially strong for boys who had been athletic leaders and girls who had been beautiful and popular in high school). [Skolnick, 1978, p. 58]

The difficulties of predicting a child's later adjustment on the basis of parent-child relationships raise serious questions about the use of foster family care as a means of preventing future adjustment problems.

It should be apparent that there is no simple answer to the question of whether foster care is harmful. Clearly, placement is necessary and helpful to some children. However, for children who are not in real physical danger and who could possibly remain with their parents, placement into foster care may create as many problems as it solves.

Will the Demand for Foster Care Increase or Decrease?

Assuming that the occurrence of problems leading to placement does not increase and the rate of placement remains the same, the demand for foster and substitute care should begin to decrease in the early 1980s because the number of children in the United States population is decreasing. It should be noted, however, that increases in the birth rate, in stress owing to unfavorable socioeconomic conditions, and in the rate of family disruption and breakup could enlarge the number of children in need of foster care. An increase in the rate of placement could offset the effect of a decreasing number of children in the United States population.

Those anticipating the future demand for foster family services and other types of substitute child care must be cognizant of

87481

College of St. Francis Library
Illinois

the fact that the American family is in a period of rapid change. Although the family as a social system will exist into the foreseeable future, the nature of that system is changing: The traditional family is becoming less common. Quotations from the studies sponsored by the Carnegie Foundation help to underscore changes underway.

> In 1948 . . . only 26 percent of married women with school age children worked at anything but the job of keeping house and raising children. Now that figure has more than doubled: in March 1976, 54 percent worked outside the home, a majority of them full time. The increase in labor-force participation is even more dramatic for married women who have preschool children. . . .
>
> . . . we have passed a genuine watershed. This is the first time in our history that the *typical* school-age child has a mother who works outside the home.
>
> . . . Today about one out of every three marriages ends in divorce and more and more of them involve children. . . . It is now estimated that four out of every ten children born in the 1970s will spend part of their childhood in a one-parent family, usually with their mother as head of the family. [Keniston, 1977, p. 4]

These dramatic changes in the American family not only will have an effect on the number of children needing substitute forms of child care but will also affect the availability of foster homes. In short, the forces contributing to a growing demand for foster care are contributing to a decreasing number of foster homes.

Are There Professional Guidelines or Standards That Can Give Direction to Decisions of Policy and Practice Related to Foster Care?

The American Public Welfare Association and the Child Welfare League of America have published guidelines on foster family services. If these were employed to guide the actions of policy makers and the everyday decisions of social work practitioners, it seems reasonable to assume that the quality of foster care would be improved and the inappropriate use of foster care reduced.

The *Standards for Foster Family Services Systems* developed by the APWA (1975) is fairly general and oriented to the public agency. (Public agencies provide 95 percent of all foster family services.) The CWLA *Standards for Foster Family Service* (1975) is more specific and detailed. Public agencies should supplement the APWA *standards* with the CWLA *standards*. It should be noted that the APWA *standards* is being revised; a new edition will be available in 1979.

What Is the Child Welfare League of America?

According to a CWLA pamphlet:

> The Child Welfare League of America is a privately supported, non-sectarian organization which is dedicated to the improvement of care and services for deprived, neglected, and dependent children and their families. [It was founded in 1920. The CWLA's] . . . program is directed toward helping agencies and communities in the U. S. and Canada . . . provide essential social services to promote the well-being of children. CWLA is an advocate for children and families, a clearinghouse and forum for . . . persons in the [child welfare] field, and a coordinating facility through which all concerned with child welfare can share . . . [knowledge and experience]. Programs of the League and its membership of over 300 affiliated public and private agencies include: accredition of agencies, adoption services, conferences, consultation, training, library/information services, publications, personnel services, public affairs and legislative programs, standards development, and surveys.

The CWLA journal, *Child Welfare,* is one of the most widely read journals of its type. The reader is urged to secure a price list of CWLA publications. Many are devoted to research and practice in foster family services.

What Other Organizations Are Sources of Information about Child Welfare?

Many organizations have an interest in child welfare. Some specialize in a single service area, e.g. day care, while others have broad interests. Listed below is a sampling of national or regional organizations concerned with foster family services.

American Humane Association
Children's Division
P.O. Box 1266
Englewood, CO 80110

American Public Welfare Association
1155 Sixteenth St., N.W., Suite 201
Washington, DC 20036

Association on American Indian Affairs, Inc.
432 Park Avenue, South
New York, NY 10016

Center for Social Research and Development
Denver Research Institute
University of Denver
2142 South High Street
Denver, CO 80208

Center for Social Service
University of Wisconsin-Extension
610 Langdon Street
Madison, WI 53706

Center for Social Work Research
School of Social Work
University of Texas at Austin
Austin, TX 78712

Child Welfare League of America
67 Irving Place
New York, NY 10003

Child Welfare Resource Information Exchange
2011 Eye Street, N.W., Suite 501
Washington, DC 20006

Children's Bureau
Office of Human Development Services
Administration for Children, Youth and Families
U. S. Dept. of Health, Education and Welfare
Washington, DC 20013

Council on Social Work Education
345 East 46th Street
New York, NY 10017

Family Service Association of America
44 East 23rd Street
New York, NY 10010

Foster Care Education Program
Continuing Education in Social Work
331 Nolte Center
University of Minnesota
Minneapolis, MN 55455

Foster Parent Training Project
Eastern Michigan University
Ypsilanti, MI 48197

Institute of Child Behavior and Development
University of Iowa
Oakdale, IA 53219

Institute for Urban Affairs and Research
Howard University
2935 Upton St., N.W.
Washington, DC 20008

International Union for Child Welfare
P.O. Box 41
1211 Geneva 20, Switzerland

Judge Baker Guidance Center
295 Longwood Ave.
Boston, MA 02115

The Midwest Parent-Child Welfare Resource Center
Center for Advanced Studies in Human Services
School of Social Welfare
University of Wisconsin-Milwaukee
P.O. Box 413
Milwaukee, WI 53201

National Action for Foster Children
611 East Wells Street
Milwaukee, WI 53202

The National Assembly of National Voluntary Health and Social Welfare Organizations, Inc.
345 East 46th Street
New York, NY 10017

National Association of Social Workers
1425 H Street, Suite 600
Washington, DC 20005

National Center for the Prevention and Treatment of Child Abuse and Neglect
University of Colorado Medical Center
1205 Oneida St.
Denver, CO 80220

National Conference on Social Welfare
22 West Gay Street
Columbus, OH 43215

National Foster Parents Association
380 Brookes Dr., Room 103
St. Louis, MO 63042

North American Center on Adoption
61 Irving Place
New York, NY 10014

The Northwest Federation for Human Services
P. O. Box 2526
Boise, ID 83701

Permanent Planning Project
Regional Research Institute for Human Services
Portland State University
P.O. Box 751
Portland, OR 97201

Project CRAFT
(Curriculum Resources for Adoptions and Foster Care Training)
Continuing Education Program in the Human Services
University of Michigan School of Social Work
1015 East Huron
Ann Arbor, MI 48109

Protective Services Resource Center
Rutgers Medical School
P.O. Box 101
Piscataway, NJ 08854

Regional Institute of Social Welfare Research
P.O. Box 152
Heritage Building
468 N. Milledge Ave.
Athens, GA 30601

CHAPTER 2

The Placement Decision

What Is the Placement Decision?

A s USED HERE, *placement decision* refers to the complex question of whether or not an out-of-home placement is necessary for a particular child. This decision precedes the use of foster family care. Frequently, the social worker does not have an opportunity to make this decision, as in the case of parents who abandon a child or a runaway adolescent who refuses to return home or whose parents refuse to let the child return. As noted by Kadushin (1974a, p. 442), "In many instances, the decision is made for him [the social worker]—by the situation (as when there is no one available to care for the child at home and substitute care is the only feasible alternative), by the limitations of placement resources, or by parental rights and strongly expressed parental preferences."

In other cases, a judge may make the placement decision; the social worker has no choice but to go along with the court's decision. In some instances, however, the social worker is in the position to make the critical placement decision or make recommendations to the court. Given the far-reaching effect of the placement decision, it must be approached in a most serious and thoughtful manner. It is a professional decision that requires a high level of knowledge and skill.

Is the Rate at Which Children Go into Foster Care the Same from Community to Community?

There appears to be great variation among communities in their rate of placement. Many factors other than the needs of the child determine whether or not a child is separated from his/her parents and placed in substitute care.

Bryce and Ryan (1977) have identified factors that reflect differences in professional knowledge and skill, agency policy, and commitment to a search for better alternatives.

The discrepancy between what is done and what is needed appears to be an honest difference in interpretation of what constitutes . . . work with family and community, and its importance to a whole and effective treatment program for a family member. Many clinics and agencies continue to recommend residential treatment, institutional placement, hospitalization, boarding school or foster care of a family member with the same frequency and for the same reasons used for the past 50 years. The number of recommendations for placement and the untold billions expended in maintaining the placement industry, undergird the neglect of . . . time, effort, finances and professional skill at the local level for the development of alternatives to placement away from home. [Pp. 11-12]

The community-to-community variation reflects personalities and philosophies of judges and county attorneys and differences in community values, traditions, and socioeconomic characteristics. In addition, communities differ in regard to the availablity of family support services. Placement rates are higher in those communities that offer few alternatives to out-of-home placements. Differences in the experience and professional training of social work staff within child welfare agencies also affect the rate of placement in a given community. Highly trained social workers use foster care less than those who have had little or no social work training. Personal bias, racism, and other forms of prejudice also may affect placement decisions.

Are the Placement Decisions Made by Child Welfare Workers Sound and Well Grounded in Data?

When must a child be removed from his or her natural home and placed in foster care? That always has been one of the most difficult issues facing the child welfare worker. While it is generally agreed that this is a serious and difficult question, it is important to realize that several studies reveal findings similar to those reported by Phillips, Haring, and Shyne (1972).

The results of the study have reenforced the initial impression of inconsistency across workers and agencies, and across cases handled by the same worker in the same agency, [and] in the information available prior to decisions crucial in the lives of the children affected. Considerable variation among practitioners, even those who are highly experienced in the service plans they consider appropriate in a particular case was also revealed. [P. 1]

There is reason to believe that critical decisions regarding child placement are being made in many ways and for a variety of reasons. However, because of the complexity of the decision, a lack of complete agreement is to be expected. In reviewing research on decision making related to placement, Kadushin (1975a) notes:

> There is considerable variation in the placement decision-making process. In one study workers given the same case to review "agreed" among themselves on slightly less than half of the decisions. . . . In a second study there were some 71 percent agreement. . . . The latter level of agreement is significantly better than chance, and is typical of the level of disagreement among experts in any complex situation—in the reading of an X-ray, in the admission of college students, in decisions concerning the necessity for surgery, and so on. [P. 423]

At present, there is no valid and reliable tool for helping child welfare workers make good decisions; unfortunately, there is reason to be distrustful of so-called common sense, because one finds so much unexplainable variation among worker judgments. What is the answer? Three things can be done. First, the social worker should be certain that he/she has adequate and accurate information before making a decision. Second, the social worker should be certain that he/she considers those factors that other experienced professionals consider important in decision making. Third, when any doubt exists, consultants and professional peers should be asked to assist in the decision-making process.

Why Is There a Pattern of Inconsistency among Placement Decisions?

There are many forces that push and pull child welfare workers and impinge on their ability to make sound decisions. Frequently, child welfare workers spend much of their time responding to crises. They also must deal with an inordinate amount of paperwork. This unfortunate reality usually is related to staff shortages or problems related to the management of the organization. When there is not time to provide or secure the support services needed by the "families at risk," their problems become increasingly severe, a crisis develops, and finally the children are placed in foster care. Pare and Torczyner (1977) make a similar point.

> Given child welfare policy's stated objectives of maintaining children in their natural family whenever possible, and given the importance of income supplementation and support service in both preventing placement and in promoting positive family functioning in order for a child to return home, one would assume that child welfare practice is directed toward improvements in these areas. It would seem likely that preventative service, income supplementation and support services to the natural family would characterize child welfare practice. In practice, however, this is not the case.
>
> In practice, despite the sound intentions of policy statements and of practitioners alike, the practitioners are confronted with a different reality than child welfare principles have allowed for. The practitioner must act often in a crisis situation with few alternative resources to apply before placement becomes the only realistic course to follow. [P. 1232]

Family support services (adequate financial assistance, day care, and homemaker services, etc.) are limited in most communities. Unfortunately, this can result in inappropriate use of foster care as a substitute for other services. Why do states and communities develop foster care services but neglect other needed services? One significant reason is that placement in foster care frequently is ordered by a court. Thus, county commissioners, legislators, and other decision makers feel compelled to support and fund foster care. Since family support services are less likely to be ordered by courts, they are given a lower funding priority than foster care.

A lack of system-wide social welfare planning results in an unevenness in the supply and demand for certain types of services. For example, in recent years, much emphasis has been placed on the detection of child abuse and neglect. Many public awareness programs have been launched in an effort to identify cases of child abuse and neglect. Less attention has been given to the development of services necessary to help abused children and abusive parents. Thus, the demand for services was increased without a concomitant increase in the supply. In part, this situation exists because public awareness or case-finding programs are relatively inexpensive, whereas treatment and support services tend to be expensive. Communities may develop the former when they need the latter.

Child welfare work, especially protective services, is demanding and stressful. Many of the factors contributing to this stress have been described by the psychiatrist Ner Littner (1957). Because of the bureaucratic and emotional demands placed on the social workers in child welfare, the turnover rate is high. Many of those who remain succumb to a form of burnout common to the human services (Maslach, 1976). Therefore, a high proportion of critical placement decisions is made by young, inexperienced individuals or by those who have become demoralized and cynical.

Many poor placement decisions are made by persons with little or no formal education in social work, specifically in the area of child welfare. At a time when there is obvious need for personnel with higher levels of skill and training, many state personnel departments are downgrading job qualifications for positions in child welfare. People are hired to be "social workers" even though they have no professional social work training. Thus, critical and far-reaching placement decisions frequently are made by untrained personnel.

When a child is in trouble, especially in situations of parent neglect and abuse, the public has little sympathy for or patience with the parent. Often there is public pressure to remove the child from the natural home. Some may want to remove the child as a way of punishing the parent. Even when a social worker wants to avoid placement, it may be difficult to resist the pressure generated by the school officials, county attorney, judge, and police. Placement may seem logical to these individuals. Many citizens and professionals do not realize that placement into a foster home does not solve the problem; at best, it presents another set of problems. The public has little knowledge about the limitations inherent in foster care.

Inappropriate placement decisions may result from inadequate information. In the research conducted by Phillips, Haring, and Shyne (1972), for example, there were indications that 47 percent of the placement decisions might have been altered if additional information had been available to the social workers. Given the seriousness of placement decisions, it is essential that such decisions be based on adequate and reliable information. Unfortunately, pressures, time limitations, and the atmosphere of crisis pervasive in child protection work preclude a systematic gathering of information. Securing adequate and reliable information is time consuming; moreover, a high level of skill is needed to collect accurate information about sensitive areas such as parenting behavior, marital and family conflicts, the child's behavior, mental and physical problems, potential resources in the extended family, and availability of other community resources.

Until greater public attention and support are given to funding and development of family support services, hiring and retention of well-trained social workers, and reduction of case loads to a more manageable level, poor placement decisions will continue to be made to the detriment of the child, his/her parents, and ultimately, to the public and taxpayer.

What Information Should Be Collected at Intake to Establish a Basis for Deciding How a Particular Case Should Be Handled?

There is no simple answer to this question because the agency or service program mode of operation affects the data that can and must be collected. Moreover, variables such as the source of the referral, time limitations, and the cooperativeness of the clients affect the data-gathering process. Emergency situations may force a decision before adequate information is available. Thus, there is a difference between the standards that should apply to "ideal" situations and those dictated by hard reality.

Except in emergency situations, the social worker should perform a basic social assessment relevant to the problem. Various semistructured interview schedules and guides can aid in this process, but they should not be used in a rigid manner—one cramping the social worker's natural style of interacting or interfering with the give-and-take of interpersonal exchange. For a discussion of the pros and cons of using outlines and other aspects of interviewing, the reader should review basic books on the social work interview; for example, Cross (1974), Kadushin (1972), and Schubert (1974).

One semistructured interview schedule designed for use in child welfare settings, *Intake Interview Guide* (1972) (*see* Appendix A), has been prepared by the CWLA. By using the *Guide*, the worker gathers data that facilitates decision making.

How Can the Social Worker Decide Whether Placement Is Necessary?

A research effort by Phillips, Haring, and Shyne (1972) attempted to answer this question by asking experienced child welfare workers to identify the factors associated with own-home decisions, e.g. not placing the child, and out-of-home decisions, i.e. placement of child into substitute care. A ranking procedure was used to identify those factors most critical to this decision-making process. Many agencies have developed checklists to use as aids in decision making. Checklists incorporate the collective experience of seasoned child welfare workers. The Report Task Force Committee prepared by the Utah Division of Family Services (1975) is one example.

The United Way of Milwaukee (1974) has issued a committee report that includes criteria for the removal of a child from his/her home and provides guidance on the differential placement decision. In using such criteria, it is important to remember that at best they are indicators pointing to the possibility that removal from the home may be in the child's best interests.

The guidelines for removal developed by the United Way of Milwaukee are as follows:

1. Pathology of family and/or environmental problems are so severe and/or persistent and the child so much involved in it that best intervention and resources available are not sufficient in degree or time to stop the ongoing damage to the child. Specifically these may be:
   a. Grossly infantile, inadequate parent(s), often severely depressed (possibly to psychotic proportions) and depleted so that adequate care cannot be given to child, e.g., failure to consistently meet physical needs, failure and/or inability to set limits.

   b. Highly self-centered, immature parents whose major energy is directed towards their own functioning with little remaining for child. Child may be used as a pawn to attempt to increase parents' self-esteem. (These parents may function quite well in other areas of life and not be seen as pathological as they are.)

   c. Parent(s) physically dangerous to child, e.g.,

     (1) violent alcoholic

     (2) violent psychotic and out of contact with reality

     (3) abusive parent who when he loses control for any reason directs anger against the child in physical attacks.

     (4) family that uses child to act out through or with or uses the child's "illness" in general as a means of maintaining their own pathologic balance to such a degree that it severely impedes the growth and development of the child. (i.e., scapegoats rather than looks at own problems, encourages a child to steal, truant.)

2. Parents are totally unable to recognize and are strongly defended against seeing their part in child's pathology.

3. Difficulty in relationship between parent and child cannot be looked at by either, unless separation for a shorter or longer period of time gives them some ability to distance and be more objective.

4. Crisis (e.g., death of a parent, severe illness, death of a grandparent who held family together, desertion of a partner, hospitalization of single parent for mental illness) is severe enough to disintegrate a family that under normal circumstances was managing at least minimally to help children grow. Family may or may not be able to reintegrate after stress is over. [Pp. 5-6]

Another set of guidelines incorporating items drawn from several sources is presented. The reader is cautioned against the misuse of such checklists. The checklist is not a validated assessment instrument; at best, it is an aid to decision making. If there are many yes answers, an out-of-home placement is suggested. However, the yes-or-no answers to these questions should be weighed against other available information and the situational context. Even if the checklist yields many yes answers, the decision to place a child should be approached with great caution. Placement should be viewed as a last resort and must be shown to be absolutely necessary and unavoidable. All other alternatives should be explored and found unworkable before placement is considered.

A yes answer to a checklist question suggests an out-of-home placement only when a less drastic alternative is unavailable. For example, a yes answer to questions 6 and 7 may indicate the need for a temporary separation of the abusing parent and child, but it need not be the child who leaves the home. It makes more sense for the offending parent to leave, permitting the child to remain in familiar surroundings.

The Need for Placement: A Checklist for Decision Making

——— 1. Is this a true emergency situation?

——— 2. Is the child clearly in need of care and supervision because his/her parents are unable to perform these tasks, e.g. death or hospitalization?

——— 3. Has the child been obviously abandoned by his/her parents or caretakers?

——— 4. Is the child unduly fearful of his/her parents or caretakers?

——— 5. Has the child been kept confined or isolated for long periods of time?

——— 6. Does the child show evidence of repeated physical abuse by persons in the home?

——— 7. Does the child show evidence of repeated sexual abuse by persons in the home?

——— 8. Is the child clearly malnourished or in need of medical attention?

——— 9. Is the child young (under five years) or disabled and consequently unable to seek help if needed or escape harm or further abuse?

——— 10. Is the child asking to be removed from the home?

——— 11. Is the parent asking that the child be removed from the home?

——— 12. Is the abuse of drugs or alcohol by the adults in the home so serious that it keeps them from providing a minimum level of care and supervision for the child?

——— 13. Is the behavior of the adults in the home so bizarre or chaotic that it keeps them from providing a minimum level of care and supervision for the child?

___ 14. Is the parent-child relationship characterized by a complete lack of warmth or affection?

___ 15. Do parents show signs of losing control or express fear of losing control?

___ 16. Do the parents lack an awareness of the child's need for attention, food, or supervision?

___ 17. In an effort to prevent an out-of-home placement, have all relevant emergency services (homemaker services, day care, respite care, and crisis intervention) been tried and found unworkable in this situation?

___ 18. In an effort to prevent an out-of-home placement, have all relevant informal resources (neighbors, friends, relatives, church groups, and Parents Anonymous, etc.) been contacted and found unworkable in this situation?

___ 19. Have the parents been approached by a well-trained and skillful social worker, informed of the serious nature of the presenting problem and offered relevant services, but still refused to explore the use of such services?

___ 20. Have other experienced social workers and professionals been consulted about the need for placement?

How Does the Social Worker Decide Whether a Situation Is a True Emergency Justifying Immediate Removal of the Child from His/Her Natural Home?

Immediate removal of the child is a matter of professional judgment. It always is a serious and far-reaching decision. The following checklist can help the social worker form that judgment. If there are several yes answers to these questions, the child may be in imminent danger.

___ 1. Is the child in danger of serious physical harm?

___ 2. Does the child need immediate medical attention?

___ 3. Is the child clearly subject to environmental danger (unsafe building, lack of heat, or danger of fire, etc.)?

___ 4. Is the child too young and/or physically unable to

escape a dangerous situation, e.g. violent parent or threatening parent with history of abuse?

——— 5. Is the parent or caretaker exhibiting severe physical or emotional problems, e.g., rage, irrational behavior induced by drugs, or hallucinations?

——— 6. Is a responsible person (parent, relative, friend, or neighbor) unavailable to care for and protect the child?

——— 7. Is the child asking to be removed from the situation?

——— 8. Is the child exhibiting severe physical or emotional problems related to the stressful situation, e.g. uncontrollable crying or vomiting?

——— 9. Is the parent(s) requesting an immediate removal of the child?

——— 10. Are other responsible and knowledgeable professionals or agencies expressing great concern about the current safety and well-being of the child and urging immediate removal?

How Are Differential Placement Decisions to Be Made?

Once it is determined that a child must be placed out of his/her home and into substitute care, the social worker must make another complex decision related to the type of substitute care most appropriate for the child. He/she must decide whether a specific child should be placed in a foster family home, ordinary group home, therapeutic group home, a residential treatment center, or in some other arrangement. Unfortunately, there are few firm guidelines that apply in all cases. Many factors must be considered, such as the child's age, the natural parents' preferences, the child's preferences and special needs (medical problems, structure to control violence, etc.). As a general rule, the child should be placed in the most normalizing and least restrictive environment possible (Wolfensberger, 1972). Increasingly, legal concerns dictate placement in the least restrictive alternative. Foster family homes generally are the least restrictive and most normal type of substitute care. Detention facilities with locked doors and residential treatment centers are the most restrictive and least normalizing types of substitute care.

There is general agreement that all normal preschool children—those under age six—should be placed in foster family homes. Mayer, Richman, and Balcerzak (1977, p. 291) state. "For the preschooler, group care is never the placement of choice. Only in emergency situations may group care be used for the normal preschool child. And even then it has to be used with great care."

The normal child between the ages of six and twelve usually should be placed in foster family care. However, there may be a few exceptions. Mayer, Richman, and Balcerzak (1977) contend that

> the placement of choice for . . . normal latency-age dependent children is the foster [family] home. In some cases, because of particular personal circumstances or because of the unavailability of good foster homes, group care can be chosen.
>
> Group care settings serving the normal latency-age child should provide individualized parental care, nurturing and privacy, together with group experiences, socialization, stimulation, skill development and habit training. It is particularly important for a child of this age to have parental figures of both sexes available in his daily life experiences. [Pp. 291-292]

Increasingly, professionals are questioning the advisability of using foster family care for adolescents. Essentially, adolescence is a period during which the individual strives to achieve independence from parental figures. Adolescents, especially those in need of substitute care, are seldom eager to form relationships with new parental figures. Foster family care demands an intensity of relationship that may be unsettling. For many adolescents, a more impersonal kind of substitute care seems advisable (a boarding or group home).

> The needs of the adolescent for identity, for peer relationships, for sexual and social experimentation, for independence and dependence, for freedom and authority, for simultaneous social immersion and withdrawal, all indicate that the adaptation to a foster family is a hard and often a futile task. Only the exceptionally normal adolescent fits smoothly into such a new "home." Only the exceptional foster home fits him. An adolescent who wants to live in a foster home possibly never had an opportunity to live in a normally functioning family. The adolescent who has lived most of his life in group care and wants to have a family experience before adulthood

degree to which a facility can work with the impulse-ridden, aggressive child and the child with severely impaired reality apperception; 4) the staff's expectation of normalcy of behavior by the new children.

Although many facilities can serve a large variety of children, a substantial number of them are faced with the problem of admitting children whose disturbances cannot be dealt with by their program. . . .

Group homes too have been found to serve disturbed children and have been used successfully as supplements and substitutes for treatment centers. It is necessary, however, to consider more cautiously the range of disturbances that can be handled in an open group home.

The severely aggressive child and the mentally sick child are of special concern to all practitioners in treatment centers. [Pp. 287-288]

Regarding the mentally ill child, Mayer, Richman, and Balcerzak observe:

Increasingly, mentally sick children are not kept for long-term care in hospital settings and increasingly they are referred to group care. . . . Unfortunately, some of the least equipped settings have accepted some of the most seriously mentally sick children.

Group care facilities can help this type of child only in conjunction with psychiatric hospitals, through contracts and agreements that include a number of provisions:

a) The hospital and the group care facility must remain in the picture at all times and work closely together.

b) They must accept each other's evaluation of the child's need for one or the other facility without new intake procedures and diagnostic studies.

c) They must expect the child's stay in either facility to be only a segment of the treatment and not charge each other with "failure" if a stay is interrupted, when, in fact, such interruptions are part of an expected course.

d) They must interpret these changes to the child and his parents in a similar way.

Psychiatric hospitals are a part of the child care and mental health system. . . . It is to be noted, however, that constructive cooperation between psychiatric hospitals and group care facilities is possible only if both facilities provide quality care. [Pp. 289-290]

Special problems exist in the case of the child who engages in violent or physically aggressive behavior.

each option and its assets and liabilities. A sound working knowledge of community resources is essential to effective social work practice.

A critical factor in any differential placement decision is the effect a given choice will have on the natural parents and the interventions needed to assist them with problems that precipitated the placement. Since the desired goal of many foster care arrangements is to reunite the child with his/her parents or at least help the child maintain a relationship with his/her natural family, it is important to select the type of substitute care that makes the achievement of this goal possible.

Below is a list of questions that may help the social worker and/or consultants decide whether a particular child should be placed in foster family care or in another type of substitute care. If several questions are answered with a yes, it is likely that foster family care is inappropriate and that a group home or residential treatment center would be more appropriate.

—— 1. Is the child fifteen or older?
—— 2. Has the child's previous experience with family life been so negative that he/she is unable to relate to parental figures?
—— 3. Is the child clearly a danger to him-/herself or others?
—— 4. Does the child engage in behavior that will invite strong negative reactions from neighbors and law enforcement officials, e.g. fire setting, abuse of children or animals, sexual exposure, or violence?
—— 5. Is the child so impulsive or so lacking in self-control that a structured environment and twenty-four-hour supervision is necessary?
—— 6. Is the controlling influence of a peer group necessary to bring about needed behavioral changes?
—— 7. Does the child have parents who are so disruptive, unpredictable, and uncontrollable (even with a court restraining order) that they will frighten and intimidate foster parents and/or other children in the foster home?
—— 8. Is the child unable to benefit from resources of the public school, even one with good programs of special

education and other special services?

—— 9. Have previous foster family placements been unsuccessful?

—— 10. Does the child require an amount of time for training, tutoring, or supervision in excess of the amount that could be devoted by foster parents involved in ordinary family activities and responsibilities?

—— 11. Is the level of knowledge and skill required to meet the child's physical, psychological, and social needs beyond that which can be provided by specially trained foster parents and those willing to work under close professional supervision?

—— 12. Is the child unable to participate in and sometimes enjoy the give-and-take of ordinary family life, e.g., sharing, tolerance, performing jobs around house, and respecting privacy of others?

—— 13. Does the child have a serious problem with alcohol or drug abuse?

—— 14. Does the child frequently engage in behavior that will offend the values and standards of even the most tolerant of foster parents (excessive stealing, foul language, outrageous dress, sexual promiscuity, seduction of children, or prostitution, etc.)?

—— 15. Does the child have a history of running away from other foster family homes?

—— 16. Assuming that the child's return to his/her biological home is desirable and feasible, would placement in foster family care, as compared to another form of substitute care, decrease the chances of the child being returned to his/her biological parents?

—— 17. In the case of a large sibling group, would it be possible to keep the children together in a form of group care but not in foster family care?

—— 18. Is the degree of attachment between the child and his/her natural parents so intensely loyal or of such a possessive nature that it will prevent the child from forming relationships with other parental figures?

—— 19. Is the child so narcissistic or self-serving that a foster family placement would create a situation where the child takes from the foster parents but gives nothing in return (warmth, appreciation, and respect, etc.)?

—— 20. Is the child opposed to placement into foster family care while expressing a preference for another type of substitute care?

—— 21. If the child is approaching adolescence and there is reason to believe that the adolescent period will be particularly stormy, is the adolescent eruption likely to exceed the coping capacities of a foster family?

—— 22. If the child has serious emotional or behavioral problems, are these of long duration in contrast to problems of recent origin or ones precipitated by a crisis situation?

It must be emphasized that the questions presented above at best are a checklist or an aid to decision making. This set of questions is not a validated instrument. The yes-or-no answers to these questions should be considered within the context of other assessment data.

What Is Meant by Social Assessment?

As used by professional social workers, the term *social assessment* refers to a study or an evaluation of an individual's or a system's, e.g. family or group, social functioning. Whereas the physician is concerned with physical functioning and the psychologist with psychological functioning, the traditional focus of the social worker has been on social functioning. According to Siporin (1975), the term

> *social functioning* [italics added] refers to the way individuals or collectivities (families, associations, communities, and so on) behave in order to carry out their life tasks and meet their needs. . . .
>
> Social functioning represents an exchange balance, match, goodness of fit, and reciprocal adaptation, between people, individually or collectively, and their environment, as in a good adjustment between a student, his family, school, and neighborhood. It therefore is a systemic product of a complementary transaction and exchange in terms of the needs, resources, expectations-motivations

and competence of people, and of the demands, resources, opportunities, and capabilities of the environment. Positive, adequate
functioning, as in completing one's life tasks, is satisfying and rewarding both to the individual and to the collectivity. However, an
individual or social system may be dysfunctional in that role performance and the nature of the situation may be frustrating, alienat-
ing, or incompetent; the personality and social system needs or
goals would then be met inadequately or poorly. Such dysfunctioning represents a lack of complementarity, a mismatching, an unequal
exchange, or ecological imbalance, between people and their environments. For both the individual and the social system, expectations
and tasks may be too stressful, undemanding, ill timed, conflicting,
or discrepant; obstacles may be too severe; resources may be lacking; capabilities or competence may be impaired or undeveloped.
[Pp. 17-18]

The concept of social role frequently is used to explain social
functioning.

Effective role performance by individuals, as in father or mother
roles, refers to the utilization of resources and the accomplishment
of tasks so that the individual and his collective, such as his family, are able to survive, grow, produce, realize themselves, and enjoy their lives. This role performance is judged by the person and
by the community to be effective or adequate, according to certain
norms and values. Social functioning is thus evaluated as to whether
it is need-satisfying and welfare-contributing to the person and to
his community, as well as to whether it is normal and socially approved. [Siporin, 1975, P. 17]

In explaining social assessment, Horner and Morris (1977)
contrast social assessment with psychological assessment and
note that

social assessment appears to have some distinct advantages over psychological assessment. By identifying relational, interactional, and
contextual components of a problematic activity, multiple points of
intervention become discernable. Similarly, the field from which to
draw resources for change greatly expands. This also appears to be
a better perspective for assessing the consequences of intervention
and thus for weighing the advantages of variety of intervention strategies. For example, intervention efforts can be assessed in terms of
their consequences for ongoing patterns of social relationships involving the client. Additionally, the interactional perspective em-

bodied in social assessment permits the development of action-re-action-action sequences in intervention planning. Perhaps the major disadvantage is captured in the saying that "it's a big world out there." That is, the assessment of social circumstances seems infinitely complex, making it difficult to know where to start, and easy to get off on the wrong track, as well as potentially time consuming. [Pp. 3-4]

The reader with an interest in more technical approaches to the assessment of social functioning may want to review Giesmar (1971) and Heimler (1967). Most basic texts on social work practice present outlines that can be used to guide the social assessment process. Such outlines are helpful in that they remind the social worker of the many elements in a complete social assessment and provide a way of organizing a written social study report. However, an assessment outline is never a substitute for assessment skills, such as involving the client in the exchange of information, sorting out contradictory information, deciding what information actually is needed, analyzing and interpreting social data, and dealing with value conflicts and biases in interpersonal communication. The social assessment outline is not unlike an outline used by a physician to conduct a physical examination. It is a reminder of the information to be gathered, e.g. blood pressure, blood chemistry, and weight, but the outline does not inform the user how to gather or interpret the data.

A social assessment is not the mere collection of information. A particular social assessment is always guided by the problem to be worked and the nature of the agency service. The information to be gathered should be relevant to a given problem or situation of concern to the client and/or social worker. For this reason, the best assessment guidelines are those that have been designed for use in specific programs or in relation to specific types of problem situations. Thus, it is suggested that the social worker construct his/her own assessment guideline or outline, one that meets his/her needs.

A sample assessment outline is presented in Appendix B. It was designed for use in assessing the social functioning of a family in which a child was experiencing difficulty. It can be shortened or modified to fit situations common to foster family services.

CHAPTER 3

The Natural Parents

What Is Meant by the Term Natural Parent and Natural Family?

A s USED HERE and in most of the child welfare literature, the term *natural parent* refers to the adult(s) who had custody of the child prior to placement into foster care. In most cases, the natural parent is also the biological parent, but there are exceptions. In some cases, the natural parent is a grandparent or other relative. In the case of an adopted child who becomes a foster child, the adoptive parent is the natural but not the biological parent.

The concept of a natural family is more complex. According to one glossary (U. S. Department of Health, Education and Welfare, National Center on Child Abuse and Neglect, 1978), a family can be defined as

> Two or more persons related by blood, marriage, or mutual agreement who interact and provide one another with mutual physical, emotional, social and/or economic care. Families can be described as "extended," with more than one generation in the household; or "nuclear," with only parent(s) and child(ren). Families can also be described as . . . "multiparent," as in a commune or collective; or "single parent." [P. 31]

In work with natural families, it is essential that the social worker identify and establish working relationships with all members of a family. In the extended families common to certain cultural groups, e.g. American Indians, many individuals—in addition to the biological parents (aunts, uncles, grandparents, and cousins, etc.)—may view themselves as parents to a specific child and therefore should be involved in foster-care-related decisions. Moreover, the child will consider many family members to be his/ her parents.

Is It Possible to Assist the Troubled Family and Prevent Out-of-Home Placements?

One of the great tragedies is that so little is done to keep families together and prevent foster home placements. Society and the child welfare agencies that reflect our commitment to families and children have not adequately developed the resources needed to assist families, especially those at risk of losing their children to foster care. In reporting his study of foster care in Massachusetts, Gruber (1977) states:

> Virtually no effort is made to keep the biological family together and to prevent children from being placed into foster care.
> There were 82% of the parents who saw a social worker six times or less before the placement, and 60% who were in contact with the foster care agency 2 weeks or less before the child was removed from home. In addition, it was shown that 23% of the children are placed in foster homes as a result of the mental illness of a parent. This indicates the lack of community-based services available to the disturbed parent who still maintains a child in his own home. Finally, though many of the parents felt that services such as day care, counseling and homemakers would have made placement unnecessary, the Division of Family and Children's Services has only minimal ability to provide them. [P. 176]

Similar conclusions are reported by Ferleger and Cotter (1976); Vasaly (1976); and in the Children's Bureau report, *Child Welfare in 25 States—An Overview* (1976). In most communities, there is a desperate need for a full range of family support services, those that could help families care for their children and thereby reduce the need for out-of-home placements. There is evidence to support the belief that skilled social workers and a full range of family support services can reduce the number of placements and shorten the length of time a child is in foster care. One of the more successful efforts to improve services for families is known as Comprehensive Emergency Services (CES), developed in Nashville, Tennessee. According to a 1977 U. S. Department of Health, Education and Welfare publication entitled *Comprehensive Emergency Services*, CES is a system of coordinated services designed to meet emergency needs of children and their families in crisis providing options in care which will protect children and reduce the trauma induced by the crisis. It provides a vehicle for cooperative program planning between agencies and involves a concentrated effort to provide quality service to neglected, dependent, and abused children on a twenty-four hour basis, including weekends and holidays. CES seeks to maintain children in their own homes during crisis situations. In cases where separation from the home environment is necessary, services are provided to children and their families insuring a more orderly, less damaging placement of children. [P. 7]

At the heart of a CES system is community-wide planning and coordination efforts that make a quick and effect response possible.

Comprehensive Emergency Services provides immediate service to a child and his family, and assures continuing service as needed. It should not be considered a "rescue" service only although it may guard the life of an endangered child. Rather CES is a well-planned, coordinated child welfare system designed specifically to

(1) Identify families and children in crisis

(2) Assess the immediate needs of the child and his family

(3) Provide twenty-four hour emergency services, by trained social service personnel, directed toward protecting the child in his own home or by making suitable placements when indicated

(4) Provide outreach and follow-up to these families to insure a continuum of service in an orderly way. [P. 11]

The CES system consists of seven basic and essential components. They are twenty-four-hour emergency intake, emergency caretakers, emergency homemakers, emergency foster family homes, emergency shelters for families, emergency shelters for adolescents, and outreach and follow-up. Two additional services, emergency neighborhood crisis centers and emergency day care, may be needed in some communities. Drawing on the U. S. Department of Health, Education and Welfare publication cited, the seven essential services are described below.

Twenty-four-hour Emergency Intake

Twenty-four-hour emergency intake is a service designed to utilize an answering service at night, on weekends and holidays, and to screen calls and refer emergencies to the caseworker on call. . . .

While the emergency intake unit must have an expert screening method for determining emergency from non-emergency situations, it must also have the capability for immediate follow-through on all identified emergencies. This unit must be manned by trained casework staff with competent skills in:

(1) Interviewing

(2) Dealing with potentially volatile situations

(3) Dealing with other people tactfully (both lay and professional persons)

Caseworkers in this unit rotate for night and weekend duty and are available immediately to handle emergency situations involving a child. In order to function smoothly there must be a plan worked out with the local police and juvenile probation officers so that they provide any needed support and protection to the worker. Without a carefully developed plan and defined roles, severe problems will result, adversely affecting the child and his family. . . .

Emergency Caretakers

Emergency caretakers are people carefully selected and trained to go into homes to provide responsible adult care and supervision for children in crisis. The primary function of the emergency caretaker is to provide care and supervision of a child in his own home at a time when supervision is lacking because parents are either temporarily absent or incapacitated.

This component provides the emergency intake worker with another option for responding to child emergencies. By using an emergency caretaker the child remains at home in an environment that is both familiar and secure. The service is terminated when the parent or a relative returns and is able to resume care or when an emergency homemaker is assigned on the next working day. Emergency caretaker service, while involved for only a brief time, is important precisely because that period is so crucial. Caretakers often provide valuable observations regarding the quality of care the child has been receiving in the home. This information can aid the intake worker in his decision to keep the child in the home or remove him for protective purposes. For this reason, caretakers need to have knowledge of children's behavior and the ability to make meaningful observations. . . .

Emergency Homemakers

Emergency homemakers are available for twenty-four-hour assignments to maintain children in their own homes until the parent is able to resume their care or until it is decided that another course of action should be taken.

While caretakers are assigned to the home at the point of initial crisis to provide child care for a few hours duration, emergency homemakers may be assigned to provide services throughout the emergency situation. The emergency homemaker service becomes an integral part of outreach services to families to maintain the family as an intact unit. The emergency homemaker works closely with the caseworker to form a team approach to helping the family cope with its problems. Once the situation reaches a point that the homemaker is needed in the home only during the day to serve in a teaching, and/or supportive role, regular homemaker service can be utilized, thus freeing the emergency homemaker for other families. (Regular homemakers should have flexible day time hours if they are to serve as a back-up service for emergency homemakers.)

Emergency homemakers can be used successfully when there is:

(1) a parent absent from the home due to emergency situations, such as physical or mental illness, desertion or some other emergency which causes the parent, usually the mother, to be away for a period of time.

(2) suspected child abuse and the parent is obviously immature and insecure in the parenting role. In these cases the homemaker often serves as the substitute parent to both mother and child. With the support of the homemaker and the teaching that occurs, the mother may become able to function in her parenting role. If not, then orderly placement of the child can be made. These cases usually require supervision for a period of time, after the homemaker is removed from the situation.

(3) failure to thrive and the parents need assistance and encouragement in the feeding and nurturing of a child. Emergency homemakers can supplement the work of the public health nurse which is usually more instructional in nature. In their assignment to such situations, emergency homemakers have uncovered in some parents a very serious lack of knowledge of infant care.

(4) gross neglect, posing an immediate threat to the children's safety as a result of inadequate nutrition and medical care. Immediate placement in an institution has been avoided by the emergency homemaker's efforts to relieve the urgency of the situation. Later assignment of a regular homemaker for teaching purposes can occur. . . .

Emergency Foster Family Homes

Emergency foster family homes provide temporary care for children who cannot be maintained in their own home. These homes are designed to minimize the emotional shock caused by removing children from their families by providing them with a home environment as an alternative to institutional placement. When emergency placement is necessary, children are returned home or placed in other appropriate facilities as quickly as possible, preferably in two weeks and in no more than one month.

Compensation

Emergency foster parents must be adequately compensated. They should be paid a monthly retainer fee plus reimbursement for the child's living costs. A paid vacation to ensure periodic relief is essential. The support system for these parents must be excellent as some of the problems and subsequent pressures of providing emergency foster care are quite different from regular foster care. The emergency foster parent is allowed no preference as to the kind of child she will take or the time of day (or night) of the placement. Many emergency placements involve children who are emotionally upset and in poor physical condition. The emergency parent has often just gotten the child settled when it is time for him to leave. Therefore, she sees little of the long range results of her work. The frequent turnover increases the demands on the emergency foster parent because of the variety of personalities and problems encountered. . . .

Emergency Shelter for Families

Emergency family shelter is a facility that provides temporary shelter for the entire family, rather than separating the children from their parents.

There are numerous ways of providing this component. An apartment or house with a limited staff in residence might meet the needs of some communities while others may wish to contract with an agency already providing this kind of service, thereby assuring space and immediate access to shelter care for families.

Some family shelter programs may provide only the physical facilities to accommodate families, and assistance in relocation. Others may include casework services to the families. When casework services are provided by the staff of the family shelter agency, the emergency service worker's function is referral, coordination, and follow-up. Agencies with sufficient, trained staff can develop highly supportive environments for parents who are abusive or potentially abusive and can deliver a wide range of therapeutic services to the entire family. . . .

Outreach and Follow-up

Outreach and follow-up provide ongoing casework assistance and supervision to families in their efforts to cope with problems. The service must be available in a formalized way for those families in need of continuing social services. Whether provided by the emergency intake worker or assigned to another caseworker, immediate contact with the family the day following the reported crisis is essential.

If during the period of emergency services the staff has been able to relate positively to the family and has involved the family in solving its own problems, then follow-up on a voluntary basis is eminently desirable. In other cases, however, the authority of the court must be used to protect the child. An absolute necessity for follow-up is that agreements and/or procedures for transfer be clearly outlined so there is no break in service to the family. At the point the emergency service worker transfers the supervision of the family to another caseworker, it is important that a case conference be held so that there is full understanding of the family's problems and needs. The parents must understand that emergency service is only temporary and that other people will be involved with them on a long range basis. They must be helped to accept the transfer of the relationship.

Any breakdown in the provision of follow-up services can negate much of what was accomplished during the emergency service phase and confirm a pattern that is all too well known in child welfare—that of working with parents only from one crisis to the next. The CES system must operate to provide successful early intervention and long term follow-through to truly help families in crisis. . . .

Emergency Shelter for Adolescents

This type of emergency care can be provided by a group home or institutional type program. Older children often have particular problems and needs which cannot be dealt with by a foster family home. Frequently these children have become detached from their families, or have had little parental supervision for a long period of time, and are resentful of adults. They often have a history of being run-aways, drug users, etc. While they may be classified as pre-delinquent or have court records of past delinquency at the point they come to the attention of the emergency intake unit, it is because of neglect, abuse, or a crisis in their home, and this must be handled as such. These are children who do not need to be placed in Juvenile Detention, which will occur if other resources are not available. These youth cannot adjust to a foster family home as they cannot tolerate the closeness of a family or the supervision provided by foster parents. [Pp. 19-31]

Services such as those provided in a CES system are needed and necessary to any effort aimed at reducing out-of-home placements. However, the development and expansion of basic social services are only a partial solution. Many of the problems associated with out-of-home placements are those on which social workers and social services can have little impact. They are large-scale social problems deeply rooted in our socioeconomic structure and values.

The problems of poor housing, poverty, lack of medical care, inadequate education, unemployment, and discrimination are the primary causes of parent-child separations in most cases. Regardless of the quality of preplacement services and supervision, these problems will exist. The fact of the matter, therefore, is that so long as dire human needs are unattended to, no amount of family services will be successful in keeping families together. [Gruber, 1977, p. 177]

Community services such as the CES system can deal with the secondary causes of out-of-home placements. Large-scale national efforts are needed to deal with the primary causes.

What Approaches Can Be Used in Work with the Multiproblem Family?

A high proportion of foster children come from so-called multiproblem families. This term often is applied to a family in which more than one family member is experiencing one or more serious social, psychological, economic, or health problems. The families frequently are poor. Problems of illness, alcoholism, unemployment, mental disturbance, family violence, drug abuse, mental retardation, and physical disability are fairly common in these families. Members of the multiproblem family usually are known to health and social service agencies. In reviewing data on the multiproblem family, Brown (1968) described

a series of studies which indicated that a small segment of families

consumed the lion's share of community services. The best known
report, of course, was on the Family Centered Project of St. Paul,
Minnesota, which said that 6% of the city's families accounted for
77% of its public assistance, 51% of its health services, and 56%
of its adjustment services—in mental health, correction and casework. Similar findings were reported from studies in San Mateo
County, California, Washington County, Maryland, and Winona
County, Minnesota. Most dramatic of all, perhaps, was the finding of
New York City's Youth Board that one percent of families were responsible for 75% of the city's delinquency. [P. 8]

Of special significance is that these serious problems coexist with
a sense of helplessness and hopelessness on the part of the family.
In short, the families are overwhelmed with day-to-day problems,
and one crisis or emergency follows another. Collins's (1969)
book provides highly readable descriptions of the day-to-day
problems experienced by these families.

Many who encounter multiproblem families express dismay
over the fact that the family members experience a great deal of
frustration and unhappiness, simultaneously demonstrating an
apparent lack of motivation to make changes in their life situation. That paradox is best explained by *learned helplessness*, a
concept borrowed from learning theory and used to explain certain forms of mental depression. Individuals subjected to pain,
whether physical or emotional, attempt to escape or fight back.
However, if repeated efforts to escape or fight back are unsuccessful, individuals eventually become apathetic. They conclude
that the situation cannot be controlled or influenced and come
to believe it is hopeless. They see themselves as helpless. Without
hope that things can be different, they give up and become
passive. Hooker (1976) notes that

> the experimental evidence indicates that learned helplessness de-
> velops when one objectively is or believes oneself to be unable to
> control the outcome of events. This cognitive disturbance gives rise
> to the motivational and emotional aspects of learned helplessness. If
> a person believes himself to be unable to control the outcome of life
> events and fails to see that his actions make a difference, he is less
> motivated to try. [P. 195]

Individuals who conclude that things are hopeless may become
angry when someone tries to help. Experience has taught them

that efforts to change are painful, and the last thing they want is more frustration.

Many individuals in multiproblem families have grown up in an environment of hopelessness. After many setbacks in life, they have concluded that no amount of personal effort could change their situations; they believe they are failures. As with the depressed individual, it is difficult to modify such a negative mind set.

Family-centered interventions designed to reverse learned helplessness must begin with helping the client work on a single, small task. Each small success is used to demonstrate that the client has some control. "A suggested technique is to start the individual on a program of behavioral change where, following a sequence of incremental steps of action, the affected individual can experience and learn the relationship between behavior and outcome" (Hooker, 1976, p. 197).

Essentially, a behavior-shaping procedure is used to raise the client's hopes. The reader will notice that this approach is similar to that used in behavioral contracting and the task-centered approach. Both place emphasis on starting with a problem of real concern to the client, focusing on small, achievable tasks, reinforcing each small success, and then repeating the process over and over again. The emphasis placed on data collection and the selection of small but measurable objectives helps the client to recognize change and success. Over time, these small achievements cause the client to reevaluate his/her beliefs about helplessness and failure. Progress is slow but change is possible.

Since the mid 1950s, a number of social work research and demonstration projects have attempted to discover or develop effective methods of assisting the multiproblem family. Results have been encouraging in some of the projects; others have failed to demonstrate effectiveness (Geismar 1972b). One of the first projects to focus on the development of social work techniques for use with the multiproblem family was the St. Paul Family Centered Project, which focused on families in which there was serious child neglect. In describing the project families, Overton et al. (1957) state that in only half (49%) of our families are both parents in the home. The number of children is large, averaging six per family. When first known to the Project 68% of the families were receiving public assistance, and 98% had at some time in the past received financial aid from the public agency. The incidence of juvenile delinquency is high. In a representative group of 100 families, 97 children from 47 families were known to the probation office. In 45 families there had been an adjudicated adult crime for either the father or mother or both. Problem drinking of one or both parents occurred in 47 families out of the 100. [P. 5]

Instead of waiting until the family problems became even worse, project workers used reaching-out techniques. The significance of the St. Paul Project is that it demonstrated that these families could be reached and engaged in an effective helping process. The approaches used were time consuming and somewhat unconventional. Of interest is the fact that twenty years ago there were social workers who used techniques described now in the literature on learned helplessness. The basic strategy was to overcome the family's fear and distrust, demonstrate usefulness, and then uncover and build upon existing family strengths. Emphasis was placed on making small, tangible behavioral changes, e.g. getting the dishes washed or making a telephone call, and then using this sense of success as a means of building hope and demonstrating that something could be done about the problems they were experiencing.

In describing the methods used in the St. Paul Project, Overton et al. (1957) observe:

> When for years a family has lacked motivation for adequate functioning, changes very seldom take place overnight. The rediscovery or development of the will to strive for a better life is in itself a major undertaking. Then there are new patterns of living to be learned and many adjustments to make. As social workers, we offer our services with all the skill we possess. The family and its members will use them as they are able. In the Project we have come to see these services as involving several casework processes by which motivation can be strengthened and guided. We start with the family by presenting plainly and firmly the basis of concern. This may serve to arouse anxiety but it will probably remain concealed under a cloak of resistance. Then we demonstrate our readiness and ability to be of immediate service. We have called this "proving our utility value." We try to give some practical and tan-

gible help with whatever problem, however incidental it may seem to us, is named by the family as their choice of a place to start. We have learned not to expect the family even to consider more distant goals until much later on. The gradual development of their trust in the worker must come first. Only then can they accept the support and recognition they need to uncover and develop their own motivation for larger positive gains. [P. 126]

. . .

This developing and shaping of goals in relation to whatever the family seeks continues throughout our work with them. We watch for signs of any discomfort or anxiety in family members which may serve as a motive for further effort to move ahead. On occasion we may even heighten their concern by bringing forcefully to their attention the implications of such behavior as gross neglect of the children. We try to share with the family our own conviction that gains can be made and our knowledge of ways and means to move ahead. Should their effort at any point lead only to failure, we stand with them in facing it, in trying to understand what went wrong and in considering what to do next. We rejoice with them whenever a step ahead is successful. Whatever happens, we try to keep always in mind that the thoughts and feelings of each member of the family are his own, developing within him in relation to how he as a person reacts to all that happens to him. . . .

It does take hope and courage for a worker to reach out to families in trouble who think they do not want his services. Returning again and again until the family dares to trust our intent and to rely upon our help requires strong faith in human nature. . . .

Early contacts will often include much watchful waiting on your [the social worker's] part while you give attention to whatever immediate worry the parents will name as needing remedy. Most families have to become sure that the worker likes them and can be trusted before they can hazard even speaking of their more personal concerns. [Pp. 122-124]

In summarizing the results of their four-year project, Overton et al. (1957) make the following observation:

What have we learned about the "how" of family centered social work with disorganized families? Here are some of the points we are more sure of:

  a) Persistent reaching out to distrustful, disorganized families is a "must." To do this requires conviction about our right to intrude, reduction of our own resistance and more skill in meeting the resistance of the family.

  b) A carefully structured approach to family diagnosis in relation to family functions and the roles of individual members has helped us understand "What's the trouble? How come? What can be done about it?'" We have found it imperative to observe family transactions in the home, and to put these observations to use in treatment. Therefore, home visits are seen as essential to the role of the worker as observer-participant in family centered treatment.

c) Emphasis on parents and upon their motivations for change opens the way for joint planning, to reduce the trouble and increase the satisfactions of family life.

d) The multi-problem family needs one worker to evaluate its total service needs, to meet as many of them as he can and to coordinate such other services as may be required. It is unfair to expect deprived families to understand the fine print of social work specialization before they can value the large print of SOCIAL WORK in the person of one general practitioner.

e) Stock taking with the family at intervals should include not only an evaluation of progress or lack of it but also the family's evaluation of the services received. [P. 159]

In the twenty years since St. Paul Project, a substantial body of professional literature has been developed around the multi-problem family. Viewpoints and techniques have changed somewhat. New approaches, such as crisis intervention, the use of indigenous workers, and self-help groups, have been introduced. In recent years, much emphasis has been placed on the teaching of specific coping or survival skills. Agencies have attempted to modify programs so services are more relevant and responsive to the real needs of these families. Most professionals now recognize that social services never are a substitute for adequate housing, income, and health care. They also recognize that social services alone cannot overcome the forces of discrimination associated with racism, sexism, and handicapism. It is clear now that interventions aimed at helping the individual family must coexist with those aimed at modifying the broader social forces that cause many of the family's problems. However, many of the original insights obtained in the St. Paul Project still are valid, especially the ones related to the process of reaching out, overcoming fears, taking on one small step at a time, and building a sense of hope. No one yet has found a substitute for the many hours needed to help the families make even small gains. Thirty to fifty hours of attention may be necessary to overcome the family's initial fears and hostility. Effective social work with the multiproblem family is time consuming and expensive.

Over the past twenty years, experience has shown that traditional approaches to psychotherapy and psychiatric treatment have little to offer multiproblem families. This is because their problems are not only psychological; they also are social, economic, and physical. In an article by Malcolm (1978), well-known psychiatrist Salvador Minuchin is quoted.

> Psychiatry sometimes presents itself as if it knew the answers to social problems, as if it could save people from the tragedies of poverty. What we do when we bring psychiatry to the slums is to put Band Aids on people. . . . We work with a mother on how to feel more competent with her children when she is living on an income that makes it impossible to be competent. If you are raising four children on three thousand dollars a year, you have problems that don't exist for someone who has thirty thousand dollars a year. We operate as if the problem were psychological because the only thing we have is Band Aids. . . . Psychiatry is the only thing we have, so that's the thing we give. We are not revolutionaries, and we are not even reformers. We are accommodators. [P. 49]

Those interested in learning about the multiproblem family may wish to read Brown (1968); Collins (1969); Feldman and Scherz (1967); Fischer (1973); Geismar (1969, 1971, 1972a): Glasser and Glasser (1970); Goldstein (1973); Haley (1976); Polansky, DeSaix, and Sharlin (1972); and Reissman, Cohen, and Pearl (1964). Many professional journals, especially *Social Casework, Social Work, Child Welfare,* and the *Journal of Orthopsychiatry,* publish articles on work with multiproblem families.

Where Does the Professional Begin in Work with the Parents of a Child in Foster Care?

Initial efforts in work with the natural parents should focus on the clarification of their rights and responsibilities and the formulation of a written treatment contract. Gruber (1977) states that the contract or agreement should specify:

a. How often the parent agrees to see the child and how long the visits will be

b. How much the parent will pay toward the support of the child while in a foster home

c. The parent's responsibility for taking the child to physician, dentist, and other appointments

d. The parent's responsibility for continuing contact with the child's school

e. The parent's responsibility with regard to participating in a treatment program for his or her own problems

f. Other responsibilities to be negotiated. [P. 191]

Given the importance of achieving permanence for the child in foster care, the social worker must give immediate attention to this issue. The emphasis on permanence is reflected in a policy statement issued by the City of New York Department of Social Services (1978).

> The highest priority, from the point of intake on, must be given to working with biological parents explicitly around the achievement of permanence. Within 60 days after placement, a service plan must be jointly developed by the agency worker, the parents, and the child, if appropriate, which identifies concrete goals and how they are to be achieved, describes what services are to be provided and by whom, makes provision for visiting, and establishes a time schedule for achieving the goals. Implementation of the service plan will require aggressive reaching out to the biological parents and extended family, consultations about the plan, arranging for and facilitating visits, directly providing or arranging for services, providing the families with opportunities to express problems and ask questions and seek support, and informing the parents of their child's progress. [P. 8]

It should be noted that permanency planning and the use of written contracts are discussed in Chapters 4 and 5.

What Should the Natural Parents Be Told about Their Rights and Responsibilities?

Clear communication and a good working relationship between the social worker and the natural parents are essential to favorable outcome in foster care. If the natural parent understands his/her rights and responsibilities, many of the problems commonly associated with foster care can be lessened or prevented. Below are some basic ideas or principles that need to be conveyed to natural parents. Several were adapted from *The Parents Handbook: A Guide for Parents of Children in Foster Care,* a fifteen-page booklet edited by Fleischmann (1977). This booklet is given to the parents of children in foster care.

It is important for you to understand that you are still your child's parent even while he or she is in placement. Your child needs you. He or she needs to know that you love and care about him or her even though you are not directly caring for him or her. Your child needs to keep in close contact with you.

It is important that you and your social worker make a "plan" and begin following it as soon as possible. If you do not work with the agency or keep in contact with your child, you could lose your rights as a parent.

The main person you talk to when your child is in placement is the . . . [social worker] at the agency caring for your child. The social worker has two main jobs: (1) to make sure that your child is getting good care and (2) to help your child return to a permanent home. This will mean either helping you to work out the problems that made placement necessary so that your child can return home, or finding another permanent home if return to your family is not possible or desirable.

You and your social worker should start to talk right away about the reasons why placement was necessary. Together, you will decide what changes need to be made by you, by your child, or by both of you and set up a "plan" for how to go about making these changes. This child care "plan" will work only when you and your caseworker work together cooperatively and keep in close contact with one another. You will be able to share information and concerns about your child. Your visits will be easier to arrange. Your social worker will be able to help you by providing advice and counseling, and by referring you to other kinds of services you may need.

Placement is a temporary period, hopefully a short one, when your child must live outside your home. But a permanent home is important to a child, and the goal always is to end placement and provide a child with permanence—either back in your home, or if that is not possible, in a new adoptive home.

The decision that it is time for your child to go home should be made together by you and your social worker. You must agree that there has been real improvement in the situation which made placement necessary. You should be visiting with your child as often as possible. These contacts will make it easier for you to prepare for his or her return, and for both of you to adjust to being together again. Together, you and your social worker should decide:

- When your child will return home
- How your child will be cared for and supervised at home
- If you need and are eligible for some financial help to get clothing and furniture for your child
- If you or your child need casework or other special services after discharge

You may decide that the only way your child can have a permanent, stable home is for you to plan for adoption. A child who is adopted goes to live with a new family permanently. This child takes the name of the new family and is legally a member of that family forever. A child can only be adopted by a new family after he or she has been made "free" for adoption. Then there must be a court order giving the new parents full responsibility and parental rights for the child.

You can voluntarily free your child for adoption by signing a legal document called a *surrender* or *relinquishment*. When you sign this document, you give up your parental rights. Since signing is a serious matter, you should think about it carefully and discuss it with your social worker and with a lawyer. After you sign a relinquishment document, you are no longer your child's legal guardian and are no longer responsible for your child's future.

When your child is free for adoption, the agency will try to find the best permanent home for him or her. If your child has lived in a foster home, his/her foster parents will usually be asked first if they want to become his or her adoptive parents. If they do not, the agency will look for other families until a suitable one is found.

It is important that you know and understand what your parental rights and responsibilities are while your child is in care. If you take full advantage of your rights and carry out your responsibilities, you can make placement a better experience for you and your child.

Your parental rights and responsibilities go together. If you do not carry out your parental responsibilities, you may lose or endanger your parental rights. If you cannot exercise your rights, you may be unable to carry out your responsibilities.

1. Your Rights:
   - To work together with your social worker in making the plan for your child.
   - To be consulted whenever a change in the plan is being considered.
   - To know what the agency expects you to do before your child is returned to you.
   - To visit your child. You and your social worker together will decide how often, when and where you should visit your child. You have the right to be alone with your child, and perhaps to have your child spend an afternoon with you outside the agency or visit you at home if that is part of the plan. However, judges and the agency social worker have the right to limit visiting if they decide that it will not be good for your child.
   - To appeal a decision limiting your visiting rights.
   - To be given carfare for your visiting, if you are financially eligible for it.
   - To meet the people who directly care for your child, such as counselors, houseparents, or foster parents.

- To get reports from your social worker on your child's health and development, progress in school, and behavior.
- To receive help and/or counseling for problems which need to be resolved before your child can return home.
- To receive help, if needed, for your children who remain at home with you.
- To have your child receive religious training if you have asked for it.
- To approve surgery or serious medical care if needed by your child, except when you cannot be reached in an emergency.
- To be notified as soon as possible of any serious medical emergency, and if any major treatment is given without your consent.
- To have your complaints listened to and responded to by the agency.
- To receive notice of and to attend any court action held about your child or about your parental rights, except if the court acts in an emergency.
- To consult with a lawyer at any time, and to be represented by a lawyer in any court action concerning your child or affecting your parental rights.

2. Your Responsibilities
    - To work with your social worker in setting up the plan for what you must do while your child is in care and for what will be best for your child's future.
    - To work toward solving the problems that prevent your child from coming home to you. If your social worker advises you to go somewhere to get help for a problem, you should follow up on that suggestion.
    - To visit your child regularly, at a time and place agreed upon with the agency social worker. This is so important that the law says that if you are able

to visit your child but make infrequent visits, you could lose your parental rights. If you cannot visit, you must tell the social worker why, and make every effort to call your child or write regularly.

- To talk about your child's care and progress with your social worker.
- To tell your social worker about major changes in your life, such as change of address, telephone number, job, income, marriage or other living arrangements and changes affecting other members of your family.
- To keep appointments with your social worker. If you cannot keep an appointment or must cancel a visit, let your social worker know.
- To answer letters that agency workers send to you. If your social worker asks for information about your child, it is very important that you provide it.
- To pay toward the cost of your child's care, if you are found to be able to do so. You must tell your social worker if your income changes.

Whenever you have a complaint or a problem, the first person to talk to is your caseworker at the agency caring for your child. An open discussion will often settle the matter. If you and your caseworker cannot resolve the problem, ask to speak to your worker's supervisor or the agency director.

Those working with natural parents may find a booklet by Rutter (1978) helpful. This CWLA publication concentrates on the needs of the natural parents.

Do Parental Visits to the Foster Child Affect Outcome?

The frequency and pattern of visits by the natural parents to their child in foster care are sensitive indicators of the child's future in substitute care. The more frequent the contact between parent and child, the greater the likelihood that the child will leave foster care and return to his or her own home. Given this relationship and an objective of returning the child to his or her natural parents, the social worker should do everything possible to facilitate visits between the parent and child in foster care. There is reason to believe that these visits are especially important early in the placement. Thus, rigid policies or rules that prohibit visiting during the first weeks of placement or otherwise limit the contact between natural parent and child tend to decrease the chance of a child leaving foster care and returning to his or her natural home.

Some important findings on parental visiting emerged from the study by Fanshel and Shinn (1978), which followed 624 foster children over a five-year period. In this study, Time I referred to the first ninety days of placement, Time II referred to a point about two and one-half years after the child entered foster care, and Time III referred to the period five years after placement. Fanshel and Shinn compared foster children who were frequently visited with those who were visited infrequently or not at all. They found:

1. Highly visited children showed significantly greater gains in nonverbal IQ scores from Time I to Time II.
2. Highly visited children showed significantly greater gains in verbal IQ scores over the full five years of the study.
3. Children who were highly visited showed more significant gains from Time I to Time II in a summary measure of their emotional adjustment as measured by the figure drawing tests.
4. Children who were highly visited showed significant changes in CBC scores (Child Behaviorial Characteristics) from Time I to Time II for the composite scores of: (a) responsibility and (b) agreeableness. From Time II to Time III high parental visiting was a positive predictor of change for: (a) defiance-hostility (negative correlation) and (b) emotionality-tension (negative correlation). For Time I to Time III, parental visiting helped predict change in: (a) agreeableness, (b) defiance-hostility (negative correlation), and (c) emotionality-tension (negative correlation).
5. A higher level of parental visiting was a significant predictor of an overall positive assessment by the child's classroom teacher. [Pp. 486-487]

Fanshel and Shinn (1978) conclude that parental visiting has a positive effect on most foster children:

In the main, we strongly support the notion that continued contact with parents, even when the functioning of the latter is marginal, is good for most foster children. Our data suggest that total abandonment by parents is associated with evidence of emotional turmoil in children. We can think of no more profound insult to a child's personality than evidence that the parent thinks so little of the relationship with him that there is no motivation to visit and see how he is faring. . . . It is our view that the parents continue to have significance for the child even when they are no longer present. [Pp. 487-488]

While these researchers offer data that underscore the positive effects of parental visiting, they recognize that visiting is not without stress. Visiting can be a stressful experience for the foster child, the natural parents and the foster parents. Fanshel and Shinn (1978) note:

It is not easy for the child to juggle two sets of relationships, and the caseworkers report that some children show signs of strain in the process. We maintain, however, that this is a healthier state of affairs than that faced by the child who must reconcile questions about his own worth as a human being with the fact of parental abandonment. [P. 488]

Why Do Parents Fail to Visit Their Children in Foster Care?

A small number of parents do not visit their children in foster care because they do not care for their children; most parents do care for their children. Yet, some of those who care greatly do not visit their children. Aside from the practical reasons that may prevent visiting, e.g. lack of transportation, lack of money for transportation, or an inability to get away from work at convenient visiting times, many parents stay away from their children for psychological reasons. They find visits to be a painful reminder of what they or others perceive as their failure as parents. Parents who have abused their children find visits to be a painful reminder of what they have done to their children. They find it difficult to observe foster parents doing for their children what they themselves should be doing or wish they knew how to do. Moreover, it is difficult for them to watch their children treat other adults as parents. In short, visits are painful experiences for many natural parents. To escape the emotional pain, they simply stay away from their children in foster care.

The pain of visiting also explains why some natural parents drink to excess before visits, are critical of the care given by the foster parents, bring their children gifts they cannot afford, or make promises that they cannot keep. These are their attempts, albeit ineffective ones, to cope with their feelings of inadequacy and failure in the parental role.

The longer the natural parents stay away from their children in foster care, the harder it becomes for them to garner enough courage to face visiting. For this reason, the social worker should do everything possible to facilitate visiting on a regular basis. It is important that visits begin early in the placement. The social worker should also explain that he/she knows that many parents find the visits unpleasant for the reasons described above. If the social worker can convey a sense of understanding of and an appreciation for the pain involved, the natural parents may overcome their resistance to visiting.

What Should the Social Worker Tell the Natural Parents about Visiting Their Child in Foster Care?

A statement by Jarrett (1977a) captures the essence of what should be communicated to the natural or biological parents. This message, of course, should be adapted to the individual needs and concerns of the parent and altered to fit the circumstances surrounding the placement. By permission of Janeil Jarrett, her statements are presented below.

> We [the agency staff] regard visiting as very important to keep family ties and to help your child feel more secure. It is important to start it soon after your child goes to a foster home and to make every effort to carry out planned visits. Visiting can be handled in many ways. Only you and [the social worker] can decide what is best for you and your child. The visits may be frequent or not, may take place at your home, the office, or the foster home. You have a responsibility to help make a plan and follow it. The more you can do to accept responsibility, such as providing transportation, keeping within scheduled times, taking good care of the child, and respecting the rights of the foster parents, the more frequent visits can usually be. When court proceedings are involved, the court may set a visiting schedule, in which case we will follow it.

Most parents worry about upsetting the children during visits or their being upset after visits. We can expect it to be an emotional time. You can help make visits easier by making them regularly so the child knows what to except, by planning an activity your child enjoys, by bringing something to eat or a gift, by not criticizing the foster parents to the child, by not engaging the foster parents in discussion of family problems, by continuing to explain to the child what the plans are, by expressing your love for the child, by not making false promises, by telling the child what you are doing toward having him/her return, and by controlling your emotions when the time comes to part again. Some of these are hard at first but can become second nature if repeated each time. Letters and telephone calls between visits can also be good. All these ways of communicating must be planned through [your social worker]. In spite of possible upset feelings, it has been shown that failure to visit and show interest in your child is more damaging. A temporary upset can be overcome much easier than feelings of having been abandoned. [P. 3]

What Should the Social Worker Tell the Natural Parents about Helping the Child in Foster Care?

Jarrett (1977a) has prepared a succinct message that should be communicated to the natural parent. It is important that this message be individualized to the needs and concerns of the parent and adapted to the parent's ability to understand.

As your child goes into foster care, it is very important for him/her to understand why it is necessary and why you are not able to care for him/her at this time. You can help by explaining that foster care will be better for him/her right now and by explaining that nothing he/she has done has caused the circumstances and separation from you. This will help your child feel less upset and feel better about himself/herself. Never think that a child is too young to understand. Even babies can sense how you feel.

Your child needs to know that you are not deserting him/her. You can help by assuring the child that you will keep in touch. This can be carried out through visiting, writing letters, and telephoning the child. Arrangements for these contacts must be made through your caseworker. You can help by planning with the caseworker about how long your child will be in foster care and explaining this plan to your child. This will help him/her not to feel abandoned.

You can help by accepting responsibility for some financial support of your child in foster care. Foster parents do not receive a salary, but we try to reimburse them for the expenses of the children in their care, such as room and board, clothing, school fees, and medicine chest supplies. It is important to your child to feel that you approve of the foster home and are helping to provide it. Helping to pay for the care is a way of showing your child that you still feel responsible for him/her. Whether you will be asked to help pay for the care depends on your ability to pay.

You can help by talking to your caseworker about your feelings about foster care and your child and by using the caseworker to help plan a permanent, secure future for the child. Your child will feel better if he/she can see the caseworker as someone who cares and wants to help the family to see that the child gets good care during a time when his/her parents cannot provide it alone.

You can help your child by keeping promises made and by explaining the reasons if you have to go back on a promise. It would be best not to make any promises you may not be able to keep. If you have to cancel a planned visit, be sure to let the caseworker know in time to explain to your child. Also be open about your plans and any change in your circumstances, so your child and we will know what to expect. Changes may include moving, taking a job, changing jobs, divorce, marriage, pregnancy—any events having an effect on your life. [Pp. 1-2].

How Often Should Natural Parents Be Allowed to Visit Their Children in Foster Care?

As a general rule, the visits should be frequent enough to maintain and enhance the parent-child relationship. Pike et al. (1977) suggest one afternoon per week as a rule of thumb and offer the following guidance:

> As a return home approaches, weekend visits can be included; however, a prolonged plan of four days in foster care and three days at home can threaten a child's sense of security.
>
> Disruptive visits may be limited to once a month, for one-half hour. [Pp. 56-57]

Where Should Visits Take Place?

Under ordinary circumstances, visits to the foster child by his or her natural parents should occur in the foster home. This natural and informal setting permits the child to show his/her parents personal possessions and hobbies, see his/her schoolwork, and meet his/her friends, etc. It also permits the parents to meet with the foster parents on a personal level and share common concerns about the child. There are two situations when it may be desirable to arrange the visits for another place: One is when the visits are highly disruptive to the child or the foster parents; the other is when there is good reason to believe that parental rights will be terminated, and the foster parents are likely to be the adoptive parents for the child now in their care. In such cases, there may be good reason to protect the identity of the potential adoptive family. This is especially true if there is good reason to believe that the natural parent will subsequently threaten or harm the adoptive parents or somehow disrupt the child's future adjustment in the adoptive home.

How Should Disruptive Visits by the Natural Parent Be Handled?

As explained elsewhere in this book, visits by the natural parents to their children in foster care are important, and they should be encouraged strongly. There are exceptions to this generalization, but they are probably fewer than commonly assumed. Disruptive visits present special problems. These may occur when the natural parents have serious behavioral problems (mental illness or alcoholism, etc.) or are so resentful of the placement that they are hostile or abusive toward all involved (agency, foster parents, social worker, and court, etc.). If the parents' behavior is vindictive and hostile, visits may be upsetting to the foster children and the foster parents. In cases where the visits are or probably will be disruptive, special adjustments are necessary.

> If the natural family member's behavior or contact is described by a foster parent as having a serious negative effect upon the placement, the worker needs immediately to find out details of what is going on and take whatever action is indicated if necessary, either limiting the contacts of the child with the natural family members or arranging for them to take place at a neutral location such as the agency office. [Aldridge, Cautley, and Lichstein, 1974, p. 331]

In short, the preferred way to handle disruptive visits is to limit the frequency and duration and, if necessary, arrange for the visits to take place somewhere other than in the foster home.

> Frequency and duration should be limited to the level the child can tolerate. In the case of open animosity and attack, visits can be restricted to once a month, in the office, one-half hour, supervised.
>
> Structure criteria for the parents' conduct in the interview; they can discuss the weather, school, fishing, etc., but they will not express vituperations against the other parent, complain of neurotic symptoms, promise the child a farm and pony, a new stepparent or imminent return home. Warn parents that violation of these expectations will result in a termination of the interview. [Pike et al., 1977, p. 57]

CHAPTER 4

Behavioral Contracting

How Are Behavioral Approaches Used in Foster Care?

INCREASINGLY, CONCEPTS of behavior modification, behavior therapy, and applied behavioral analysis are used within the field of child welfare. An interest in this approach was apparent in the early 1970s. In a special issue of *Child Welfare* devoted to behavioral approaches, Schoenberg (1973) noted that "interest in behavior modification theory is rapidly picking up speed in the child welfare field, with application of techniques following. Social work journal articles that tell of practice experiments in agencies are appearing ever more frequently."

The use of behavioral contracting with natural parents and foster parents is one obvious application. In addition, behavioral approaches are used with children and adolescents who have emotional and behavioral problems, with handicapped children who need special training, and in ordinary child management. While a sizable book is required to describe adequately the basic behavioral techniques and procedures, an attempt is made in this chapter to familiarize the reader with underlying assumptions and common terms and provide the reader with direction for additional study.

Behavioral approaches differ significantly from the more traditional models of intervention based on psychodynamic explanation of human behavior, but both models are concerned with changing behavior. The psychodynamic approach presumes that behavior change follows the modification of subjective feeling and increased self-understanding. In contrast, the behavioral model focuses directly on the behavior. Stuart (1974) applies the term *information therapist* to those professionals holding the psychodynamic viewpoint and *action therapist* to those with a behavioral orientation.

Information therapists tend to initiate the behavioral change process by seeking to change thoughts and feelings first, with changes in behavior and social experience following. . . .

The action therapist, on the other hand, seeks either to promote changes in the client's behavior directly (eliminating the necessity to make accurate inferences about the client's thoughts and feelings) or to "reprogram" key people in the client's environment to act differently toward the client (eliminating the problem of translating therapeutic information into action). For the action therapist, then, the chain of actions culminating [in modified client behavior is shortened considerably, eliminating] several potential obstacles to change. Success or failure thus occurs more promptly and hopefully more reliably than is true for information therapies. [Pp. 401-402]

In general, behavioral approaches emphasize interpersonal factors and the immediate social environment. Compared with those with a psychodynamic orientation, behaviorally oriented professionals place less emphasis on intrapsychic factors. It is assumed that behavior is learned and maintained because other people or forces in the environment reinforce and punish some human behaviors but not others. Behaviors that are reinforced tend to be repeated; behaviors that are not reinforced tend to decrease. This emphasis on the social environment is compatible with social work's traditional focus on social functioning, i.e. the interaction between the individual and his/her environment.

Behaviorally oriented professionals depart from the medical model and view behavior as adaptive or maladaptive, rather than healthy or sick. Some reject the concept of mental illness. They begin with the assumption that all behavior—whether adaptive or maladaptive—is learned and that the learning of behavior follows certain basic principles. By applying these same basic principles, it is possible to help an individual learn adaptive behavior and reduce or eliminate the occurrence of maladaptive behavior. Professionals with a behavioral orientation generally think in terms of specific behaviors rather than symptoms or personality traits. They find such terms as *passive-aggressive, character disorders, neurosis,* and *schizophrenia* too vague to be useful and believe that the use of such labels may do more harm than good.

It must be recognized that there are many behavioral approaches. In a recent book on the casework method in social work, Schwartz and Goldiamond (1975) note that ". . . there are many kinds of behaviorism just as there are many kinds of dynamic orientations." In recent years, developments in the various behavioral approaches, especially the cognitive approaches, have begun to bridge the separation between covert thought and overt behavior, between concepts of the dynamic orientation and the behavioral orientation. Mahoney (1974) observes that "As perceptual processing factors began receiving attention from behavioral quarters, it soon became apparent that the naive realism . . . [of the early proponents of behaviorism] was functionally untenable in human behavior. An individual responds—not to some *real* environment—but to a *perceived* environment. . . . Data from several different lines of research offered converging evidence on the critical role of cognitive factors in human behavior." Also, concepts of self-reinforcement are emerging. These developments also help bridge the more traditional dynamic approaches and the behavioral orientations.

A characteristic of the behaviorally oriented approach is the emphasis on clearly stated goals of intervention and the use of data as a means of planning and evaluating intervention. This is consistent with those developments in the human services that emphasize accountability and evaluation.

The social worker wanting to learn more about behavioral approaches has abundant resources on which to draw. Books written by or for social workers include Arkava (1974); Derek, Hardiker, Yelloly, and Shaw (1972); Fischer (1978); Fischer and Gochros (1975); Gambrill (1977); Rose (1977); Schwartz and Goldiamond (1975); Sundel and Sundel (1975); and E. Thomas (1974). Other references include DeRisi and Butz (1975); Goldfried and Davison (1976); Gottman and Leiblum (1974); Kanfer and Goldstein (1975); Krumboltz and Krumboltz (1972); Lazarus (1971, 1972); Mager and Pipe (1973); Patterson (1971); Schmidt (1976); Sharp and Wetzel (1969); Stuart (1970); and Thoreson and Mahoney (1974). These references can help the social worker become familiar with basic concepts and terminology such as operant behavior, respondent behavior, consequences, positive reinforcement, negative reinforcement, punishment, shaping, forward chaining, backward chaining, extinction, behavioral deficit, behavioral excess, schedules of reinforcement, modeling, etc.

The effectiveness of behavioral approaches has been impressive, especially for clearly defined problem behaviors. Like any type of intervention, thorough knowledge of technique and procedure and proper application are essential. Uninformed applications or the misapplication of principles can do more harm than good. It also is important to recognize that some concerns of the social worker do not lend themselves to a behavioral approach. Fischer and Gochros (1975), two of the most respected writers on the application of behavioral theory in social work, state:

> Many of the goals and activities of social work practice are either outside the boundaries of behavior modification as an intervention strategy, or are in early stages of development in behavior modification. For instance mobilizing, modifying and providing material resources is a major area of social work activity. Assisting individuals to make decisions—within the context of nurturing interpersonal relationship—is perhaps one of the unique and best developed areas of social work practice and is a major component of most social work helping. A whole range of common social work interventive practices involving community and societal change remain virtually untapped in the behavior modification literature. [P. xviii]

Because it is useful in many areas of child welfare practice, the social worker should possess basic skills in the application of behavioral techniques. One should not expect, however, that these techniques will prove useful in all situations or provide an easy answer to all complex problems.

What Are Behavioral Contracts?

Sundel and Sundel (1975) define a behavioral contract as "an agreement between two or more individuals in which the expected behaviors of each are specified along with the consequences for their performance or nonperformance." DeRisi and Butz (1975) explain:

> Contracting is a technique used to structure behavioral counseling by making each of the necessary elements of the process so clear and explicit that they may be written into an agreement for

behavior change that is understandable and acceptable to everyone involved. . . .

From the counselor's standpoint contracting is both a goal and a method. It is a goal because a new contract is the end result, the permanent product of each counseling session. It is also a method for reaching the other goals of counseling. The contract and its elements are the focus of sessions with clients; data collected in contracting process are indications of the relative success of counseling efforts. And records of past contracts can tell the counselor when to abandon strategies that are unsuccessful before too much time and effort are wasted. [Pp. 1-2]

Increasingly, contracts are used in social work practice (Maluccio and Marlow, 1974; Rhodes, 1977). For example, contracting is an important element of the task-centered approach, a model of social work intervention developed over the past ten years (Reid and Epstein, 1972).

[The] use of contracts help avoid certain perennial problems in social work practice: misunderstandings between worker and client as to the nature of the former's intention and the latter's difficulty . . . ; lack of clarity on the part of both as to what they are to do together; drift and scatter in the focus of treatment. Contracting, as do most things in social treatment, works best when the client has an active interest in getting help and some notion of what he wants to accomplish. Unfortunately many if not most of the clients of social work do not fall into this category. Forming contracts become far more difficult when the client is reluctant to accept the services of a social worker or is uncertain about the nature of his problems or the kind of help he wants. Although contracts are hard to develop with such clients, we would argue that they are even more important with this group. . . . Most important, use of contracts with the unmotivated or uncertain client provides some assurance that he will not be treated "behind his back" for conditions that have not been made clear to him. [Reid and Epstein, 1977, p. 9]

How Are Behavioral Contracts Used in Foster Care?

Behavioral contracting has been applied in foster care, especially in the area of intervention with biological parents of children in foster care. These applications have shown promising results (Salmon, 1977; Stein and Gambrill, 1977; Stein, Gambrill, and Wiltse, 1974, 1977).

The Alameda Project is one of the most extensive research efforts on the use of contracting in foster care. This research focused on 227 foster children in an experimental unit served by M.S.W.-level social workers and 201 foster children in a control group served by county child welfare workers. The social workers in the experimental unit utilized with biological parents behavioral contracts as a means of encouraging their participation in planning for their child in foster care, as a tool for helping parents make necessary behavior changes, and as a basis for deciding when the agency should seek legal custody of the child. Statistically significant differences in the outcome of foster care were found between the experimental and control groups. In terms of the percentage of children leaving foster care, a significant difference was found in favor of the experimental intervention (79% compared to 40%). Unrelated to outcome were family composition; the child's age, sex, and ethnicity; type of placement; and reason for placement. However, the number of years in placement was related to outcome in that there was less likelihood of movement out of the system following three years in foster care. A statistically significant difference also was found in the number of identified problems resolved. The social workers in the experimental unit were more successful in resolving problems.

A recent 228-page book describes the specific techniques and procedures used in the Alameda Project: Theodore Stein and Eileen Gambrill, *Decision Making in Foster Care: A Training Manual* (1976).

Why Are Contracts Useful in Work with Neglecting and Abusing Parents?

Not infrequently, cases of child neglect and abuse reach court, where a decision of permanent custody must be made. A decision so serious as the termination of parental rights must be based on solid evidence. Written behavioral contracts can serve as evidence in legal decisions. For example, they can be used to prove that the parents are making changes that will reduce the likelihood of subsequent neglect or abuse or that the parents have failed to make necessary changes.

Bennett and Nofen (1975) note the practical importance of contracts in custody hearings.

Contracts be they good or bad, just or unjust, well-written or scrambled, are, nevertheless, held in high esteem by the judiciary. Therefore, the prior existence of a contract unfulfilled by a family greatly enhances your possibilities for winning a case in court, particularly if it is an extreme one in which permanent custody is likely to be an alternative.

For some reason judges like broken contracts better than the best-kept casework log.

Contracts are viewed fondly by defense attorneys and they will work hard to get a contract signed by the client and entered into a court record as a way of avoiding a court hearing. [Pp. 1-2]

Because contracts are valued by judges and sometimes given more weight than they deserve, their improper use can result in unfair treatment of natural parents.

What Are the Basic Steps in Using Behavioral Contracting with Natural Parents?

Stein and Gambrill (1976) have outlined the basic tasks of behavioral contracting. While a careful reading of their book plus special training is necessary preparation for the use of behavioral contracting in foster care, a brief review of these tasks will give the reader a clearer picture of the contracting process. It is important to note that while the process is described in terms of steps, the actual process seldom unfolds so neatly or in this exact sequence. There is considerable overlap among the various steps or tasks.

In Step 1, the parents and social worker meet to identify the parents' objective relative to their child's future. Depending on the situation, the goal may be to place the child out of the home or, if the child already is placed, to have him/her restored to the parents' care. One to three interviews may be needed to help the parent arrive at the goal.

Step 2 involves constructing a problem profile, i.e. identifying those changes that are needed or the problems that must be solved to accomplish the goal selected in Step 1. The problems and changes may be identified by the parents or the social worker, or they may be ones revealed in case reports and court records. It is important that the problems be described in behavioral terms, operationally defined in simple, clear language.

Step 3 involves the additional clarification and analysis of the problem with particular attention to understanding the situational context of the problem. Special attention is given to the identification of those situational factors that give rise to the problem, aggravate it, or are present when the problem occurs. This serves to identify environmental factors that contribute to the problem or that reinforce the problem behavior. Such an analysis also provides some clues as to how the behavior might be modified by changing the environmental context.

In Step 4, the parents and social worker select a few problems, e.g. one to three, that are related directly to the parents' goal for their child (Step 1). These are the problems of highest priority, those that must be successfully resolved if the parents' goal for their child is to be reached.

Step 5, one of the most complex, involves the detailed specification of objectives, including a statement of subgoals and client assets or strengths. In keeping with the behavioral approach, the desired outcome objectives may involve the acquisition of a new behavior, the increase of desired behaviors, the decrease of undesirable behaviors, the elimination of an undesirable behavior, the maintenance of a desired behavior, or the variation of behavior. It is essential that all objectives be written in behavioral terms so that everyone knows exactly what is meant and so the outcome can be measured. For example, an objective such as "improve housecleaning" is too vague. Objectives such as "wash all dirty dishes once a day" or "scrub bathtub each Friday" are more useful.

Step 6 involves the gathering of baseline data that permit the measurement of progress. Once the objectives have been specified, Step 7 focuses on the formulation of a written treatment contract.

When the basic contract is operational, the social worker or parents may discover that some aspect could be improved or is unworkable. Thus, Step 8 involves the specification of additional objectives relevant to the overall goal. In Step 9, the contract is amended to meet unanticipated circumstances.

Finally, Step 10 focuses on locating environmental resources to assist the client and providing reinforcers that help the parent make the necessary changes and sustain motivation to work on the problems.

What Should Be Included in a Behavioral Contract?

In discussing behavioral contracting, DeRisi and Butz (1975, pp. 43-44) state that the exact form of the contract is almost unimportant, but it always should include the following:

1. Date agreement begins, ends, or is renegotiated
2. The specific behavior(s) targeted for change
3. Amount and kind of reward or reinforcer to be used to encourage or maintain change
4. Schedule or plan for the delivery of reinforcer
5. Signatures of all those involved (e.g., clients, parents, social workers and others participating in contract)
6. Schedule for review of progress
7. Bonus clause for sustained or exceptional performance by client
8. Statement of the penalties that will be imposed if specific desired behavior is not performed.

Behavioral contracts used in court proceedings are almost certain to include other elements. In describing the behavioral contracts used in the Alameda Project, Stein, Gambrill, and Wiltse (1974) state:

> in the project, contracts have been defined as written documents specifying particular agreements between the . . . [agency] and the county worker, and a client. There are two parts to a contract, the first of which contains the following statements:
>
> 1. The client's objective (e.g., restoration of a child on a permanent basis or for a specified time period, such as a trial visit);
>
> 2. The goals for a treatment program focusing specifically on the identified problems to be remedied prior to the return of a child or upon goals to be accomplished during a trial visit;
>
> 3. The agreement of both the project and the county workers to support the parent's objectives (number 1) by making the appropriate recommendation to the juvenile court provided that problems are remedied;
>
> 4. A statement of the potential consequences of nonparticipation by the parent (e.g., that the objectives cannot be recommended to

the court) and that alternative planning for the child's future will have to be considered;

5. The time limits within which the treatment goals are to be accomplished.

The second part of the contract focuses upon the specific treatment methods to be employed and includes:

1. The steps to be engaged in to achieve the goals that are outlined as point number 2 above;

2. The tasks of the client and others in the client's environment who may be involved in treatment;

3. The environmental resources that will be brought to bear in addressing the problem; and

4. The role of the caseworker in achieving the specified goals. [Pp. 21-22]

While the concept of contracting is relatively simple, the actual use of behavioral contracting is complex. It is unlikely to be an effective tool for the social worker without some special training in this area. Considerable knowledge and skill are needed to select feasible objectives, write clear and measurable statements of objectives, specify workable programs of treatment or behavior change, set realistic time limits, and select and clearly describe the consequences of compliance and noncompliance. The selection of a treatment program and the setting of time limits, for example, require a knowledge of existing intervention methods for specific problems, an understanding of the amount of time usually required to make a specific behavior change, and an ability to plan a temporal sequence of behavior-change efforts.

Behavioral contracts are not always effective in helping a client make desired changes. They are almost always ineffective when they are imposed. Any attempt to impose a contract is a violation of the concept and reflects a misunderstanding of proper contracting procedure and the underlying behavioral principles. DeRisi and Butz (1975, pp. 58-60) provide a number of questions that can be used to evaluate contracting procedure. Some of the questions appear below. If proper contracting procedure were followed, the answer to each should be yes.

1. Was the target behavior clearly specified in the contract?

2. Did the contract provide for immediate reinforcement of the desired behavior?

3. Did the contract ask for small approximations to the desired behavior rather than a large, dramatic or complete change in behavior?
4. Was reinforcement frequent and in small amounts?
5. Did the contract call for and reward accomplishment rather than obedience?
6. Was the desired behavior rewarded after its occurrence?
7. Was the contract fair?
8. Were the terms of the contract clear and understandable to the client?
9. Was the contract honest and free of coercion?
10. Was the contract positive with an emphasis on do's rather than do not's?
11. Was the contracting method used systematically?
12. Was the contract mutually negotiated?
13. Was the penalty clause reasonable, inviting hope rather than fear?

The proper and effective use of behavioral contracting requires a good grasp of the professional literature on the topic. Books cited previously in this chapter will be of assistance in developing a better understanding of contracting.

What Do Contracts Look Like?

While each contract is or should be unique and individualized to the client and his or her situation, a few examples may further clarify the content and typical form of such behavioral contracts. Below are two examples taken from Stein and Gambrill (1976):

. . . *Sample Contract Between Client and Worker Regarding Trial Visit*
. . . This contract is entered into by Mr. C., social worker for .... county department of social services, and Ms. D., mother of J.D., at the present time a dependent child of the .... juvenile court. The *objective* of this contract is to have J.D. reside in his mother's home for a two week period of time, beginning on .... through ....
. . . This contract is in effect for 8 weeks, beginning .... and ending .... During this period of time the mother agrees to visit with her son, and the worker agrees to observe a sample of these visits as per the following schedule.

. . . Ms. D. agrees to visit with her son on the following schedule:

(1) for the first four weeks, beginning . . . . Ms. D. will visit her son on Saturday from 9:00 a.m. to 5:00 p.m. Ms. D. will pick up her son at the foster home, and return him to the foster home as per the above timetable.

(2) for the final four weeks, beginning . . . . Ms. D. will visit with her son from 9:00 a.m. on Saturday through 5:00 p.m. on Sunday. Ms. D. will pick up her son at the foster home and return him to the foster home as per the above timetable.

Mr. C., the caseworker, agrees to do the following:

(1) to assist Ms. D. in developing a schedule of planned activities for those visiting periods;

(2) to take Ms. D. food shopping for the weekend visits and to assist her in menu planning;

(3) to observe the mother and child for a minimum of . . . . . . hours during these visits. The objectives of these observations will be to identify both strength and weaknesses in parent-child interaction.

a) Should any problems be identified, these will be shared with the client, and the worker agrees to develop programs to resolve any problems that are identified.

(4) If no problems are identified, or if identified problems are either resolved or, in the worker's estimation close enough to resolution so as to not threaten the stability of the trial visit, she agrees to obtain an ex-parte order from the . . . . juvenile court permitting J.D. to reside in his mother's home for the two-week period of time.

. . . It is understood by Ms. D., that should she fail to maintain any of the above visits, or fail to participate in resolution of any identified problems, that the planned two-week-long visit cannot take place.

Signatures: . . . .

          Ms. D.   Mr. C.

. . . [Sample] *Restoration Agreement*

This contract is entered into between . . . . Social Worker for the Alameda Project of Children's Home Society, ..., Child Welfare Worker, Alameda County Human Resources Agency, and . . . . father of . . . . and . . . . at present dependent children of the Alameda County Juvenile Court.

In keeping with the wish of the father of . . . . and . . . . to have his sons returned to his home on a 90-day trial basis, both . . . . and . . . . agree to recommend such a trial return to the Alameda County Juvenile Court contingent upon attainment of the three goals listed below. It is understood by the father that failure to comply with these goals will result in a statement to the Alameda County Juvenile Court that, in the opinion of both social workers, such a return is not feasible at the present time. The general goals of the program are as follows:

(1) The father is to visit his children on a regular schedule established by both social workers and the father. (schedule attached);

(2) The father agrees to be at his home, with his children, during a portion of each of these visits. The objective here is for the worker to observe and assess parent-child interaction; (See attached plan for details)

(3) The father agrees to establish a plan for substitute care for his children on any occasion on which he is absent from the home, other than those times when the children are attending public school. (See attached plan for details)

This contract will be in effect for one month from January 27, 1975 to February 28, 1975.

Signed: . . . .
          Father   Social Worker
                             Alameda Project

. . . .
          Date   Child Welfare Worker
                       Alameda County Human
                Resources Agency [Pp. 32, 35]

A contract mutually negotiated and entered into by both client and social worker should clearly state what each is to do and what each can expect within a certain time frame. These points are illustrated in the sample agreement by Pike et al. (1977).

[Example of] 90-day Agreement Between (Client) and (Child Welfare Agency)

I, (Client), have stated my interest in regaining custody of my child, (Child), and in order to work toward that goal, I agree to the following conditions:

1. I agree to visit my child, (Child) every Wednesday from 1:00 p.m. to 3:00 p.m. in the (Child Welfare Agency) office.

2. I agree to meet with my caseworker, (Caseworker) every Wednesday at 3:00 p.m. in the (Child Welfare Agency) office to discuss my visit with my child, to review planning concerning my child, and to discuss changes in my situation as well as any other relevant matters.

3. I agree to participate in weekly meetings with a counselor from

the County Mental Health Clinic.

4. I agree to keep (Caseworker) of (Child Welfare Agency), informed at all times of my whereabouts and home address.

I, (Client), understand that failure to meet the terms of this agreement may result in a petition for termination of parental rights to my child, (Child).

(signed)   (date)

. . . .

(Client)

I, (Caseworker), acting on behalf of (Child Welfare Agency), agree to assist (Client) in her efforts to regain custody of her child, (Child), and in order to work toward that goal, agree to the following conditions:

1. I agree to have (Child) at the (Child Welfare Agency) office every Wednesday at 1:00 p.m. for visits with her mother, (Client).

2. I agree to meet with (Client), each Wednesday at 3:00 p.m. in the (Child Welfare Agency) office.

3. I agree to arrange transportation, upon request, for (Client) so that she can attend weekly meetings with the mental health clinic counselor.

4. I agree to maintain (Child) in foster care until a permanent plan can be accomplished for her.

5. I agree to keep (Client) informed of any significant matters relating to her child, (Child), such as illnesses, school progress, etc.

(signed)   (date)

. . . .

(Caseworker)

It is jointly understood and agreed between (Client) and (Caseworker) that this agreement will continue in effect for a period of 90-days (unless jointly modified) and will be reviewed by (date), to evaluate progress toward meeting the stated goals. [Pp. 50-51]

CHAPTER 5

Permanence Planning

What Is Permanence Planning?

DEFINITIONS OF FOSTER FAMILY care emphasize that such care is to be a planned service. Too often a child enters foster care and remains in foster care without a clear plan or goal being set for him/her. Too often the foster child remains adrift in a legal limbo. The problem of drift is of growing concern to child welfare experts. Increasingly, permanence planning projects are attempting to address this problem. In the western United States, for example, two well-known permanent planning projects are the Oregon Project and the Alameda Project. The first is described in Regional Research Institute for Human Services (1976), the latter in Stein and Gambrill (1977).

Basically, permanence planning refers to efforts directed toward developing and implementing plans and goals for children in foster care. The purpose of permanent planning is to prevent drift and provide the foster child with a greater sense of permanence and security. Clearly, a predictable future is a basic need of all children. In discussing permanency planning, Pike et al. (1977) state:

> *Permanence* describes *intent.* A permanent home is not one that is guaranteed to last forever, but one that is *intended* to exist indefinitely. When the expectation of permanence is lacking, a child experiences doubt, uncertainty, and hesitancy. Permanency planning means clarifying the intent of the placement, and, during temporary care, keeping alive a plan for permanency. When a temporary placement is prolonged, foster care may have the appearance of permanency, but it lacks the element of intent that is critical to permanence.
>
> Permanent homes give commitment and continuity to the child's relationships. To become emotionally stable adults, capable of giving love to others and of making lasting, trusting relationships, children need consistent nurturing by adults who really belong to them. A permanent home is one that holds together through many kinds of

family crises. Such disruptions as prolonged sickness, changes of residence, unemployment, marital problems, and conflicts between parents and child are weathered and resolved within the framework of the family itself. Friends, relatives, and community services may help families during times of stress, but a family crisis in a permanent home does not usually cause the child to be moved to a family he does not know, for an indefinite length of time. It is no derogation of the love and commitment of foster parents to say that their role, the expectations of the agency, and legal authority, do not permit the kind of commitment and continuity permanence is made of. [P. 1]

Pike et al. (1977) observe that ordinary foster care is necessary and important but it is not a substitute for more permanent arrangements.

Foster care placements serve a needed purpose when they exist for a planned period of time. The planned period can be quite temporary while a permanent home is being arranged, either with the child's own or with adoptive parents. For the child who should remain with his foster family until he is grown, the temporary placement can be made permanent by a formalized long-term foster care arrangement of foster parent adoption. When used in these ways, foster care fills a needed place in the spectrum of child welfare services. Difficulties arise when foster care placements intended to be only temporary extend indefinitely and become substitutes for permanent homes. [P. 3]

While there is obvious logic to the permanent planning approach, the reader should not conclude that the implementation of such a program is inexpensive or easy. The barriers to permanent planning are many and complex. Experiences reported by the Regional Research Institute for Human Services (1976) indicate that successful permanent planning requires specially trained social workers, reduced case loads, additional legal and community resources, and usually, new legislation. In spite of the many barriers to permanent planning and the resources needed to overcome these obstacles, data gathered in the Oregon Project provides evidence that permanent planning is cost-effective.

The reader should be alert to the potential destructiveness of poorly planned and underfunded permanency planning projects.

A cheap or poor imitation of the successful and well-run Oregon Project, for example, may create more harm than good. There is a danger that legislators or administrators with little awareness of the realities of child welfare may endorse permanency planning simply because they believe they can cut the cost of foster care. They may overlook the fact that permanency planning touches directly and forcefully on one of the most significant of human relationships—the relationship between a child and his/her biological parents. Short-sighted or inept efforts to terminate parental rights to free a child for adoption can harm the parent and child. There is a danger that permanency planning projects staffed by poorly trained individuals may run roughshod over the rights and wishes of foster children and biological parents. Fanshel and Shinn (1978), the authors of a ground-breaking research report on children in foster care, express a similar concern:

> While we are concerned with the problem of "drift" in foster care, as revealed by our data, we do not support the increasing tendency of many critics of the foster care system to make short shrift of natural parents who have failed their children. Lifting the banner for foster parents and adoptive parents, there is a much too cavalier readiness to early terminate the rights of natural parents, even when there has been no real effort to assist these hapless victims of poor service delivery. . . .
>
> In addition to our concern for the well-being of the foster children who have need for their own parents, we are also concerned with the rights of the adults involved. *The termination of parental rights reflects one of the most extreme forms of state power. It should be used most gingerly and judiciously. People should not be penalized because they are poor, because they are mentally ill, or because they are afflicted with drug addiction or alcoholism. They should not be penalized because it is less expensive for society to terminate their rights and allow others, endowed with better economic means, to replace them as parents to their children.* [Pp. 489-490]

What Are the Obstacles to Making More Appropriate Arrangements for Children in Foster Care?

There are many interrelated reasons why children remain in foster care when it is known that they will not return to their natural parents and would be better served by adoption or planned long-term foster care. Pike (1976) has observed that there are many factors that perpetuate the status quo in foster care. "These may include, for example, overburdened caseworkers; lack of case management procedures or case review mechanisms; lack of commitment on the part of the agency and workers to change the characteristics of foster care practice; the absence of statutory authority or a poor statute upon which to seek termination of parental rights decisions; and lack of skills in preparing cases for courts" (p. 24). A recent survey by Claburn, Magura, and Resnick (1976) of state child welfare agencies found that legal problems—particularly courts that are unable or unwilling to act on questions of custody and insufficient legal staff—were the most frequently mentioned obstacle to permanent planning for children. Various types of agency problems (insufficient staff, high staff turnover, poor attitudes among staff, etc.) were the second most frequently mentioned obstacles to permanent planning. Third in importance were child characteristics (age, physical or emotional problems, etc.) that hampered permanent planning. Fourth in importance was a lack of resources, e.g. family support services or adoption resources. Parental uncooperativeness was the final category of obstacles. Given the actual data reported in this study, it is apparent that considerable attention must be given to legal and staff problems. It should be noted that these problems often are interrelated.

An important finding reported in *Barriers to Planning for Children in Foster Care: A Summary* (Regional Research Institute for Human Services, 1976) was that there were many institutional barriers to permanent planning. In fact, nonclient variables seemed to have more effect on permanent planning decisions than did client variables, e.g. age, behavior problems, or parent-child bonds.

> Simply by knowing in *which* county cases occur one can predict how workers will decide which permanent plan a child shall have. Thirty-nine percent of the variance was accounted for in this way. This county variation, in turn, was found to be attributable to differences in worker attitudes toward permanent planning, in optimism and pessimism about what can be done for children of each

age group, and in caseworker perceptions of what can be accomplished in their county. For children 0-11, 82 percent of the variance of permanent planning decisions was predicted by *non-client* variables; that is, by worker attitudes and institutional barriers; 57 percent for those 12 and over. Institutional barriers partialed out most of the effects of the client predictors, suggesting that caseworker attitudes and the general climate regarding what is possible in a county determine how these caseworkers rate the condition of and prospects for their individual clients. [P. 8]

Research has shown that the rates at which children go into foster care, e.g. number per 1,000 children, differ widely from one jurisdiction to another. These differences also may reflect variation in organizational structure and prevailing opinion. It is noteworthy that worker attitudes, which varied from county to county, were found to be a significant barrier to permanent planning. The staffs in some counties were optimistic about being able to arrange permanent plans, whereas staffs in other counties were pessismistic about what could be done. Attempts to deal with problems in foster care must take into account these county-by-county differences in organizational structure and administration.

> Systematic county differences in plans for children were happenstance for the child; they represent differences in what can be accomplished in a particular county environment. Each county has its own climate of opinion about what is possible or not possible and these prevailing climates can be substantial barriers to permanent planning over and beyond the attitudes of individual workers. It suggests the need to address the system of services in each county as a unique challenge. [Regional Research Institute for Human Services, 1976, p. 18]

Some of the variables that constitute the attitudinal barriers were as follows:

1. A negative attitude toward termination of parental rights
2. Pessimism about being able to find adoptive homes for older children
3. Pessimism about the options available to a child who has been in foster care for a long time and/or one who has experienced several replacements
4. Pessimism about local judges' and county attorneys' willing-

ness to consider or work toward the termination of parental rights

5. Reluctance to make a decision about a child's future and a tendency to drift with the status quo.

Interestingly, the study found that workers with the most experience in attempting to terminate parental rights, thereby freeing a foster child for adoption, were the ones least likely to pursue this option. Apparently, the process of terminating parental rights is so distasteful to social workers that they are reluctant to try it again. Unsuccessful attempts to terminate parental rights are especially distasteful. A worker who arrives at the decision to ask a court to terminate parental rights needs guidance in preparing the evidence, a good grasp of legal procedures, competent supervision, and a great deal of moral support from others equally concerned about the child's future. Involvement in the termination of parental rights is an emotional and agonizing experience. Frequent involvement contributes to worker burnout and causes many to leave child welfare practice.

What Is Needed to Implement a Program of Permanency Planning in Foster Care?

In answer to the question, "What is required to change existing practices and to implement planning for permanency?" Emlen (1977) has identified several prerequisites:

> Social workers, with manageable caseloads, who are decisive about the best future placement for the child, can be effective by intervening from the time a child first enters foster care; by planning regular visits between parents and child, by structuring time-limited rehabilitation efforts for parents, and by organizing legal evidence for court action to terminate parental rights. Knowledgeable attorneys, committed foster parents, expert witnesses to evaluate parental condition, homemaker and other community services, are all needed participants.
>
> Yet effort spins if its direction is not supported administratively. Top-level *agency endorsement* of permanency policies, and expert supervision and consultation, can reinforce direction and purpose.
>
> So much for staff resources, which cost money and appear on budgets because they take staff time. Another key element is the *institutional framework*, including a sound statute that authorizes al-

ternatives to foster care; a supporting body of case law; established pathways for exit from foster care, such as subsidized adoption; caseload screening and review procedures; and client information systems.

Lastly, permanency planning requires *a body of knowledge,* the content and method to guide practice. [P. 1]

A final report on a research and demonstration project in New York, *Barriers to the Freeing of Children for Adoption,* prepared by the Temporary State Commission on Child Welfare (1976), provides additional perspectives on what is needed to implement an effective program of permanency planning for children in foster care. The report listed many recommendations. Some are relevant only to New York, while others undoubtedly apply to most states. Some of the latter are listed below.

design a standard investigation form for use by all agencies in providing information at foster care review hearings. . . .

. . . greatly restrict the practice of prolonging foster care review by issuing a series of time consuming orders and requesting a series of follow-up reports.

. . . sponsor joint meetings of judges, attorneys and social services agency staff in order to develop greater interprofessional respect and cooperation.

. . . Consideration should be given to . . . [legislation] to require the appointment of a law guardian to represent the child in a foster care review proceeding.

. . . The period of time Family Court judges remain at one assignment in . . . should be substantially increased, thereby reducing delays in adjudicating termination of parental rights and foster care review cases caused by rotation. . . .

. . . inform . . judges in a timely fashion of statutory changes affecting foster care, adoption or termination of parental rights. . . .

. . . undertake a detailed study of visitation by natural parents of children in foster care. Following this, . . . [the public agency] in consultation with appropriate public and voluntary child care agencies, should promulgate regulations setting forth, among other things: a minimum periodicity of visitation, how visitation may be encouraged, and conditions under which visitation may be stopped. Such regulations should contain sufficient flexibility to be responsive to individual situations, and also should provide for a uniform state policy on reimbursement for parental transportation costs as well as inclusion in agency case records of a record of parental visits.

. . . The written agreement for placing a child in foster care should include specifics on periodicity of visitation and a statement of parent and agency responsibilities for visitation and the consequences of parental failure to visit. This agreement should be explained and put in the court record. . . .

. . . develop guidelines within the "diligent efforts" requirement of the permanent neglect statute, on casework and other services to be provided to families of children in foster care. These guidelines should spell out circumstances when efforts to re-establish the parent-child relationship would not be in the best interest of the child within the meaning of that statute.

. . . The role, rights and obligations of parents and agency to work together to plan for the child should be spelled out in the written agreement for placing the child in foster care and read into the Court record. . . . This agreement should also inform the parent of his obligation to keep the agency apprised of his current address and should impose obligations on the agency, when the parent phones or visits, to inquire as to the parent's current address.

. . . assure that up-to-date service information and referral resources are available to local agency personnel. Within available funds, additional emphasis should be placed on development of training opportunities for social services personnel. . . .

. . . review the basis for current foster care reimbursement rates in order to encourage agency services to reunite families. . . .

. . . develop criteria and promulgate guidelines to assist agency personnel in making decisions on permanent planning for children. . . .

. . . sponsor demonstration projects to assess the impact of various planning techniques, the use of specialized staff and methods of management control.

. . . encourage, where child welfare legal caseloads so merit, the establishment of welfare attorney positions in local departments of social services.

. . . develop training programs to teach caseworkers fundamental provisions and principles of law, including the constitutional concept of "due process," the law of evidence and related matters, so that caseworkers may better understand theirs' and others' and responsibilities in the process of terminating parental rights. . . . Prepare and up-date . . . compendium of child welfare laws, and interpretations of court decisions.

. . . provide for the development of better, more standardized and less time consuming agency case records to serve the dual purpose of determining need for services as well as providing a basis for evidence in judicial proceedings. . . .

. . . meet with the State Department of Civil Service to review and revise standards for the selection of caseworkers and develop a separate testing device for child welfare workers. . . .

. . . consult with schools of social work to determine the need for additional formal graduate training for child welfare workers. . . .

. . . clarify existing adoption subsidy regulations to eliminate difficulties encountered in their implementation and . . . work . . . to resolve report delays in approval of subsidy applications. [Pp. xiv-xviii]

It should be apparent that an effective program of permanency planning requires a willingness and a commitment to change from all parts of the child welfare system, e.g. agency administrators, judges, attorneys, social workers, supervisors, staff trainers, civil service administrators, and legislators.

Does an Adoption Subsidy Increase the Chances of Adoption for the Foster Child with Special Needs?

Evidence supports the belief that a program of subsidized adoption increases the chances that adoptive homes can be found for children who otherwise would remain in foster care. For example, in one demonstration project (Washington State Department of Social and Health Services, 1975), 534 children were assigned randomly to a subsidized adoption group and a nonsubsidized adoption group. At the conclusion of the project, 41 percent of the children in the subsidy group had been adopted, while only 19 percent of the nonsubsidy children had been adopted. This shows that a program of adoption subsidy increases the possibility of finding adoptive homes for children with special needs or the so-called hard to place, e.g. children who have severe medical problems or physical or mental handicaps. A program of subsidized adoption is necessary to support the goals of permanency planning for children in foster care.

It is important to note that there are a number of reasons why people may refuse to adopt a child they deeply love and cherish. Some people do not trust the stability of government adoption subsidies. For example, they fear that in the future funds for the program will be cut back and/or that the subsidy will not keep pace with inflation. If that happened, it would place the adoptive family in a difficult financial situation, and they might not be able to provide the special services needed by the child. Thus, some people would rather remain foster parents to a child rather than becoming the child's legal parents.

It is also important to recognize that adoption gives the adopted child a right to inheritance. Some people are more than willing to enter into an agreement to provide long-term foster care but will not consider adoption because of inheritance problems or issues. In some cases, other natural children or relatives object to the legal adoption because it would result in further division of an estate or perhaps the loss of certain control over a family business or farm.

It is important to equate permanency planning with the provision of stability for the child who can never return to his/her natural family. It should not be equated with the process of finding an adoptive home for every foster child free for adoption. Adoption is not possible or even desirable for all children needing permanency.

What Is Case Screening in Permanency Planning?

Case screening refers to an ongoing process of reviewing each foster care case to determine whether permanent planning should be initiated. A simple screening tool, applied on a regular basis, e.g. bimonthly, can identify those foster children who are unlikely to return to their natural homes and need more permanent and stable living arrangements, such as adoption or planned long-term foster care.

Emlen et al. (1977) developed a simple screening tool. A slightly modified version of their case screening questionnaire is presented below.

CASE SCREENING TOOL FOR FOSTER CARE

County/District . . . . Foster Child's Name . . . .
Social Worker's Name . . . . Child's Birthdate . . . .
Case Number . . . . Age (Years) . . . .
Instructions: Check the *one* that applies to the child named above. Do not check more than one statement.

———— 1. It is very likely that this child will return to his/her own home very soon.

—— 2. It its likely that this child will return to his/her own home, but there are obstacles that must be overcome.

It is likely that this child will not return to his/her own home and will be adoptable:

—— 3. By his/her current foster parents.

—— 4. By other adoptive parents.

—— 5. This child is already free for adoption and awaiting placement.

It is likely that this child will not return to his/her own home and will not be adoptable. He/she needs:

—— 6. Permanent foster care with current foster parents.

—— 7. Permanent foster care with other foster parents or relatives.

—— 8. Other type of setting, e.g. institutional or residential treatment.

—— 9. This child is no longer in foster care.

This screening tool also can be used to monitor social work practice in foster care. For example, if item 2 is checked, it follows that action is required to deal with the obstacles. If items 6, 7, or 8 are checked, it follows that action is required to free the child for adoption or design a plan for permanent foster care. If such items are checked but appropriate action is not underway or planned, it is apparent that practice in this case is unsatisfactory.

What Is the Role of the Social Worker in Permanency Planning?

A variety of professionals must be involved in permanency planning efforts.

The job of placing a foster child in a permanent home requires the talents of many people. If the parents need rehabilitation or other help in order to make a home for their child, they may need services from mental health workers, job counselors, physicians, psychiatrists, psychologists, homemakers, alcohol or drug rehabilitation clinics, and many others. If legal action is necessary, juvenile court counselors, lawyers (sometimes as many as three or four) and judges will be involved. Foster parents are always part of a permanent planning effort, and step-parents, absent spouses, grandparents, and biological fathers, as well as the child's legal parents, may be participants in arranging a permanent home for a foster child. [Pike et al., 1977, p. 5]

Given the complexity of the permanency planning efforts, one professional must be responsible for coordination. This task is usually assumed by the social worker. According to Pike et al. (1977), the social worker

has the central and indispensable role of coordinating the activities of these people and service agencies. It is safe to say that without the interest and expertise of a knowledgeable caseworker, a child adrift in foster care will simply continue to drift. If planning is to begin when the child first enters foster care, it is nearly always the caseworker who will set the plan in motion. And the responsibility is just as great, if more onerous, if the child has been in foster care for a long while with no plans made for his future. [P. 6]

The social worker must possess a variety of skills, especially ones associated with tasks such as brokering, advocating, counseling, and consulting. Pike et al. (1977) have identified permanency planning tasks that must be performed by the social worker.

To set in motion planning activities and to keep the momentum going until the child is permanently settled. To do this, the caseworker must be constantly willing to initiate and keep track of all activities. If referrals to other agencies are necessary, the caseworker will be the one to make them. The same is true for arranging parent's visits with their children, for initiating court action, and for all other actions necessary to implement a plan.

To coordinate all service activities related to permanent planning. The caseworker will ensure that the parents have access to all services that they need, and will coordinate referrals to other services so that they follow a coherent case plan.

To keep all activities focused on the need of the child for permanency. In this respect, the caseworker acts as an advocate for the child. The worker may be the only professional involved who will be mainly concerned with the child's need for permanence.

To be willing to make decisions, and to exercise judgment in doing so. To a large extent, permanency planning involves decision-making. The decisions are very often difficult to make, because they require judgments on what is likely to occur in the future, in situations where all the facts are not, and never can be, known. Decision-making in permanency planning involves risks, and the gravity of the risks are compounded by the serious implications the decisions will have on the lives of parents and children. But timidity in the face of difficult decisions will not achieve a stable future for the foster child. The caseworker does not make these decisions alone . . . , but does have responsibility for seeing that they are made, and made with as much judgment and knowledge as possible. [P. 6]

As indicated above, the social worker must be ready to make some difficult decisions. He/she must possess a high degree of skill in social assessment and an ability to collaborate with others who need to be involved in the decision-making process.

Effective planning for children in foster care requires the ability and willingness to make decisions. Very often no solution is obvious, and no plan without disadvantages. In these instances, all factors must be carefully weighed, and the plan chosen that has the best chance of success under the circumstances. The serious consequences of permanent planning decisions mandate that no one person take full responsibility for making them; responsibility should be shared with others who have knowledge and insight about the case. [Pike et al., 1977, p. 7]

In the process of making permanency planning decisions, the social worker should consult with and gather information from professionals having knowledge of a particular foster child and his/her natural family. This would include other social workers, homemakers, teachers, court workers, physicians, psychologists, psychiatrists, and attorneys. In addition, nonprofessional persons such as family friends and relatives may be a valuable source of information necessary to sound decision making.

When Should the Social Worker Begin the Permanency Planning Process?

As soon as the child enters a foster home, serious attention should be focused on the child's future in substitute care and the need for permanency planning.

Permanency planning can be done at any point in the foster child's career, and it is certainly better to undertake it even after a period of years has passed than not to undertake it at all. But the difficulties inherent in permanency planning can be mitigated by starting work on a permanent plan as the child is entering foster care. [Pike et al., 1977, p. 4]

The advantages of early permanency planning are rooted in basic concepts of social work practice and the dynamics of human adjustment to change. Pike et al. (1977) have identified many advantages of starting permanency planning as soon as a child enters foster care.

A structured treatment plan, initiated immediately after placement, provides the best opportunity for the child to return home. The literature shows that visits between child and parents are particularly crucial to returning children to their homes from foster care (Fanshel, 1975).

Immediately after the child has been placed in foster care, parents and worker can more easily identify and agree on the reasons that the child was removed. Parents have not yet adjusted to their loss and are motivated to change in order to regain their child, and perhaps to prove to themselves and others that they are fit parents. If intensive casework does not begin immediately after the child has been placed in foster care, the original problem may become obscure. Parents may have adjusted to life without children and be unable to reincorporate children into their homes without major changes, or they may resist treatment because they are reluctant to reopen old wounds and to face the possibility of again failing to meet society's expectations of parents.

If the parents have deserted, it will be easier to find them and make a plan with them about the future of their child. If you wait, they may disappear altogether, in which case you will first need to locate them, and then, perhaps, face the handicap of evaluating from a distance their potential to care for their child. This can be time consuming, and results are often inconclusive.

The child hasn't settled into a relationship with his foster parents. On the other hand, if the child has been in a good foster home for a long time, he may have developed firm ties to his foster family and have little memory of his own parents. But these parents are now visiting regularly as part of a case plan which may, from his point of view, take him from the only home he knows. Any plan that entails removing the child from his long-term placement may be resisted by foster parents, who, understandably, sometimes resent the disruption of an arrangement they have come to enjoy. They may well be possessive of the child after providing years of care. This is desirable in a permanent placement but can make them unable to cooperate in a plan that may result in a severe loss to them.

If the restoration plan is unsuccessful, the documented effort to treat, and failure of the parents to respond, become part of the case for terminating the parents' rights so that the child can be adopted.

If the foster placement has been successful and the foster parents want to adopt, an early adoption in that setting is better for the child than the status of foster child.

If adoption in another home is indicated, the move for the child is easier, because he spent only a brief time in foster care. [Pp. 4-5]

Where Can the Social Worker Obtain Information on the Specific Techniques and Procedures Used in Permanency Planning?

An excellent source of information on step-by-step procedures of permanency planning is a 1977 publication, *Permanent Planning for Children in Foster Care: A Handbook for Social Workers,* by Victor Pike, Susan Downs, Arthur Emlen, Glen Downs, and Denise Case. This 142-page book can be secured from the United States Government Printing Office, DHEW Publication Number (OHDS) 77-30124, or from the Children's Bureau, Administration for Children, Youth and Families, Office of Human Development Services, United States Department of Health, Education and Welfare, Washington, D. C. 20201.

What Is a Case Plan?

A written plan should be prepared for each foster child and his/her family, i.e. the natural or biological family. By definition, a plan should be forward looking rather than a report of what has already happened. A case record may describe what has happened, but a case plan describes what will happen or what is intended. A good case plan is a working document, one designed for ongoing day-to-day use by the social worker and others concerned with the child in foster care and the biological family. A good plan—one that facilitates the delivery of service—satisfies certain criteria determining who participates in the development of the plan, what it contains, and how it is written. The model developed by the Joint Commission on the Accreditation of Hospitals (1973) for individualized plans of this type is relevant to foster care. An individualized plan should be developed for each person accepted for service. . . . The plan should be based on individual assessment data and on other data that assist in understanding the client's situation, and it should be developed by the relevant staff of the agency serving the client, with the participation of the staff of other agencies involved in serving the client, and with the participation of the client and his family. . . . Long- and short-term objectives should be stated separately and within a time frame, and they must be expressed in behavioral terms that provide measurable indices of progress, and that enable the effectiveness of interventions to be evaluated. Modes of intervention for the achievement of the stated objectives must be specified, and agencies capable of delivering the needed services should be identified. The individual program plan must be modified as goals and objectives are, or are not, attained. Review and appropriate revision of the plan must be a continuous and self-correcting process. The plan must help all concerned to coordinate their efforts and activities, so as to maximize services to the client. [P. 17]

It is noteworthy that a case plan is to be based on assessment data. Since each situation and problem are unique, each case plan is unique. It also is important to recognize that it is not the social worker alone who develops the case plan. Rather, it should be a team approach with all relevant individuals and agencies participating in the planning process. The foster parents, foster child, and biological parents are key participants in the planning process.

In describing case management procedure used in a foster care-related parent counseling program, Johnston (1976) applies the term *initial team meeting* to a group discussion among foster child, natural parents, social worker, foster parents, and others. Such a meeting is designed to begin the formulation of a case plan. Johnson (1976) states that this team meeting should occur as soon as possible after placement and that the meeting has the following purposes:

—to assist all involved to share their feelings about the situation that exists (i.e., the child in a parent counsellor home)
—assist in establishing a working rapport among all present
—observe the child and natural parent interact in an attempt to learn more about the child
—identify why all participants are present
—introduce the parent counsellor program
—discuss each person's role during placement

—indicate that the first month is getting acquainted time

—introduce the goal setting procedure which will occur in a month

—assist the natural parents in recognizing their responsibility to prepare for the return of the child

—indicate they will meet again in six weeks and if possible set date. [P. 121]

As should be apparent, the parent counselor approach to foster care, developed and used by Johnston and others in Alberta, Canada, is designed to keep the child's parents actively involved in foster care and in making those changes that allow the child to return home if possible.

Subsequent to the initial team meeting, a goal-planning meeting is held. According to Johnston, this meeting occurs two to three weeks after the placement and includes those who attended the initial team meeting and all others—professionals and agencies—who may be involved with the child and/or the natural family. The purpose of the goal-planning meeting is

—to orient to goal plans for child and family

—to review strengths and weaknesses summary

—to review child's goal

—to establish goals

—to determine method of working towards goals including time estimates

—goals will be set for approximately three months

—set time for periodic review. [P. 121]

According to Johnston (1976, p. 122), once the goal reviews have been established, case conferences are used to "(1) review goal attainment progress, (2) reassess goals and methods, and (3) establish new goals and/or methods where required." A case plan should be written in functional language that is understandable by all concerned, especially the clients. Professional jargon should be avoided. Moreover, the objectives must be stated in a manner that permits evaluation. Writing this kind of plan may require some new skills and new ways of thinking on the part of some social workers. In particular, it requires a behavioral orientation and an ability to communicate in a clear, simple, and precise language.

Persons new to the preparation of behavioral objectives make two common errors: (1) They formulate objectives in terms of what they will do rather than what the client will do, and (2) they use vague terms and therefore create objectives that are unmeasurable. Examine the following objectives:

1. John should acquire a better attitude toward school.
2. Social worker will provide counseling (one hour per week) to John relative to school performance.
3. Between March 1 and March 31, John will increase school attendance from an average of three times per week to an average of four times per week.

The reader will note that Objective 1 would be nearly impossible to measure. To evaluate an attitude change, it is necessary to describe the proposed change in behavioral terms, such as school attendance, getting to school on time, improved grades, or a decrease in times reprimanded by the principal. Objective 2 states what is to be done with John (counseling) but says nothing about the change expected in John's performance. In this sense, it is the social worker's objective but not the client's. It focuses on the input or the means (counseling), but not the end or output. Objective 3 is behaviorally specific and provides a time line. It would be relatively easy to evaluate whether or not the objective was reached.

What Is Case Management?

In recent years, increasing attention has been given to the development of techniques for case management. In part, the effort has been an attempt to deal with excessive case loads and the complexities of human service bureaucracies. Most developments in case management have occurred within public welfare organizations.

Case management systems essentially are management strategies that employ management techniques. While the use of flowcharts, computer technology, and management by objectives (MBO) may seem confusing, a close examination of well-developed case management systems reveals that they fundamentally are applications of the basic problem-solving process familiar to trained social workers. Numerous basic social work texts use the similar problem-solving framework to explain social work methodology (Goldstein, 1973; Loewenberg, 1977; Reid and Epstein, 1972; Siporin, 1975; and Whittaker, 1974).

If the modern systems of case management can be faulted, it is in relation to a tendency to oversimplify the helping process and describe it as if it always unfolded in neat, clearly defined steps or phases. A process involving people, dynamic human interactions, and complex social problems seldom proceeds in a predictable sequence shown on a flowchart. The better case management systems recognize this reality and the necessity for flexibility and individualization in service provisions. The poorly designed systems approach the human services as if the people needing and seeking these services had the same motives and behaved like people using a supermarket, department store, or shopping center. For this reason, approaches to case management borrowed from business or industrial organizations have limited application in the human services. For example, they do not give adequate attention to the difference between client requests and client needs. A supermarket can assume that need and request are the same. A human service agency cannot or, at least, should not.

Consider the mother who approaches the agency and requests that her children be placed in foster care because she no longer can cope with the stress and strain of parenting. Careful exploration by a skilled social worker may reveal that the mother does not really want to be separated from her children; what she needs and wants is some type of assistance or a support service that will help her cope with the demands of parenting and obtain occasional relief from her burdens. We see that an initial request or want may be different from the need. Frequently, persons who request help from a social agency do not know what they want or need simply because they are not aware of possible choices or have not had an opportunity to examine carefully their situation with someone skilled in the process of helping. Moreover, emotional stress and crisis situations may distort perceptions and cause people to make requests that they later find unacceptable. For this reason, skilled social workers should occupy the key intake positions. If the intake worker lacks the knowledge and skills needed for careful exploration and assessment, some clients may be directed toward an inappropriate service.

Poorly designed case management systems can create numerous technical and personnel problems. This is especially likely when case management systems are imposed on local social service programs by a higher level of administration or when the line social service personnel have not had a part in designing the case management system. Such unilateral decision making is a violation of basic MBO methodology. Pflanczer (1977) recently described many of the practical problems associated with the implementation of case management systems.

The case management model developed by the Regional Institute of Social Welfare Research (1977) is sensitive to the many practical problems and issues associated with systems of case management.

> Case management is like everything else in the public arena; it cannot be imposed. Rather, agreement about its value and commitment to its methods must pervade the full scope of its attempted implementation.
>
> Even if consensus about the desirability and usefulness of the model is reached in an organization, it is not realistic to bring everybody on board at once. For one thing, the dominant interests and values of the system need to be clarified before the full extent of case management can be deployed. Consequently, a preferred option may be to identify an agency or subsystem most attuned to meeting case management requirements, and begin there on a pilot or early-implementation basis.
>
> On both counts, the implementation of the model is a matter of gradual unfolding. [Vol. I, pp. 23-24]

A three-volume report prepared by the Regional Institute of Social Welfare Research (1977) describes one of the better-developed systems for case management. Selected quotations drawn from the report give the reader added perspectives on case management systems.

> Briefly defined, case management comprises a series of steps or activities which describe the interrelationships among service workers, agency administrators, service vendors and clients. Conceptual-

ly, and in systems terms, it is one of the essential functions of a service delivery system. In this context, and from the standpoint of individual service workers, it intends to give focus to a definable order of events and staff responsibilities. . . .

. . . Case management is best understood as a process made up of a series of interconnected steps. These steps reflect the various objectives of case management and, as such, constitute a frame-work for the activities and tasks which account for the agency/worker and client relationship. In this way, the process can function as a guide for making case decisions and for doing the job(s) required by the delivery system. . . .

While case management may mean different things to different people, it is commonly recognized as a way for addressing the many complications of "the system" in a manner that does not require radical change. Even though radical change (including the simplification and rationalization of policies, regulations, and rules) may be indisputably in order, it is also self-evident that such a dramatic turnabout will not take place. Instead we look for compromise solutions rather than all-out reorganization and reform. In this sense, while it is by no means an instant solution, case management is advanced as the best approach to establishing the routines and checkpoints necessary for guiding service delivery system case activities. . . . [Pp. 1-5]

Approaches to case management utilize management techniques such as management by objectives and emphasize the clear definition of responsibility and accountability.

Finally, it should be mentioned that case management touches directly on the philosophy and methods of management by objectives (MBO). Setting objectives on a case-by-case basis and making the objectives work or finding out why they do not work, is a theme throughout the process. Also, the pin-pointing of responsibility and its definition is essential to case management operations. . . .

This case-by-case emphasis does not mean a paternalistic patronizing caseload approach. On the contrary, one of the essential methods of case management is the calculation of client needs and requests in terms of the concrete factors which affect the care and the agency's abilities to respond. The governing idea is to keep the program lines clear and the relationship functional throughout the process. . . .

As a structure or set of requirements around which work can be organized and carried out, case management is made up of a series of seven separate but interconnected sets of activity:

—Evaluation of Request/Need
—Eligibility Determination of the Client/Applicant
—Planning for the Arrangement and/or Provision of Services
—Arranging for Service Delivery
—Provision of Services
—Overseeing
—Recording [Vol. 1, pp. 3-8]

As reported above, the term *case management* often means different things to different people. The term is used differently within various fields of practice. A 1978 U. S. Department of Health, Education and Welfare publication, *Interdisciplinary Glossary on Child Abuse and Neglect: Legal, Medical, Social Work Terms,* defines case management as follows:

Coordination of the multiplicity of services required by a child abuse and neglect client. Some of these services may be purchased from an agency other than the mandated agency. In general, the role of the case manager is not the provision of direct services but the monitoring of those services to assure that they are relevant to the client, delivered in a useful way, and appropriately used by the client. To do this, a case manager assumes the following responsibilities:

1) Ascertains that all mandated reports have been properly filed.
2) Informs all professionals involved with the family that reports of suspected child abuse or neglect have been made.
3) Keeps all involved workers apprised of new information.
4) Calls and chairs the initial case conference for assessment, disposition, and treatment plans; conference may include parents, physician, probation worker, police, public health nurse, private therapist, parent aide, protective service and welfare workers, or others.
5) Coordinates interagency follow-up.
6) Calls further case conferences as needed. [P. 7]

As used in the field of child abuse and neglect, case management is similar to what others have termed *case coordination.* After discussing differences between case coordination, case load management, case management, interagency coordination, and team models of practice, Bertsche and Horejsi (1978) define case coordination as

a direct service provided by a professional, sanctioned and planned by an interprofessional and interagency team, designed to mobilize and coordinate all significant resources, formal and informal needed and desired by a particular individual and his/her family in their efforts to deal with a specific problem or a set of interrelated problems. [P. 7]

Somewhat related to the concepts of case management and case coordination is case load management. In a discussion of social work supervisor-social worker relationships, Kadushin (1976) explains the concept of case load management:

The total caseload might be reviewed and some decision made as to those cases on which minimum effort might be expended because the situation is stable and not subject to much change. Other cases might be selected for more intensive consideration. The client in such cases may be more vulnerable, or the client and social situations may be open to positive change in response to active intervention by the worker. At the same time the supervisor can make clear to the worker where the agency's preferred priorities lie, which cases should receive service if time and energy are limited. [P. 43]

From this brief discussion of case management, it can be seen that it is a complex concept and one that still is evolving. Nevertheless, conceptually clear and well-designed approaches to case management are badly needed, especially in the practice of child welfare.

How Can Citizens Assess the Adequacy of Foster Family Services and the Need for Permanency Planning?

Social workers should urge and assist local and state-wide service organizations and interested citizens to study child welfare services, especially the foster care system. By doing so, citizens become better informed about the needs of children and families, more supportive of social services, and advocates for needed changes within social welfare structures.

A recent U. S. Department of Health, Education and Welfare publication provides a set of nontechnical guidelines that can be used by interested citizens and community groups. The publication, *Action for Foster Children: Community Self Evaluation Chart* (1974), is based on the ten-article Bill of Rights for Foster Children developed by the National Action for Foster Children. A slightly edited version of the guidelines is presented.

Article [I] . . . *Every foster child has the inherent right to be cherished by a family of his own, either his family helped by readily available services and supports to reassume his care, or an adoptive family or by plan, a continuing foster family.*

What services does your community provide to avoid unnecessary separation of children from their natural families?

Does your community provide twenty-four-hour emergency services for children in crisis?

What percentage of children are returned within reasonable time limits to improved family situations?

What percentage of children are placed for adoption? How long are they in care before they are adopted?

What percentage of children with special problems are placed in adoptive homes, either according to the usual plan or through the subsidized adoption plan?

What percentage of children are in permanent foster family care with signed agreements?

What is the average length of placement of foster children according to purpose of placement, i.e. emergency placement, return to natural family, placement for adoption, or permanent foster family?

Article [II] . . . *Every foster child has the inherent right to be nurtured by foster parents who have been selected to meet his individual needs and who are provided services and supports, including specialized education, so that they can grow in their ability to enable the child to reach his potential.*

Are there sufficient numbers of foster homes to allow for matching the qualities of each foster home to the child's special needs and developmental difficulties, such as adolescent, behavioral, emotional, and retardation problems?

Is there . . . [an aggressive, creative and] year-round challenging [foster home] recruitment program?

What is the foster care maintenance rate in your community? Does this [amount of money] cover the total cost of raising a foster child [or are foster parents dipping into their own pockets]?

Do foster parents receive a salary with fringe benefits?

Are foster parents given preservice and ongoing education for fostering? Who provides it? What does it include?

Article [III] . . . *Every foster child has the inherent right to receive sensitive, continuing help in understanding and accepting the reasons for his own family's inability to take care of him, and in developing confidence in his own self-worth.*

Where parental rights have not been terminated, how is the natural family involved in all major decisions affecting the child?

How do agency staff, including foster parents, respond to visiting by [biological] parents and significant family members?

What percent of natural family members visit . . . [their children in foster care on a regular basis]?

Are discussions held routinely with the foster family regarding the natural family and the reasons that made placement necessary?

Are discussions held with the child regarding the natural family and the reasons that made placement necessary?

Does agency staff including foster parents utilize . . . ways of helping [that assist] the foster child develop [self] confidence . . . [and a sense of] self-worth?

Article [IV] . . . Every foster child has the inherent right to receive continuing loving care and respect as a unique human being—a child growing in trust in himself and others.

Are foster families selected for parental abilities and qualities of warmth, acceptance of differences, and concern for foster children and their natural families?

Is there mutual trust between foster parents and social workers?

How often are children moved from foster home to foster home?

Are social workers changed at a rate that is harmful to the child?

What is the retention rate of foster families?

Do foster parents and social workers identify the foster child's talents, special abilities, and personal goals and secure special resources to develop them?

Article [V] . . . Every foster child has the inherent right to grow up in freedom and dignity in a neighborhood of people who accept him with understanding, respect and friendship.

Is there a community program to provide information for citizens about the needs of foster children? Who runs it?

Are there organized opportunities for citizens to express responsibility and commit themselves to become advocates for improved foster family services?

Are there programs which provide opportunities for citizens to be trained for and to work as volunteers with foster children and natural parents?

Do foster children have the same standing as other children in schools, recreation and neighborhood activities?

Article [VI] . . . Every foster child has the inherent right to receive help in overcoming deprivation or whatever distortion in his emotional, physical, intellectual, social and spiritual growth which may have resulted from his early experiences.

Is [the] social work staff qualified and experienced and effective in producing improvements in the above areas?

Is there provision for professional consultation (psychiatric, educational, psychological, etc.), as needed?

Are the preventive health, medical, dental, and optical needs of foster children being met? Are adequate financial resources available to meet these needs?

Does the agency have working agreements with other community groups to secure needed services?

What are the resources and services needed for foster children which are not available in your community? (list)

Article [VII] . . . Every foster child has the inherent right to receive education, training, and career guidance to prepare him for a useful and satisfying life.

Are there efforts to help school personnel understand the special stresses on foster children and to provide resources to help the child achieve?

Is there a planned program of determining education levels and for securing tutoring, if needed?

Is there a regular program of career counseling and guidance for foster children?

How many scholarships for college, vocational training, etc., were provided foster children last year?

Are community resources available for educating foster children with special handicaps, such as mental retardation, blindness, etc.?

Article [VIII] . . . Every foster child has the inherent right to receive preparation for citizenship and parenthood through interaction with foster parents and other adults who are consistent role models.

Are special efforts made to help each child remain with the same foster parents as long as helpful, to enable the child to adopt values and useful patterns?

Does interaction between [the] foster child [and] foster mother and father provide the child with consistent role models of good citizenship and parenthood?

Are other adult models available to the [foster] child?

Is the social work relationship helpful to the foster child?

Are foster children appropriately involved in group activities?

Article [IX] . . . Every foster child has the inherent right to be represented by an attorney at law in administrative or judicial proceedings with access to fair hearings and court review of decisions, so that his best interests are safeguarded.

Does the agency policy recognize and describe the legal status and rights of natural parents and the foster child?

Does the agency describe fair hearings and grievance procedures for natural parents and the foster child, and are these procedures regularly interpreted to parents and the foster child?

Is legal representation available to natural parents and foster child, especially for those who cannot afford it?

Is there provision for appropriate court review of agency decisions?

Article [X] . . . Every foster child has the inherent right to receive a high quality of child welfare services, including involvement of the natural parents and his own involvement in major decisions that affect his life.

Is funding sufficient to provide a good quality of foster family services?

Are there adequate employment procedures for prospective foster parents?

Are there licensing requirements for foster families which safeguard the child's well-being?

Are the number of foster children and their current problems limited to those each foster family can manage?

Is there a diagnostic conference and plan developed for each child by social service and foster parent staff?

Are foster parents involved individually and in conferences in the development of plans during placement and for termination of placement by return home, adoption, etc.?

Are foster parents given adequate agency help and support in carrying out their special roles in achieving goals determined in the social service diagnostic conference?

Does the supervising social worker develop a team relationship with foster parents in carrying out their respective roles?

Is there an immediate study involving natural parents and children when appropriate, for developing tentative diagnostic goals and time-limited steps to reach goals?

Does the social worker begin immediately to help the natural parents improve their situation?

Is the group method also used to improve the relationship between the natural parents and foster child?

What percent of natural parents whose rights have not been terminated were in conference with the social worker last month?

Is there an immediate development of a working relationship with the child?

Were diagnostic goals and intermediate time-limited steps established and carried out?

Is there a routine review of success in meeting goals?

Are workloads established according to the type of child and family problems and limited to a size (from 30-35 children for usual care situations) to enable workers to provide good services?

What percentage of natural families and foster children do not have a worker assigned?

Is there orientation and ongoing education for all staff?

Are there provisions for fair hearings and grievance procedures which are routinely interpreted for staff including foster parents?

Are there adequate procedures for semiannual or annual evaluations?

Are supervisors professionally qualified, experienced, and expected to supervise no more than six workers?

Are direct service workers selected for knowledge useful in helping people, personal qualifications, and interest in helping natural parents and foster children?

Answers to these questions provide a great deal of information about the strengths and weaknesses of foster family services. Adherence to the ten articles of the Bill of Rights for Foster Children would do much to reduce the problems experienced by children in foster care.

CHAPTER 6

The Child in Foster Care

What Are Some of the Common Problems Experienced by Foster Children?

FOSTER CHILDREN experience all of the normal problems of growing up. In addition, they experience special problems associated with the status of being a foster child. Within the context of discussing the problem of "drift" in foster care and the need for permanency planning, Emlen and others (1977) present striking examples of these special problems.

> Foster families often ask that the foster child be removed when a crisis occurs, even if the child has been there a long time—for instance, when the foster father dies or is laid off, or the foster mother becomes pregnant; she's tired and the extra room is needed.
>
> If a child changes families and schools during primary school years, his reading disabilities or poor vision may go unidentified and untreated.
>
> It may be difficult for a child to turn out for sports, because he is not in the same school throughout the season.
>
> It's not uncommon for foster children not to have up-to-date immunizations or to have the same ones two or three times because of frequent moves. Records aren't always accurately kept.
>
> Not all doctors wish to participate in the public medical assistance program, so foster children often go to a different doctor from the rest of the family.
>
> A foster child may not know until the last minute where he will spend important anniversaries or holidays. A foster boy soon to be five years old, on being told that he would be adopted by his foster parents, said, "Oh, now I know where I'll be on my birthday."
>
> At the beginning of the school year when the registration fee is due, the gym fee, school annual, student body card, etc.—delays in the agency's payment system identify the foster child as different. Special extras at school which cost money may also be passed up.
>
> Foster children always have a different name from the family and other children they live with, for which they have no simple explanation.
>
> Foster children in the same home often compare the actions of

their various natural parents. They often ask why one child sees his parent every other week-end, while another child visits only once in six months. One parent gives presents and another doesn't.

Foster children are often caught in jealousies between foster and own parents, and are torn in their loyalties to the families. As a result they miss out on many family functions such as birthdays, picnics, camping, etc. For instance, if a foster family birthday party conflicts with a week-end visit with a parent, the child won't ask for a change of week-ends because he knows how angry his own parents might become at the suggestion. [P. 12]

In addition to these concrete and practical problems, foster children typically experience psychological and emotional conflicts.

What Conflicts Does the Foster Child Experience?

Since each child is different, it is difficult to predict children's reactions to foster care. There is danger in believing that all foster children experience this or that feeling or personal struggle. However, persons who have had many years of experience with foster children have identified many concerns that frequently are troublesome to foster children. They may or may not apply to a given child. Some of the more commonly reported concerns are presented below in the form of questions that the foster child asks himself/herself.

1. Why am I in foster care? Does this mean I am somehow different from other children? Is there something wrong with me?

2. Why couldn't my parents take care of me? Did they really try? Would they have been able to care for me if I had not misbehaved?

3. Did I do something so bad that my parents could not or did not want to keep me any longer? What did I do to deserve this? Am I being punished?

4. If my parents could not do a good job of raising me, does that mean that I will not be a good parent when I grow up? Will I have the same problems? Are those problems inherited?

5. What is my future? Will I ever go home to my parents? Will they ever want me?

6. What is happening to my parents? Have they forgotten me? Do they still care?

7. Will I be moved to still another foster home if I do not please my foster parents? How will I know what they expect?

8. Who am I supposed to believe? My parents tell me one thing, my foster parents tell me something else, and my social worker gives me a third opinion!

9. I wish I could get back at my parents for hurting me. They do not care for me and I hate them! Yet, I know I should not hate my parents.

The reader will recognize that many of the above statements express common human feelings and reactions to separation and emotional conflict. The more completely the child understands the real reasons why he/she is in foster care, the easier the adjustment will be. If the reasons are unclear, the child undoubtedly will create a fantasy or jump to conclusions that help make sense out of his/her current life experience. Except in the case of small children, it is best for the social worker to be open and honest about the child's situation.

What Is Meant by the Statement That the Foster Child Has Multiple Parents?

Most children have a single set of parents. Unlike other children, foster children have several sets of parents. Reistroffer (1974a) states that the foster child

> has multiple parents, parents who have impact from his past, have important involvement in his present, and portend much for his future. These multiple parents cannot be erased or ignored and we must help the foster parents and the foster child understand them and cope with them because they affect the child's daily life and his future. [Pp. 1-2]

First, a foster child has biological or natural parents. The child usually refers to his/her natural parents as his/her "real parents."

> The biological parents exist for the foster child whether or not they are involved in his present life. Even if the child has no recollection of them, has had no good or bad experiences with them, never mentions them or is not currently in contact with them, they are real and directly affect his life and his adjustment. . . . Even if he has no memory of these blood parents, they affect him because the simple fact that he is *not* with them means much in his mind

and feelings. It means that he thinks—and feels—he is some kind of unloveable creature who was too unacceptable to be kept with them, that he is basically a "bad character" who likely caused the breakup with his family, and that he will be whole only when he is "found" by his biological parents. . . . If his feeling memories . . . include bad treatment by his biological parents, his life is worsened because this is confirmation of his essential badness and unacceptability. [Reistroffer, 1974a, pp. 2-3]

As described above, foster care can be a situation fraught with confusion and conflict for the child. The uncertainty and subjective meaning of foster care can be a source of anxiety for many children. In an effort to make sense out of his/her situation and deal with anxiety, feelings of unworthiness, and guilt, the child may create still another set of parents, what some writers refer to as imaginary parents or the dream parents. "The dream parents of the foster child are the kind typical of all children, who when vexed or angry with parents, imagine they have 'other parents someplace.' They are, however, more significant and meaningful for the foster child because they are, touchingly, the parents he *wishes* he had" (Reistroffer, 1974a, p. 3).

Most people recognize these fantasy experiences of childhood. Children commonly have fantasies about being adopted. The child thinks, "If these were my real parents they would treat me much better, so somewhere out there I must have parents who really love me." Such human experiences are more complex and confusing to the foster child because he/she really does have another set of parents. While a certain amount of fantasy and make-believe is a normal way to cope with stress and confusion—especially for children—excessive fantasy can hamper adjustment to reality.

One of the basic arguments advanced for visits by natural parents is that they provide the foster child with information—a sense of reality—about his/her real situation. Such visits can be painful and upsetting for the child, particularly if the parent is drunk, abusive, or embarassing, but such visits may present the child with an accurate picture of why he/she is in foster care and what his/her parents are like. Furthermore, it may help the child understand that he/she is not guilty or responsible for breaking up his/her family. It is believed that the child is better off struggling to understand and adjust to a harsh reality than living with an unreal fantasy, e.g. his/her mother no longer drinks to excess, lives in a big white house on the hill, and will soon rescue him/her from the foster home.

Foster parents are a third set of parents in the foster child's life. They may be far from perfect human beings and cannot measure up to dream parents. The life of the foster child is further confused by the fact that each family has its own rules, values, and ways of dealing with life. The foster child, especially one subjected to replacement, will be exposed to a variety of models and asked to conform to many different and often conflicting sets of expectations. In many ways, the social worker and the agency represent additional parental figures insofar as they exert control over the child's destiny.

What Is Meant by Regression of the Foster Child?

Essentially, regressive behavior refers to behavior that would be expected of a younger child at an earlier stage of biological and psychosocial development. If a child regresses, he or she slides backward in development. It is fairly common in children who find themselves in stressful situations. For example, a child completely free of bed-wetting may resume wetting as a reaction to placement in foster care. Regression may be manifested as eating problems, sleep disturbances, temper tantrums, or whining and clinging behavior, etc. In most cases, it is time limited. Once the child begins to feel secure, regressive behavior diminishes.

What Is the Honeymoon Period?

Some children have extreme reactions to foster care placement and the separation that immediately precedes it. A few children—especially older ones—may react with overt anger and aggression. Some run away. Most experienced foster parents recall placements that were "pure hell" for the first few weeks. Not all children, however, react overtly. Some children may have a different type of reaction—one in which they do not exhibit the problem behavior that seems natural to such a stressful situation. Writing from a psychodynamic perspective, Kline and Overstreet (1972) state:

> Some children, in direct contrast to those who react to placement with overt disturbance, present a superficial picture of adaptation to the entire placement experience with a notable absence of the kinds of behavior that make adults uncomfortable. Even symptoms known to exist before placement may suddenly disappear. This phase has sometimes been called the "honeymoon" period. It may last for a few weeks or a few months. It is reassuring to the adults involved to see the child accept the loss of his previous environment without overt distress and take on the new environment with apparent ease. . . . It is exceedingly tempting to accept the child's behavior as a reflection of true adaptation. In most instances, however, the initial conforming adjustment is not a reflection of adaptation; on the contrary, it may reflect a degree of anxiety that the child cannot master except by total repression and denial. Only as he becomes increasingly safe in the new situation can he tolerate the anxieties that threaten him; then the pseudomaturity may break down into symptomatic behavior, sometimes after weeks or months of placement. [P. 79]

In situations where the foster child's reaction to placement appears to be that of a pseudoadjustment, the social worker should make a special effort to explain the honeymoon phase to the foster parents and prepare them for the eventual breakdown of the child's good behavior. If this is not done, the foster parents may conclude that they have done something wrong or become demoralized by feelings of personal failure.

It is noteworthy that the honeymoon period overlaps with the period when the social worker can be of greatest help to the foster parents. Aldridge, Cautley, and Lichstein (1974, p. 13) state that "one recurring relationship throughout the analysis of the data of this study was that input during the first few weeks of placement was crucial." It is the first few weeks of a placement that are pattern setting.

What Is the Mourning Reaction in Foster Children?

Foster children separated from their parents and familiar surroundings and placed with a strange family frequently experience a reaction that some authors refer to as grieving or mourning and others describe as a separation reaction (Bowlby, 1962; Didier, 1977; Littner, 1956; Thomas, 1967; and Walker, 1971). While the child's age, circumstances surrounding the placement, and other factors affect how he/she reacts to separation, it is possible to offer a few generalizations.

First, it must be recognized that separation from familiar people and places is difficult for most people, adults and children. People find security in familiarity and sameness. Even in cases of severe child abuse, most children would rather remain with their abusing parents than move to a physically safe but strange environment. In such cases, losing the emotional or psychological security that comes from being in a familiar and predictable situation is more fearsome than occasional physical pain.

When the children are separated from parents, their reactions often resemble those of persons who have lost a loved one through death. Sometimes the reaction occurs in stages such as shock, denial, anger and protest, despair and depression, and, finally, resolution or adjustment. It is interesting to note that these reactions, long observed in foster children, are similar to those described in recent books on dying (Kübler-Ross, 1969). The reactions also are similar to those commonly described in the literature on crisis theory and crisis intervention. For many children, separation and placement precipitate a genuine psychological crisis. The reader interested in exploring the relationship between crisis theory and separation reactions should consult the professional social work literature of crisis intervention (Darbonne, 1973; Golan, 1974; Kaplan, 1973; Lukton, 1974; Oppenheimer, 1967; Parad, 1977; Parad, Selby, and Ouilan, 1976; Pasewark and Albers, 1972; Porter, 1973; and Rapoport, 1970).

Shock is a typical first reaction to separation and placement. The child shows little emotion and appears docile. Shock may explain the honeymoon phase frequently observed early in the placement. A period of denial also is typical. The child may talk as if his or her return home is imminent and as if the placement has not really happened or is a mistake soon to be corrected. When the reality of the situation is finally acknowledged by the youngster, he or she may react with anger toward the foster parents, natural parents, social worker, and anyone else associated with the painful situation. As the child tries to fight his or her way out of the placement, temper outbursts, crying, and running away may occur. When the child realizes that he or she cannot return home and that anger and protest do not change the situation, he/she may enter a phase of depression or despair accompanied by a loss of interest in friends, hobbies, play, and school. Some children experience disturbances in patterns of sleeping and eating. Regression also may be apparent.

In time, the child begins to put the separation into perspective and understand why the placement was necessary. Finally, the placement—while not a happy situation—is at least something that can be lived with, and he/she picks up on previous interests and reaches out to others, resuming his/her former pattern of behavior.

Even though some of these common reactions have been described as if they progressed through definite phases, the reader should be aware that they are not predictable. The stages may overlap and/or deviate from the order presented. Some stages may not be evident at all. In addition, some children move through the reactions within a matter of days, while others may struggle with these conflicting feelings for several weeks or even months. Ordinarily, however, one would expect to see the initial turmoil of placement decrease gradually and reach resolution and acceptance within two to three months. If the adjustment reactions continue longer, it may signal the existence of psychological problems requiring psychological or psychiatric consultation. The continuation of adjustment problems also may indicate that the match between foster child and foster family is contributing to the difficulty.

In the vast majority of cases, visits by the child's parents facilitate the adjustment. If a parent has been hospitalized, for example, a visit to the parent helps the child understand the reasons behind the separation and placement. Even disruptive visits by drunk or mentally ill parents help the child to more accurately perceive reality and understand that his or her parent is not able to provide a home at this particular time. If the child is not given an opportunity to confront and struggle with the reality related to placement in foster care, fantasy may delay or distort the adjustment process. A discussion of disruptive visits by the natural parents appears elsewhere in this book.

What Are the Common Goals in Direct Work with Foster Children?

Those working with the foster child should attend to four basic goals. First, every effort should be made to stabilize the child's life so that development and learning can proceed at a normal rate. Excessive anxiety and insecurity can interfere with normal development and learning. Second, efforts should be made to compensate for current learning or developmental deficits caused by previous life experiences. For example, if the child has nutritional deficits, special attention should be given to the child's diet and eating patterns. If the child has fallen behind in basic skills such as reading, remedial programs should be made available to the child. A third goal is to help the child come to terms with and make a realistic adjustment to his/her current life situation, understanding the events that led to placement in foster care. Reistroffer, an expert on foster care, describes this process as helping the child come to peace with the past. Finally, every effort should be made to help the child develop a relationship with at least one other person who really cares about him/her and can affirm the child's worth. The latter goal is especially important because the foster child typically questions his/her worth and feels unloveable. It makes little difference whether the child forms such a relationship with the foster parent, a teacher, the social worker, or a relative. The important point is that a meaningful relationship does much to counter the child's feelings of being different and rejected and provides an opportunity to talk about personal concerns and conflicts.

In an article on the preparation of foster children for adoption, Chestang and Heymann (1976) have stated that the first step in working with foster children is "to clarify for the children that they are not bad; that parents are human beings who sometimes have problems; that they cannot always handle their problems;

and that it is not the children's fault that placement becomes necessary" (p. 35). This objective is similar to Reistroffer's notion of helping the child come to peace with the past.

Some of the work with children typically includes a review of past events and a working through of old conflicts. Many hours and a high level of social work skill and sensitivity are required to form a trusting relationship with a child and help him/her deal with these conflicts.

> While it is possible to establish a trusting relationship by focusing on events in the present, review of the past is necessary as a means of working through children's unrealistic guilt feelings about responsibility for family breakdowns and their being sent away. . . . Children's questions about why they are in foster care and what happened to their parents provide the content for these discussions. Through this process children are helped to achieve a realistic picture of the reasons why they are not able to live with their own families and the guilt surrounding this fact is attenuated. [Chestang and Heymann, 1976, p. 35]

Useful information on the specific skills and methods of building relationships and communicating with children can be found in Axline, 1947; Della-Piana, 1973; Ginott, 1965, 1969; Gordon, 1970; Redl, 1966; Rich, 1968; and Zwerdling, 1974.

Nonverbal methods are especially important in work with children. In their work with "hard to place children," Unger, Dwarshuis, and Johnson (1977) have used concrete visual aids such as scrapbooks and life books.

> During their preparation for adoption, many children are able to discuss important issues and provide answers to questions which help workers locate an appropriate available family for each child. Some children, however, especially those who are very young or who have been badly hurt emotionally, may not be able to express their feelings directly or to respond to expressions of feelings. In working with these children, the Spaulding [agency] staff have learned to use "concrete," rather than "abstract," methods of communication. These simple, visual communication aids are invaluable resources for the worker who is committed to helping the child adjust to himself and his new placement situation. [P. 83]

Since play is a primary means of expression for children, it is a useful nonverbal communication technique. Puppets, dolls, drawings, and toys can be used to help a child express or act out thoughts and feelings.

What Is a Psychological Parent?

One of the basic conflicts experienced by foster children—especially those who have been in foster care for many years—is that of being torn between feelings of affection toward the foster parents and the desire or longing to have a meaningful relationship with the biological parents. Research on parent-child bonding, searches by adopted children, and other recent developments have focused increased attention on the importance of the biological parent, even in cases where the past parent-child relationship was characterized by abuse, neglect, and severe conflict. On the other hand, it also is apparent that children develop meaningful relationships with substitute or surrogate parents. The disruption of close relationships between foster child and foster parent can be a painful experience.

Some writers apply the term *psychological parent* to the parent figure who is of central importance to the child. Goldstein, Freud, and Solnit (1973) define the term as follows:

> A psychological parent is one who, on a continuing, day-to-day basis, through interaction, companionship, interplay, and mutuality, fulfills the child's psychological needs for a parent, as well as the child's physical needs. The psychological parent may be a biological, . . . adoptive, foster, or common-law . . . parent, or any other person. There is no presumption in favor of any of these after the initial assignment at birth. [P. 98]

In discussions of permanency planning and the termination of parental rights, increasing weight is given to the relationship between the child and the psychological parent. The recognized importance of the psychological parent has resulted in a reevaluation of policies that discourage the legal adoption of a foster child by foster parents.

How Can the Foster Child Be Helped to Maintain Ties with His/Her Parents?

Considering the importance of preserving the relationship between foster child and his/her natural parents, efforts should be made to help the child maintain parental ties. Simple acts can serve this purpose, for example:

1. Help foster child make or buy gifts for parents.
2. Help foster child make birthday cake or treats for parents.
3. Help foster child plan birthday party for parents.
4. Encourage child to show parents grades, awards, school projects, etc.
5. Help foster child write letters or send cards on Mother's Day, Father's Day, and other holidays.

What Is Meant by the Term Replacement?

Replacement refers to the movement of a foster child from his/her current foster home to another foster home. While replacement is sometimes necessary and unavoidable, professionals agree that it is undesirable and should be avoided if possible.

Replacement increases the child's insecurity and sense of being rootless. It reactivates painful feelings of rejection and further reinforces the child's belief that he/she is unwanted by and unacceptable to others. Replacement hampers the child's development of a sense of identity, i.e. who am I, and where do I belong? It increases the child's distrust of parental and other adult figures, e.g. the social worker, and reinforces fear of separation, causing the child to avoid close attachments. It increases the chances of adjustment problems that will, in turn, decrease the chances of success in a subsequent placement. Thus, a vicious cycle is set in motion. Replacement contributes to the development of an adult behavior characterized by shallowness in affect and limited capacity to form meaningful and satisfactory human relationships.

Given the disadvantages of replacement, the social worker should approach such decisions with extreme caution. To prevent the need for replacement, additional time and resources must be devoted to maintaining the current placement.

How Is a Foster Child's Life Book Helpful?

Not infrequently, foster children have problems of personal identity. This is especially true of the child who enters foster care at an early age and subsequently loses contact with his or her natural family. Such children are curious and sometimes puzzled about their roots. It is normal and natural for them to want to know about their parents and relatives.

A well-kept scrapbook or life book can help the foster child preserve a connection with the past and establish a sense of personal identity. Included in the scrapbook should be pertinent information about the child's parents, grandparents, brothers, sisters, and other significant persons; e.g. birthdates, nationalities, hobbies, interests, and talents. The child's birth certificates, baptismal records, and school records also should be included. Since family photographs are especially meaningful to the foster child, the social worker should make a special effort to obtain photographs of the natural parents, siblings, and relatives. In addition, pictures of the foster child and the foster parents should be taken on a regular basis and included in the scrapbook. The foster child should be helped to secure and preserve scrapbook entries. The scrapbook belongs to the foster child, not to the social worker, agency, or foster parents. It may be his/her only link with the past.

Whenever possible, relevant information about diseases experienced by the natural parents or close relatives, causes of their deaths, or unusual physical characteristics should be recorded. Such information may be of importance to the foster child later in life.

What Is a Genogram?

The genogram, a tool used by many family therapists, has been adapted by Dr. Ann Hartman of the University of Michigan School of Social Work for use in dealing with the questions or problems of identity common among foster children and adopted children. According to Hartman (1976), "The genogram is a simple picture of a family through time which captures and makes available for observation the life history of a family and helps to surface the family transmissions, assignments, secrets and projections." A variety of symbols and notations may be used in the genogram to record names, dates of birth and death, occupations, place of birth, current residences, talents, interests, personality characteristics and structural information on the family. Hartman notes:

> The genogram organizes and records a vast amount of information about a family system as it exists through time and may be used in any practice situation where such family information would be useful (e.g., a child in long term foster care, an aged person involved in life review, an adolescent struggling with identity issues, a person unable to parent). [P. 2]

The genogram is used by many Michigan child welfare workers and has been found useful as a recording device.

CHAPTER 7

Recruitment of Foster Families

What Is Meant by Recruitment?

RECRUITMENT IS primarily a process of reaching out to the public, explaining the need for foster homes, and enlisting new foster parents into the foster family care systems. The purpose of recruitment is to strengthen and replenish the resource pool from which a particular foster home can be selected to care for a specific foster child. The larger the pool, the greater the opportunity to select a foster home that will meet the needs of a particular youngster. This notion is expressed in the guidelines developed by the American Public Welfare Association (1975).

> A sufficient number of foster families shall be selected for personal qualities and foster parenting ability so that each individual child's needs will be met and objectives for the child and his family will be achieved. Family composition, number of children in a family, age of the foster parent(s), health, income, employment, moral, ethical, and spiritual development, physical facilities, location of the home, and comfort and privacy shall be expected to sustain the highest level of foster parenting. [P. 43]

A program of effective recruitment is of critical importance because a shortage of foster homes can result in an inappropriate match between the needs, desires, and abilities of the foster parents and the needs of a foster child and/or his or her natural parents. Such a mismatch creates frustration for all concerned. Frequently, a high rate of replacement and burnout among foster parents is a sign of poor matching caused by a shortage of foster homes.

> The shortage of [foster] homes limits the deliberate care with which the social worker can select a home for a particular child. Despite the [professional] practice view that priority should be given to the child's needs, in actuality not need but resources available often determines the decisions. [Kadushin, 1974a, p. 457]

A shortage of good foster homes is a problem frequently reported by child welfare agencies.

Why Is the Recruitment of Foster Homes So Difficult?

At the core of foster parenting is a major personal decision—a decision to spend one's time and effort being a foster parent rather than devoting time and effort to something else. The foster parent freely chooses to take on and struggle with the problems and frustrations that accompany the parent role. Because many foster children have severe problems, foster parenting can be stressful. Making the situation even more complex is the fact that the child's natural parents, the social worker, and the agency also are involved. All take time and place demands upon the foster parents. To become a foster parent, an individual must believe that the rewards outweigh the frustrations, and to continue in the role, the actual experience must provide more rewards than frustrations.

It is reasonable to assume that there is a finite limit to the number of foster homes that can be developed in a given community. In any community there is a limited number of people who can or will become foster parents. This number can be termed the *foster parent pool,* which consists of actual foster homes (those already in service or licensed) and potential foster homes (those yet to be recruited). Sociocultural variables, e.g. economics and family values, determine the size of the pool. The pool is larger, for example, in those communities that place high value on family life and parenting and devalue women working outside the home. Because there are community-to-community differences, a recruiting approach that works in one community may fail in another. Recruitment efforts should be individualized to the community.

How Long Do People Remain Foster Parents?

There is a constant turnover among foster parents. Some are foster parents for a short time; others continue in the role for twenty or more years. The average length of service by foster parents caring for physically normal children is from four to six years. While good comparison data are not available, there is reason to believe that the average length of service for foster parents servicing children with special problems, e.g. mental retardation or physical handicaps, is less than four years.

Because of the turnover among foster parents, recruitment efforts must be continuous. To maintain and retain foster homes, it is probably necessary for agencies to move toward the concept of professional foster parents, including elements of a career ladder, respite care, paid vacations, special training, and various supportive services. The professionalization of foster parenting provides additional rewards and enhances the image and status of foster parents. It also increases the cost of foster family care.

How Can People Be Attracted to Foster Parenting?

Studies indicate that, of the people who make an inquiry about becoming foster parents, only a small number actually become foster parents; usually less than 10 percent and rarely more than 20 percent. This fact underscores the reality that those responsible for finding homes must reach a large number of people to find a single foster home.

The child welfare literature on recruitment suggests that continuous recruitment efforts are more effective than sporadic bursts of intensive recruitment. Therefore, one should recruit constantly, day after day, year after year. Blitz efforts, because they must make heavy use of the media (television, radio, newspaper advertisements, etc.) rather than the slower person-to-person, informal channels of communication, seldom are effective, and attrition rates are high. A media campaign attracts many inquiries about foster care, but most applicants drop out. Because of the need for a continuous, ongoing recruitment effort and the expense involved, full-time recruitment coordinators or home finders usually are necessary. Cooperative multiagency efforts are most cost-effective. Recruitment efforts should be concentrated on those groups or neighborhoods most likely to contain potential foster parents. For example, a speech before the local professional women's club probably is a wasted effort, while a presentation before a home extension group is likely to reach those whose personal values center on home, family, and childrearing, and are more likely to consider seriously becoming foster parents.

In conducting research on foster care, Gruber (1977) asked a sample of 147 foster mothers what it would take to interest others in foster parenting. Several suggestions were offered by these foster parents.

> The most frequent suggestion was to increase publicity and public awareness of the need for foster parents. This was mentioned by 58.5% of the respondents. Almost half of the foster parents, however, felt that the most important single necessary change was to make better services available to them. The third most frequent response was to allot more money per child, again mentioned by almost half of the parents. This response was made in spite of the fact that most foster parents previously mentioned that finances was not a consideration when deciding to become a foster parent. Related to this about ⅓ of the foster parents thought salaries for foster parenting would interest more people. [P. 173]

Advertising experts know that image is critical. Those who want to recruit foster homes also must pay attention to image. The public image of foster children, foster parents, social workers, social services, and all that is associated with foster family care has much to do with whether people are attracted to foster parenting. People want to be valued; they will avoid placing themselves in situations where a negative image spreads to them. Thus, enhancing the image of the social agency, social services, the foster care program, and the professional staff, etc., makes recruitment easier but not easy. It must be realized, however, that the cultivation of a positive image is a slow, continuous process. Attractive office space, competent performance, favorable publicity, and appropriate educational credentials are some of the components of a favorable public image. Those involved in foster home recruitment must create a positive image of themselves as professionals and of the program they represent. They must believe in the value of foster family care and convey this conviction to the public.

A variety of approaches should be used to make citizens aware of the need for foster homes: television and radio spots, leaflets, posters, shopping bag stuffers, newspaper advertisements and articles, and speakers, etc. It generally is recognized, however, that the most effective recruitment is done by other foster parents. A useful technique, therefore, is to have foster parents present the recruitment message to the public. They should be encouraged and helped to make presentations before appropriate groups. Audio- or videotapes of interviews with foster parents can be used when foster parents are unavailable for in-person appearances.

Recruitment speeches should be accompanied by a slide show or other visual presentation of happy foster children and foster parents and other pictures that portray a positive yet realistic image of foster care. It is important to mention the frustrations of foster parenting, but they always should be balanced with attention to the rewards of foster parenting. The first step in recruitment is to get people to think about the possibility of becoming foster parents and to seek additional information. Subsequently, attention can be addressed to the task of screening out those who are hopelessly naive, overly idealistic, or unsuitable for other reasons.

To the greatest extent possible, the foster home recruiter should use a one-to-one or a small-group context to discuss the need for foster homes and describe foster parenting. This permits the recruiter to individualize his/her presentation and respond to concerns or questions. The recruiter must realize that he/she is dealing with a great deal of ambivalence in those who have a spark of interest in becoming foster parents. Once interest is aroused, the recruiter must nurse it along with information, empathetic listening, straight answers to their questions, and assurances that resources are available to help them cope. Such individualized attention should be given in a face-to-face situation. It is nearly impossible to individualize the recruitment effort within the context of a large-group meeting. Thus, as a general rule, it is better to meet with many small groups rather than one large group. Moreover, it is better to talk privately with an individual or couple than to talk with them when they are members of a small group.

The recruiter should arrange recruitment presentations to allow ample opportunity for informal, friendly chats and individualized communication with those in attendance. On the other hand, it must be realized that some interested people are cautious in their approach. They may wish to hang back, size up the situation, gather more information, and think it over. The recruiter must not appear pushy. He/she must be courteous, positive, and realistic. Moreover, the recruiter must avoid communicating the impression that the agency is so desperate for homes that it will place a child with the next person who walks through the door; such an attitude frightens prospective foster parents. People want to be protected from making bad decisions. They expect social workers to help them think through the pros and cons of becoming a foster parent: that is the social worker's job. The social worker must be open and friendly but professional in his/her approach to people who are making an inquiry. As used here, the term *professional* refers to systematic and objective assessment and decision making based on knowledge.

One approach to creating an opportunity for individualized conversations with potential foster families is for the recruiter to announce (radio, newspaper, church bulletins, etc.) that he/she will be at a particular place, e.g. church hall, bank meeting room at a given time, e.g. between 1 and 5 PM on Sunday, and invite people to stop by and talk about foster parenting and foster care. Refreshments and a short film may offer added attraction. Baby-sitters or child care arrangements may be necessary to get the adult's undivided attention at such a meeting.

If someone makes an inquiry about becoming a foster parent, the recruiter should respond quickly with an interview or other follow-up. Those who make an inquiry usually are ambivalent about foster parenting. If a response is delayed, e.g. if the recruiter is slow to return a telephone call, their interest diminishes. An in-person follow-up interview is the preferred response. If that is not possible, the telephone should be used. Many potential foster parents are lost because they are kept on the string for weeks. It is important for the recruiter to reinforce moves toward further exploration of foster parenting.

As previously indicated, face-to-face and word-of-mouth communication, especially from other foster parents, are the most effective means of attracting potential foster parents. However, some media work is usually necessary. It is advisable to consult

with a journalist or advertising specialist to develop effective
written recruitment materials (posters, newspaper advertisements,
classified advertisements, and fliers).

What Is Meant by Reaching Out, or Assertive Recruitment?

Most recruitment strategies are passive. In an advertisement
campaign, for example, the message is put before the public; the
recruitment staff then waits for people to respond and express
an initial interest in foster parenting. This is not unlike the advertising done by a department store, where the purpose is to get
people to come to the store so the salesmen have a chance to talk
with the potential buyers.

An opposite approach might be called *reaching out,* or *assertive
recruitment.* In this approach, the recruiter identifies an individual or couple who might be interested in foster parenting, approaches them directly, and asks if they might like to learn about
foster parenting. Such an approach resembles that of the sales-
man who works on leads. Martin and Keltner (1975) used such
an approach to recruit Navajo foster families. They state that

> The task force did not content itself in recruitment to the mere
> usage of posters and public advertisements to encourage Navajo
> families to make application for foster parenthood. Using informa-
> tion solicited from our staff, trading post operations, chapter and
> tribal officials and staff of related social service agencies, we ap-
> proached families referred to us as stable family and community
> members inviting their participation to learn more of our efforts in
> foster care. Many of these families became foster families. [P. 160]

The assertive approach to foster home recruitment is especially
useful in communities where people are reluctant to respond to
advertisements or, for one reason or another, are hesitant to
contact agencies and seek out additional information. There is
reason to believe that the assertive approach to recruitment is
especially useful in small communities or rural areas. In such
areas, it is fairly easy to identify those families who might be
receptive to the idea of foster parenting.

Is There a Relationship Between the Level of Foster Home Payments and the Ease of Foster Home Recruitment?

There is tremendous variation in the amount of money paid

for foster care. In 1975, for example, monthly foster care payments ranged from a low of $65 in New Mexico to a high of $263 in Alaska. Culley, Healy, Settles, and VanName (1977) state that "virtually every state has a different payment schedule. Some states elect to vary payments on the basis of the foster child's age, while others pay a fixed amount per child or vary payments according to where the child is located in the state or what year of school the child is in" (p. 222).

A statistical analysis by Simon (1975) suggests a positive relationship between foster care payments and the number of available foster homes. Since money influences behavior in many areas of life, this finding is not surprising. The success of subsidized adoption programs provides further evidence for the belief that a more realistic monthly payment makes foster parenting attractive to a larger number of people.

In one empirical study of money as an attraction, a school of social work placed two newspaper advertisements a month apart. The first advertisement appealed for foster parents and mentioned "modest financial remuneration." This advertisement attracted five couples who were potential foster parents, most of whom were deeply religious. The second advertisement was identical except for the fact that "reasonable financial remuneration" was offered. A total of 185 people responded to the second advertisement. This is further evidence that money makes a difference.

The social worker looks for many qualities in potential foster parents, and those persons interested only in money should not be selected. However, there is no evidence to support a belief that the quality of foster parenting lessens as the size of payment increases. There is also reason to believe that a higher monthly payment reduces the turnover. Many foster parents must dip into their pockets to meet the normal costs of foster parenting. It is not unusual for foster parents to use their own money to buy their foster child a class ring, school pictures, a yearbook, or clothing. Such a situation adds to the normal frustrations of being a foster parent. Few foster parents expect to make money, but it is unfair when they must lose money in order to perform a vital task for society. Settles, Culley, and VanName (1977) discuss the actual costs of caring for a foster child.

Is It Possible to Find Foster Homes for Adolescents?

While many of the adolescents in need of substitute care are best served in group homes, others can adapt to foster family homes. The recruitment of foster family homes for adolescents is difficult.

Bonlender (1977) has outlined an approach to the recruitment of homes for teenagers that makes heavy use of advertisement. The approach uses a variety of methods to reach large numbers of people (newspaper articles, news releases, radio spots, questionnaires placed in banks, radio talk shows, grocery stuffers, and pamphlets, etc.). According to Bonlender, these techniques were designed to accomplish the following:

1) Generate interest and questions about adolescent foster care
2) To activate people already interested in foster care into action
3) To allow for an informative, educational exchange of information about foster care
4) To deal with the myth, stigma, and stereotyping of foster care
5) To increase the number of licensed adolescent foster homes available. [P. 1]

Two techniques, a questionnaire and a grocery bag stuffer, are novel and may be of special interest to the reader. The recruitment questionnaire that was placed in banks is presented below.

"WOULD SOMEONE HELP ME UNDERSTAND THE WORLD I LIVE IN?"
"I don't understand. My parents say they love me, but they're always yelling at me."

Adolescents are in urgent need of foster homes in your community. Maybe you can help.

	Yes	No
Do you enjoy helping guide adolescents into adulthood?	___	___
Do you have extra time to spend with someone who needs to be cared about?	___	___

Do you understand what is important to an adolescent?	___ ___
Do you have room in your home for one more?	___ ___
Would your family be accepting of an adolescent foster child?	___ ___
Are you open-minded and fair?	___ ___
Can you be firm and kind at the same time?	___ ___
Are you willing to listen to someone who needs to talk?	___ ___
Do you care about the young people in your area?	___ ___

Foster parents come from all walks and professions of life. They are people who care about young people. Good foster homes already exist within your community, but we have more kids than we have homes.

If you are able to answer "Yes" to the above questions or would like more information, please contact Debbie or Nancy at Sherburne County Society Services at 441-1711, 253-2384, or 662-2524.

We have kids who need you now. [Bonlender, 1977, P. 15]

The grocery stuffer was placed in customers' grocery bags as they left the checkout counters in supermarkets. It, too, can serve as a model.

SHOPPER'S CHECKLIST
10 lbs. of guidance
2 dozen boxes of time
30 lb. of understanding
1 room
1 bag of acceptance of adolescents
1 gross of open-mindedness
12 tons of fairness
16 lb. of firmness
Lots of kindness
Indefinite amount of listening skills
20 gallons of concern and caring

Foster parents come from all walks and professions of life. They are people who care about young people. Good foster homes already exist within your community, but we have more adolescents than we have homes.

If you are able to complete this checklist or would like more information, please contact Debbie or Nancy at Sherburne County Social Services at 441-1711, 253-2384, or 662-2524.

A film and meeting will be August 23rd at 7:50 p.m. at the Elk

River Public Library. If you are interested please call or come to the meeting.

Adolescents need homes too! [Bonlender, 1977, p. 20]

How Can the Public Be Made Aware of Problems and Issues Related to Foster Family Services?

Individuals interested in informing the public can find ideas on both method and content by studying the efforts of agencies that have developed successful public information programs. Organizations such as the Child Welfare League of America and the American Public Welfare Association are sources of such information.

A recent 304-page book by Bast and Crass (1977) provides detailed descriptions of newspaper columns and radio programs used to recruit foster homes in Wisconsin. The book is a rich source of innovative ideas on how to reach the public and inform them about foster care and other social services.

CHAPTER 8

Selection of Foster Families

What Is Meant by Selection?

A S USED IN THIS chapter, the term *selection* refers to a screening process that follows recruitment. It involves the assessment and preparation of applicants for the task of foster parenting. Individuals or couples selected to be foster parents are then licensed by a state social services agency. Those licensed have met the basic requirements for being foster parents. Subsequent to selection, a matching decision must be made relating to the question of whether a particular child should be placed in foster home A or foster home B.

What Personal Qualities Should Foster Parents Possess?

The CWLA *Standards for Foster Family Service* (1975) suggests that foster parents should be persons—

—who care about others and respond to them
—who enjoy being parents
—who are able to give affection and care to a child without expecting immediate returns
—who show flexibility in their expectations, attitudes and behavior in relation to the age, needs and problems of children, as well as an ability to use help when needed to meet problems of family living
—who are able to accept the child's relationship with his parents and with the agency
—who have worked out satisfactory and stable adult relationships, without severe problems in their sexual identifications or in handling angry feelings
—who are able to maintain meaningful positive relationships with members of their own families and with persons outside the family
—who are emotionally stable and able to function adequately in relation to family responsibilities and employment, as indicated both currently and in the history of the family

—who have reputable characters, values and ethical standards conducive to the well-being of children. [P. 54]

Few would disagree with the importance of these qualities. However, there are many problems associated with the task of determining whether a particular foster home applicant possesses the desired qualities.

What Are Unacceptable Motives for Foster Parenting?

Motivation can be viewed as a hope-discomfort balance. In other words, people are motivated to take a certain action because they think it will give them something they want and/or because they wish to escape a situation with which they are not completely satisfied or with which they are uncomfortable. They move toward that which they desire (hope) and away from that which is somehow distressing (discomfort). Applying this simple but useful model to foster parenting, one would assume that people interested in becoming foster parents hope it will give them something they value and desire, e.g. money, feelings of self-worth, status or recognition, conformity to religious ideals, or a sense of meaning in life, and/or because they believe foster parenting will help them escape from a less than satisfactory life situation. Among unacceptable motives for foster parenting are the following:

1. To preserve a shaky marriage
2. To conform to expectations of others (spouse, friends)
3. To prove to self or others that one can be a successful parent or a giving person
4. To make up for past wrongs, whether real or imagined, or to counteract feelings of guilt, e.g. for abandoning parent to nursing home or for having done a poor job with one's own children
5. To live out a "rescue fantasy"
6. To secure a playmate or a friend for another child

What Is the Potential for Foster Parenthood Scale (PFPS)?

According to its developers, Touliatos and Lindholm (1978, p. 1), the *PFPS* "is a measure that is designed to express, quantify and summarize the evaluations by caseworkers of persons who are applicants for foster parenthood." This rating scale is based on the 1959 Child Welfare League of America *Standards for Foster Family Service*. It consists of fifty-four items distributed across nine clusters: (1) health, (2) employment and adequacy of income, (3) availability of time to parent, (4) opportunities for the cultural and intellectual development of the child, (5) opportunities for the religious and spiritual development of the child, (6) stability of marriage, (7) ability and motivation, (8) flexibility, and (9) ability to work with the agency and the child's parents.

In using the PFPS, the social worker rates each applicant separately, e.g. both husband and wife, on a four-point scale and on each of the fifty-four items. A total score is derived by simple addition. Scores of 216 or above indicate excellent potential. According to the *PFPS Manual*, an example of a "good" or "excellent" applicant is as follows:

> This person is in good health. He/she is successfully employed and has an income that is more than adequate for care of the child. He/she has enough time to give the child proper supervision and care. He/she would be able to contribute to the cultural and intellectual development of the child. He/she could provide opportunities for religious and spiritual development which would not conflict with the broad preferences of the child's own parents. He/she is emotionally stable. He/she has had good relations with children, spouse, family members, and persons outside the family. He/she is a caring and loving person. He/she is a responsible person with ethics and values that would be conducive to the well-being of the child. His/her motives for becoming a foster parent are positive. He/she is free from problems in sexual identification. He/she is a flexible person in regard to children's needs, their expectations, and use of help if necessary. He/she would be able to work with a social agency and with the child's natural parents and would not be overpossessive of the child. [P. 2]

One of the major weaknesses of the PFPS is that it requires the rater to form subjective judgments about the applicant. For example, the rater must judge whether the applicant "can give love to meet a child's needs" (Item 28) and "would enjoy being a foster parent" (Item 37). There always is a danger that this type of rating and scoring procedure results in a facade of precision or that the user forgets that the overall score is merely a summary of individual subjective judgments. In short, a scale of this design is only as good as the rater's ability to form accurate judgments.

From both a research and a user's perspective, the rating scales for the selection of foster parents developed by Cautley and Lichstein (1974) are stronger than the PFPS developed by Touliatos and Lindholm. By design, Cautley and Lichstein attempted to avoid items calling for subjective judgments. Where such judgments are necessary, they provide detailed guidance on how to form the judgment. The Cautley and Lichstein guidelines are built on a data base far superior to that used as a basis for constructing the PFPS. It is noteworthy that, while Touliatos and Lindholm cite foster care literature through 1977, they make no mention of the 1974 to 1975 publications by Cautley and Lichstein. One can only conclude that they were unaware of the significant research on the selection of foster parents conducted at the University of Wisconsin Center for Social Service.

In spite of limitations inherent in the PFPS, some social workers may find it to be a useful tool, especially as a sort of checklist and a way of summarizing information. For example, a completed PFPS might be attached to the social study report. The PFPS is published and distributed by the National Foster Parent Association.

What Are the Cautley-Lichstein Guidelines for Foster Parent Selection?

As a result of extensive research on foster parent applicants and foster parents during their first experience in caring for a foster child in the six-to-twelve-year age range, Cautley and Lichstein (1974) have developed an instrument that can help the social worker select those foster parents likely to be successful. This tool is a semistructured interview schedule designed for use with prospective foster fathers and foster mothers. Responses to the questions and case vignettes presented to the applicants by the social worker are coded and assigned a numerical weight. The total score obtained serves as a predictor of success or failure in foster parenting. A high score signals probable success; a low score indicates probable failure in foster parenting.

The instrument grew out of an analysis of data obtained over a four-year period from 1,102 applicant families and thirty-eight social agencies. Six out of every ten applicant families became foster parents and were studied further to determine placement success or failure. Certain parent characteristics were associated with the successful and unsuccessful foster parenting of six-to-twelve-year-olds.

In describing the results of their study, Cautley and Lichstein (1974) state:

> no single characteristic by itself is of any help in identifying a "promising" foster parent. A considerable number of characteristics must be considered together in any attempt to do this. . . . From a very detailed study of the wide variety of information obtained in the initial interviews with these families when they were applicants, we found that a number of their characteristics, taken together, can be used to identify with a fair degree of accuracy those who turned out to be "more successful" than those who were "less successful." And although somewhat different characteristics were significantly related to the evaluations of success made by the social workers on the one hand and the research staff on the other, there was considerable overlap. This has increased our confidence in the findings. The accuracy with which such information could be used in advance to predict the eventual success of a new foster family is sufficient to be of value to homefinders. And if this information regarding the prospective foster parents themselves is combined with other information which an agency has available at the time it considers placement of a particular foster child in a specific foster home, the accuracy of prediction is increased. [Pp. 1, 3]

While instruments such as the one developed by Cautley and Lichstein are far from perfect, they are more objective and reliable than individual judgments based on intuition or common sense. A good deal of research indicates that projection, bias, prejudice, and guesswork enter into the usual approaches to foster home selection. Social work research, such as that by Cautley and Lichstein, attempts to develop a more objective approach to selection. This does not mean that the social worker or homefinder should not trust his/her best judgment, especially if it points in the same direction as that based on a more systematic approach. If it points in the opposite direction, however, the home should undergo closer study.

Those involved in the selection of foster homes should study the 116-page book prepared by Cautley and Lichstein, *The Selection of Foster Parents: Manual for Homefinders* (1974). It can be ordered by writing to the Center for Social Service, University of Wisconsin-Extension, Madison, Wisconsin.

According to the Cautley and Lichstein Research, What Characteristics Are Associated with the Successful Foster Parenting of Six-to-Twelve-Year-Olds?

A brief summary statement cannot do justice to this complex research. Thus, the reader is urged to carefully read the manual prepared by Cautley and Lichstein (1974). Excerpts from an article by Cautley and Aldridge (1975), however, provide some idea as to how the findings can be used in the selection process.

> Four characteristics found useful in predicting success might be termed "degree of familiarity of the applicant with child care." Two describe the mother: (1) the number of siblings she had as a child combined with a code summarizing her position in the family (the most weight is given to her being oldest or among the older children with a number of siblings, and the lowest to being the youngest or only child) and (2) a five-point scale indicating the length of time the foster mother has had a child, not her own, stay in her home overnight (ranging from a high score for a period of over a month to a low score for not at all). Two measures describe the father: (1) the number of siblings he had as a child and (2) a code summarizing his position in the family (was he an only child, the oldest, or neither of these?). Being the only or oldest child is related negatively to success. Thus, in general, the greater the familiarity with child care, the more promising the applicant. [P. 51]

It should be noted that these predictors, e.g. number of siblings, are objective and do not require a fine discrimination or a subjective judgment. Moreover, such data are readily obtained. Cautley and Aldridge (1975) reported on the importance of additional characteristics of the foster father.

> One predictor, related positively to success, is the extent to which he reports his own father as affectionate toward him, combined with

the warmth he expresses in talking about his father while answering other questions regarding strictness, discipline, his father's confidence in him, and the like. Another predictor is the degree of formal religiousness of each of his parents combined. . . . A report of the parents' high formal religiousness was correlated negatively with success. . . . The husband's report that he and his wife together made such decisions is correlated with success, whereas the wife's attributing more influence to her husband is so correlated. . . .

Three other characteristics of the foster father are related positively to success. The first, "attitude toward social worker's supervision," refers to the foster father's willingness to have the worker visit his home regularly once a child is placed and to have the worker make suggestions about handling the foster child. These two attitudes are not highly related, but together give a greater representation of a cooperative attitude toward the worker than either one alone. The second, "foster father's flexibility," is a sum of the ratings of the extent to which he has changed because of his experiences with children and his self-awareness. The third, "concern for foster child," consists of two ratings of the foster father's answer to the question, "What will be difficult about being a foster parent?" Both ratings reflect a concern for the child, rather than for the foster father's own convenience, privacy, and time. [Pp. 51-53]

Several social work writers have emphasized the importance of the foster father and argued that social workers must devote additional time and attention to him. This research provides added support for such a viewpoint.

The Cautley-Lichstein (1974) instrument used vignettes as a means of getting applicants to share their attitudes and viewpoints on child rearing.

A number of predictive items consist of scores describing the prospective foster parent's responses to various behavioral situations likely to occur in most families with school-age children and to problem behaviors more likely to occur with foster children. These reliable measures are on the whole not highly related to each other but represent different strengths. In general, the measures . . . describe the ability of the foster parent to cope with the common problems of school-age children—prompt and appropriate handling of problems, without harshness or excessive discipline, and understanding the reasons for certain behaviors (such as why a child might deliberately break the toy of a younger brother in anger, take money from the mother's purse to go to the movies with friends, or be careless with clothes and furniture). [P. 53]

An important predictor was the degree to which a prospective foster mother could individualize her own or some other child. Those who could provide detailed descriptions of a child—ones who identified uniqueness—tended to do well as foster parents. Those who could not see much individual differences among children did poorly as foster parents.

> The foster mother's "differentiation in regard to her own children" is based on ratings of the following: To what extent does she consider each of her own children as a distinct individual when describing what pleases and concerns her about each? If she has no children, what about those she has worked closely with? These ratings are related positively to her success as a foster mother. [Cautley and Aldridge, 1974, p. 53]

It is important for the reader to recall that the work by Cautley and Lichstein focused on the foster parenting of six to twelve year olds. The findings may or may not apply to children younger than six and those who are teenagers. Equally rigorous research is needed, especially regarding the selection of foster homes for teenagers.

Should Factors of Age, Health, Physical Disability and Income Be Considered in the Selection of Foster Families?

According to *Standards* proposed by the APWA (1975), the age, health, and physical condition of the applicant should be considered only insofar as they may affect the capacity to parent and care for a specific foster child. Thus, such factors should be considered on a case-by-case basis.

Regarding the factor of income, the APWA *Standards* (1975) state:

> When the agency does not have a plan for paying foster families a salary it shall determine that the foster family's income is stable and sufficient for the maintenance of the family and that reimbursement for the foster child's maintenance is not needed for the foster family's own expenses. [P. 44]

In other words, the foster home payment, while necessary for the maintenance of the foster child, should not be an essential source of income for the family.

The question of working foster parents also must be considered in the selection of a foster family for a particular foster child. The *Standards* proposed by the APWA (1975) provides the following guidance for decision making.

> In two-parent homes it is preferable, in most instances, that both foster parents shall not be employed outside the home so that one parent is available for the parenting that the child requires. The Agency shall make decisions regarding such situations on the basis of what is in the best interest of the child.
>
> When both parents in a two-parent home and when single parents are employed, it is preferable that the home be used for school age children, and only when there are suitable plans (approved by the Agency) for care and supervision of the child after school and during the summer while parent(s) are at work. [P. 44]

What Home Characteristics Need to Be Considered in the Selection of a Foster Family?

The physical safety of the foster child is of obvious importance. Thus, the home's physical characteristics and condition should be such that it does not present a hazard to the foster child. Appendix C includes a checklist that may be used to evaluate basic factors of physical safety.

In regard to issues of basic physical comfort and privacy for the foster child, the guidelines proposed by the APWA (1975) state:

1. It is preferable for no more than two children to share sleeping rooms.
2. The sharing of sleeping rooms by children of opposite sexes is undesirable, especially for foster children who may be experiencing difficulties in the development of their sexual identities, attitudes, and behavior.
3. Children, other than infants and during emergencies (illness), shall not share sleeping quarters with adults in the household.
4. Individual space shall be provided for the child's personal possessions.
5. In all instances when exceptions are necessary, these shall be for children under two years of age or when special cultural, ethnic, or socioeconomic circumstances create a situation in which such exceptions will not be to the detriment of the child. [P. 45]

In Addition to Personal Qualities of the Foster Parents, What Is Important in the Selection of a Foster Home?

The Potential for Foster Parenthood Scale, the Cautley-Lichstein guidelines, and much of the professional literature on the selection of foster homes emphasize personal characteristics and relationships among family members. While such factors are important, factors external to the applicant family also should be considered, since they may exert more influence on the foster child than do the foster parents.

Parents—whether biological or foster—are less powerful than many have believed. Skolnick (1978, p. 56) states that "increasing evidence suggests that parents simply do not have much control over their children's development; too many other factors are influencing it." Similar conclusions were reached in the five-year study conducted by Carnegie Council on Children (Keniston, 1977). The behavior of the foster parents is influenced by a wide variety of forces external to the family. These dynamic forces have a strong impact on the ability of foster parents to care for the foster child.

> The parent-child relationship does not exist apart from other social contexts. . . . Parent's behavior toward children is based not so much on beliefs and principles as on a "horde of apparently irrelevant considerations": work pressures, the household work load, the availability of other adults to help with household tasks and child care, the design of houses and neighborhoods, the social structure of the community. All these influences, over which parents usually have little control affect the resources of time, energy, attention, and affection they have for their children. [Skolnick, 1978, p. 60]

Given the importance of factors external to the foster family, those involved in the selection of foster homes should look carefully at the environmental influences and opportunities that may or may not be associated with a particular foster home, for example: school programs, community cultural activities, health care programs, characteristics of available peer groups and role models, social services, self-help groups, sport and recreational resources, community and neighborhood values, and other adults associated with foster family.

What Factors Should Be Considered in Selecting Foster Homes for Handicapped Children?

There is evidence to support the belief that there are differences between typical or conventional foster family homes and those that provide care for children with physical or mental handicaps. The special problems and demands associated with a handicapped child must be considered in the selection of foster families.

Arkava (1977) compared forty-three specialized foster homes serving developmentally disabled children with a random sample of foster homes serving normal children. Several statistically significant differences were reported. The handicapped children were younger than those in "conventional" foster homes. As compared to the normal foster children, the handicapped children experienced a higher rate of replacement in foster care. Of the handicapped foster children, 60 percent were male, compared with 50 percent in conventional foster homes. The handicapped children were more likely to be on medication, especially anticonvulsants and sedatives, and they had significantly more difficulty in the areas of mobility, feeding, dressing, toileting, and communication, both receptive and expressive. The specialized foster parents spent significantly more time in such activities as preparing special foods, cleaning up spills and soils, and dealing with disputes and crises. Moreover, they incurred greater expenses, e.g. special foods, toys, appliances, homeowner costs, and especially baby-sitter costs. Compared with the conventional foster parents, the specialized foster parents experienced greater restrictions on their personal freedom and mobility. On the basis of his data, Arkava (1977) makes the following suggestions to those responsible for recruiting and screening foster homes for developmentally disabled children:

> carefully select parents who are willing to make long-term care commitments to minimize the possibilities of replacement of children.
> . . . prospective [specialized] foster parents should be realistical-

ly informed of the likelihood that they will be extensively involved in the following activities: (a) dispensing anticonvulsant medication, (b) feeding, (c) dressing, (d) toileting, (e) moving children around and (f) cleaning up spills and soils. A careful assessment of their capacities to provide these services should be made before placing a child in care.

Prospective . . . [specialized] parents should also be informed of the restrictions in personal mobility that may result from difficulties in finding babysitters. A careful assessment of their capacities to handle the extra costs and reductions in mobility should also be made before placing children in care. [P. 5]

In his book summarizing an extensive study of foster care in Massachusetts, Gruber (1977) offers many recommendations on how to improve foster family care. Several relate to the care of handicapped children and the use of specialized foster homes. He states that children with severe behavior problems and those with serious physical or mental handicaps should be cared for by specialized or professional foster parents.

It is recommended that specialized foster homes be those which employ professional foster parents, defined as one who assumes the role of foster parent on a full-time basis. Compensation must be commensurate with time and effort. In addition, each professional foster parent must successfully complete a prescribed training program. . . .

The professional foster parent should also be required to participate in on-going . . . programs [of training] and be required to complete periodic reports on their activities and changes in the children under their care. [P. 196]

Horejsi and Gallacher (1977) have developed a set of guidelines for the selection of foster parents for developmentally disabled children. While these guidelines incorporate many of the factors considered in the selection of conventional foster homes, some specifically relate to the problems and tasks associated with the care of severely handicapped children. For example:

1. Do the prospective foster parents understand and accept underlying assumptions of normalization and appreciate the "dignity of risk," i.e. a certain amount of physical and psychological danger and risk are involved in all new learning, and overprotection prevents the child from learning?

2. Does the parent have experience with developmentally disabled and/or physically handicapped children?

3. Can the prospective foster parent be objective about his or her behavior and the characteristics of the home environment (systematic home training of handicapped children requires the parents to step back and look at how they are affecting the child)?

4. Is the prospective parent willing to do systematic training, keep detailed records, and work under professional supervision?

5. Does the prospective foster parent have sufficient time for direct training with child (probably will need at least one hour per day)?

6. Is the couple's marriage relationship stable enough to take the stress and strain of caring for a handicapped child?

7. Is the couple's financial situation adequate so as to avoid extraordinary worry about making ends meet?

8. Do the couple's own children understand and accept the foster parenting of a handicapped child? Do they realize that it will have an effect on their lives? (Children should be included in the decision making.)

9. Is the prospective foster parent willing to participate in orientation and training sessions and willing to learn and practice behavioral technology?

10. Is the age of the foster parent such that it creates a normal family appearance, e.g. parents in their mid fifties might have a teenager but not an infant as a child? Normalization requires attention to the concept of age appropriateness in the selection of foster parents for a particular child.

11. Do the prospective foster parents express an interest in long-term foster care? Ideally, the parents should be committed to the care of the child until he or she can move on to greater independence in a group home or semi-independent living, etc.

12. Can the foster parents cope with negative community pressure, public misunderstandings, and prejudice against handicapped persons, etc.?

13. Does the foster parent see the need for and is he/she willing to be supervised by the agency?

14. Does the foster parent see the need for having the bio-

logical parents involved, understanding that while some parents simply cannot cope with the demands of a child they still care deeply for him or her?

15. Is a school program available to the child in the applicant's neighborhood or community?

16. Are local teachers and school officials willing to work with the foster parents, case manager, or home trainer, etc.?

17. Are suitable medical and dental resources available in the community (including physicians willing to cooperate with agencies and nonmedical professionals)?

18. If needed, are physical or occupational therapy resources available?

19. Is the immediate environment free of architectural barriers and extraordinary physical dangers?

20. Is an effective case management service available to coordinate the various specialized services needed by the child?

21. Is respite care available to prevent burnout of foster parents?

22. Is transportation, including emergency transportation, available to the family?

23. Are appropriate speech and hearing services available?

24. Is a normal peer group available to the foster child?

25. Are useable and affordable recreational opportunities available to child and foster parents?

26. Can necessary training and supervision be made available to the foster parents?

27. Can informal service systems (Association for Retarded Citizen groups, foster parent groups, and other foster parents, etc.) be enlisted to provide help to new foster parents?

Some of the factors mentioned above also should be considered in the selection of foster homes for children with other handicapping conditions, e.g. physical handicaps or severe behavior problems.

What Is a Foster Home Study?

The term *foster home study* refers to a process designed to select those foster home applicants likely to perform successfully.

Because a child welfare agency has a serious ethical and legal obligation to provide the best possible home for children needing foster care, the agency cannot avoid difficult decisions related to the screening of foster home applicants. Each year, a number of foster children are subjected to child abuse and neglect by foster parents. Others receive poor-quality care. This reality underscores the importance of the selection process. Moreover, the agency has a responsibility to protect applicants from situations with which they cannot cope or that are disruptive to valued family relationships, e.g. husband-wife or parent-child.

For the most part, persons who express an interest in foster parenting are stable psychologically and concerned about the foster child's well-being. There are exceptions, however. A few persons applying to be foster parents have serious psychological problems. Some are attracted to foster care because they hope it will somehow solve their personal, marital, family, or economic problems. Other applicants are stable and well meaning but naive about the care of children, especially children who have problems. A good home study procedure eliminates those who could not perform adequately, while helping the others prepare for the difficult job of foster parenting.

A traditional approach to the foster home study includes the use of individual interviews that focus on the applicant's personal stability, motivation, and past experience with children, etc. Wiehe (1977) raises questions about the traditional approach used in foster home studies and reports on the use of group methods. Essentially, he argues that the approaches used by many agencies place too much emphasis on evaluation and too little emphasis on preparation. The major disadvantages of emphasizing evaluation are as follows:

1) The foster home study becomes focused on eliminating those not fit to be foster parents which is a small percentage of the applicants who follow through after the initial screening process.
2) Individuals who are good candidates for serving as foster parents benefit little from the foster home study apart from having been engaged in an investigation or evaluation exercise.
3) A climate is set up between the agency and foster parents in which the latter must prove their ability to serve as foster par-

ents. This attitudinal climate may persist throughout the placement of foster children thereby discouraging foster parents to use their natural intuition and skills in child rearing and to relate to the agency in a dependent fashion.

4) An opportunity for preparing foster parents is lost when the primary emphasis in the foster home study is placed on evaluation. [Pp. 2-3]

An alternative conceptualization of the foster home study is primarily as a method of preparing applicants for foster parenting and secondarily as a method of identifying and screening out those who, for one reason or another, are unsuitable for this role. Most of those who are unsuitable will withdraw their applications once they have been presented with a realistic picture of foster parenting and an opportunity to examine their motives for wanting to become foster parents and their abilities to deal with foster children. Various techniques are used in the home study approaches that emphasize preparation rather than evaluation. These include presentations by experienced foster parents, foster children, and natural parents, discussions of case vignettes, films, video tapes and role play, and question-and-answer sessions, etc. The purpose of these techniques is to help applicants understand common problems in foster care and learn methods of dealing with these problems. Wiehe (1977) notes that the

> areas in which preparation should occur can be identified by foster parents participating in the foster home study, by social workers from their practice experience as well as from research on the outcome of foster placements. . . .
>
> A foster home study focusing on preparation for foster parenthood provides a climate in which the prospective foster parents and agency work together to provide care for children in need of temporary placement. [P. 12]

There is reason to believe that agencies will move toward approaches that place primary emphasis on preparation and give secondary attention to the screening process.

Can Home Study Information Be Secured by a Questionnaire?

A questionnaire can be used to secure certain basic information. A well-designed questionnaire also can be used as a springboard for in-depth discussion and exploration with the applicant.

As used here, the term *questionnaire* refers to a set of written questions to which the applicant responds in writing or by checking certain precoded responses. This type of data-gathering tool is different, for example, from the semistructured interview schedule developed by Cautley and Lichstein (1974). Their interview schedule is used within the context of a face-to-face interview and is filled out by the social worker rather than by the applicants.

A questionnaire, even a well-designed one, is not a substitute for skillful interviewing by a trained social worker. Questionnaires should not be used in a rigid manner. They need to be adapted to different groups of applicants. They should be used selectively; they may be useful in work with some applicants but confusing and frustrating to others. Appendix C presents a set of questionnaires designed for use in home studies with applicants interested in becoming foster parents to a child who is developmentally disabled. This set of questionnaires is intended to gather basic factual information, e.g. educational level or employment status, but, more importantly, to elicit and identify the questions, concerns, and worries of the applicants. The social worker then uses the completed questionnaire as a point of departure for in-depth interviews with the applicants. The reader can use these model questionnaires to develop questionnaires relevant to a particular group of applicants.

How Are Vignettes Used in Foster Home Studies?

During the interviews that are part of a foster home study, the social worker helps the applicants express their feelings, concerns, and questions about foster parenting. By getting to know the applicants as individuals with strengths and weaknesses, the social worker can deal with their real concerns, provide relevant information, and prepare them for the difficult job of being a foster parent. A friendly and open exchange with the applicants helps the social worker to assess their abilities to parent a particular child with certain problems and characteristics.

How does the social worker encourage applicants to express their feelings, concerns, and views on parenting? He or she, of course, could ask direct questions: "Do you believe in spanking a child when he/she misbehaves?" "How do you feel about children who wet the bed?" Such pointed questions, however, tend to elicit rather factual and superficial responses that do not probe the deeper levels that play such an important part in parenting. An alternative approach is to use a series of carefully written vignettes as springboards for discussion and exploration. Basically, a vignette is a sketch or a brief description of a real-life problem or situation in foster care. This method is non-threatening to most applicants. It provides an indirect method of gathering useful information and facilitates the expression of personal views.

The social worker should prepare vignettes for individualized use with potential foster parents. Applicants with children of their own, for example, might be asked to discuss a vignette that describes recurrent fighting between foster child and biological children. Obviously, such a vignette would reveal little if used with applicants who have no children. Vignettes also should be tailored to the age-group or the problems of foster children likely to be placed with the applicants. Eleven sample vignettes are presented below.

Sample Vignettes

1. Mr. and Mrs. Brown are foster parents to Johnny, age five. Johnny is mentally retarded and has poor arm and hand coordination. Consequently, he has some trouble eating. Because today is Mrs. Brown's birthday, the Browns decide to go out for an evening meal at the 4B's restaurant. While eating at the 4B's, Johnny drops food on the floor and generally is messy. In addition, he has a temper tantrum, cries, and throws food. This gets stares and disapproving looks from the other people in the restaurant.

    a. What do you think of this situation?

    b. How should this behavior be handled?

2. The Pattersons are religious people. They have been foster parents to fifteen-year-old Alfred for the past five years. The Pattersons go to church service and participate in other church activities on a regular basis. It means a lot to them. Until a few months ago, Alfred went to church with them, even though he was raised in another religious denomination. Now Alfred re-

fuses to go to church. He says that religion is foolishness and besides he should not be forced to go to the Pattersons' church when his parents belonged to a different one. The Pattersons feel that religion is central to their life and they expect everyone living in their family to participate in religious activites.

    a. What do you think of this situation?

    b. How should a conflict of this sort be handled?

3. Mr. and Mrs. Jones are foster parents to Jim, age ten. Jim is mentally retarded and has poor physical coordination. He likes to explore new things. Mrs. Jones is home alone when Mr. Smith, a next door neighbor, brings Jim to the door. Mr. Smith is angry because he found Jim in his garden pulling up tomatoes and flowers.

    a. How should Mrs. Jones, the foster parent, deal with this situation?

    b. How should she deal with Jim's behavior?

4. Jacob is a fifteen-year-old. He was expelled from school for smoking marijuana in the school restroom. He may get back into school next semester. Jacob's foster parents, Mr. and Mrs. Thomas, suspect that Jacob smokes marijuana around home and in the garage, but they have never caught him. Jacob says he does not smoke marijuana at home. The foster parents are afraid that Jacob will get into trouble, and they are angry because they feel that Jacob is lying to them.

    a. How should the foster parents respond to this situation?

5. Mary is a ten-year-old foster child. Mary's foster parents are Mr. and Mrs. Johnson. For the past few weeks Mary has been balking at mealtime and refusing to eat what is served. The foster parents decide to offer Mary her meal, and if she has not started to eat after one-half hour they will remove her plate and offer her no food until the next mealtime. Today Mary's teacher called Mrs. Johnson and expressed anger and alarm over the fact that Mary is hungry at school. The teacher accuses the foster mother of not feeding Mary.

    a. How should the foster mother handle this situation?

    b. What do you think about the training procedure selected by the foster parents?

6. The social worker is to visit with foster parents on a regular basis and make sure that the foster child is receiving needed services and that the foster parents are not having any unusual problems. The Andersons are foster parents. They must go out of state in eight days to attend a relative's wedding. Since it is impossible and too expensive for them to take their foster child on this trip, they talked to the social worker about finding someone to look after the foster child while they were out of town for five days. That was two weeks ago. The social worker said he would look into it, but the Andersons have not heard from him. They are starting to worry since they are scheduled to leave in a week.

    a. What should the Andersons do?

    b. How should they deal with the problem of an unresponsive social worker?

7. Emil is a sixteen-year-old high school junior. Basically, he is a good kid. Recently he has become interested in a girl friend and wants to date on a regular basis. The problem is that dating is expensive. The foster home payment simply is not enough to cover the extra costs of dating. The foster parents think it is unfair to have to spend their own money on the foster child.

    a. What do you think of this situation?

    b. How would you handle this problem?

8. Suzie lives with Mr. and Mrs. Gallager, her foster parents. Suzie is in the fourth grade. Mrs. Gallager has visited the school and Suzie's teacher a couple of times. Mrs. Gallager's personal reactions are less than positive. She is uncomfortable around the teacher and feels that the teacher doesn't want her visiting the school. Moreover, it seems as if neither Suzie nor her classmates care for the teacher. Suzie has made good progress at home and has not had unusual behavior problems. She is good natured and outgoing. She behaves well at home. The only time Suzie acts up is in the morning as she is about to go off to school. Today, Suzie's teacher called Mrs. Gallager, complaining about Suzie's behavior at school. According to the teacher, Suzie is having temper tantrums and will not obey.

    a. In view of the fact that Suzie's behavior is all right at home but bad at school, how should Mrs. Gallager, the foster mother, deal with the teacher's concern and complaint?

b. Do you have any other ideas on how foster parents should interact with their foster child's teacher?

9. Bobby is a ten-year-old foster child. For the past six months Bobby has been living with foster parents, Mr. and Mrs. Redding. Bobby has some rather unusual behaviors, probably because he spent so many years in an institutional setting. These behaviors (hand flapping, rocking, and head banging, etc.) bothered Bobby's teachers, and they recommended that Bobby be seen by the psychiatrist at the Mental Health Center. After observing Bobby for fifteen minutes, the doctor concluded that it had been a mistake for Bobby to be placed out of the institution. The doctor recommended to the foster parents and the school officials that Bobby be sent back to an institution.

a. What should the Reddings do?

b. Should they try to get Bobby back into an institution?

10. Mr. and Mrs. Green have been foster parents to Betty, age six, for about two months. During that time Betty's mother has visited three times. The problem is that the mother is usually drunk when she visits and makes promises to Betty that she cannot keep. The Greens are starting to think that the visits do more harm than good.

a. What should the Greens do?

b. What are your thoughts about visits by the foster child's parents?

11. Mrs. Gregg is a foster parent to Ann, a six-year-old child who is mentally retarded and has cerebral palsy. A home trainer comes to the Gregg home twice a month to help Mr. and Mrs. Gregg to learn techniques for teaching Ann to eat by herself. Mrs. Gregg has been working with Ann, and there has been some progress. The problem is that the home trainer gives her advice and asks Mrs. Gregg to keep detailed records on the training program. Keeping the records seem like a pain in the neck to Mrs. Gregg, and she feels that the time spent on paperwork should be spent with Ann. In addition, Mrs. Gregg is wondering whether the home trainer, who sees Ann only a couple hours each month, has any right to give directions on how to teach Ann.

a. What is your reaction to this situation?

b. If Mr. and Mrs. Gregg disagree with what the home trainer has to say about teaching Ann, how should they handle this problem?

It is noteworthy that Aldridge, Cautley, and Lichstein (1974) employ several vignettes as part of their semistructured interview schedule used to evaluate potential for foster parenting. A review of their instrument may give the reader additional ideas on the use and construction of vignettes.

How Are Sentence Completions Used in Foster Home Studies?

Like vignettes, a series of carefully written sentence completions can be used to elicit thoughts and feelings about foster parenting. The use of sentence completions, as described here, should not be confused with the various sentence completion tests used in psychological assessment. There are no right or wrong or preferred answers to these sentence completions. Responses may be oral or written. The usefulness of sentence completions lies in their ability to elicit responses for serious discussion. An example of a sentence completion is presented below. Note that it begins with a message to the applicant completing the form.

On Becoming a Foster Parent

Being a foster parent is a rewarding but difficult task. Some of the frustrations of foster parenting can be avoided or prepared for; others cannot. Most people interested in becoming foster parents have ambivalent feelings: They are attracted to it; at the same time they are a bit wary. It is important for the social worker to learn of your personal concerns and feelings about foster care. This will permit him/her to give you information that would be especially helpful. In addition, by being aware of your personal concerns and feelings, the social worker is in a better position to identify the type of foster child that would fit into your home and lifestyle.

Below are a number of sentences that are incomplete. You are to finish them. Simply write down what first comes to your mind. It is important to realize that this is not a test. There are no right or wrong answers. Rather, it simply is a tool to help you identify and express feelings and concerns about foster parenting. After you have completed the sentences, you and your social worker can review your responses and use them as a springboard for further discussion and exploration.

1. The one thing I find most attractive about being a foster parent is _____

2. When I think of myself being a foster parent I worry most about _____

3. The one behavior problem that I know I could not handle is _____

4. My relatives think being a foster parent is _____

5. My spouse (husband, wife) thinks that being a foster parent is _____

6. As a foster parent I would probably need help with _____

7. I would stop being a foster parent when _____

8. The biggest problem I would probably have with a female (girl) foster child is when she _____

9. The biggest problem I would probably have with a male (boy) foster child is when he _____

10. When my spouse (husband, wife) and I talk about being foster parents we disagree most about _____

11. The one thing I really want to know about being a foster parent is _____

12. When I think about the foster child's parents visiting in my home I feel _____

13. I might find it difficult to ask for outside help with a foster child because _____

14. If the social worker and I were to establish a good working relationship, he/she would have to _____

15. When I think about the possibility that the foster child may have a physical handicap I _____

16. When I think about two possibilities—becoming a foster parent or becoming an adoptive parent—I _____

17. The biggest problem I would probably have with a teen-aged foster child is _____

18. The biggest problem I would probably have with a grade-school-age child is _____

19. If I were to establish a good working relationship with the social worker I would have to _____

20. If I am told that I cannot become a foster parent I _____

What Do Applicants Experience When Deciding Whether to Be a Foster Parent?

The prospective foster parent faces a basic decision. "Should I try to become a foster parent?" Below are some thoughts and feelings that prospective foster parents struggle with while they try to decide.

"I would like to be a foster parent because. . . . Are those good and normal reasons?"

"I am scared of being a foster parent because. . . . Should I really be scared of that?"

"Basically, I am uncertain; I am ambivalent. One minute I say yes and the next minute I say no."

"Will I be happier and more satisfied as a foster parent than I am now? Maybe I should leave well enough alone."

"What if I try and fail? What will others think of me? I want to do a good job, but I don't know if I can."

"Will other members of my family (spouse, children) be happier and more satisfied if we care for a foster child, or will doing so create problems for them?"

"What if the care of the foster child adversely affects my relationship with my spouse, my other children?"

"The agency and other professional people say they will provide assistance and support service, but will they really? How do I know for sure? What if I am left high and dry—trapped in a miserable situation without the necessary help?"

"I know there is a lot of staff turnover in public agencies. I like this social worker but what if he/she leaves? What if I cannot get along with the people from the agency? Then I am really stuck!"

"I know the foster child needs a home, and homes are not easy to find. If I don't do it who will? Oh God, why did I even ask about becoming a foster parent?"

"I know there is a big push to get handicapped kids into foster care. How do I know they just won't dump an impossible child on me?"

"If I care for a foster child, will my in-laws, relatives, neighbors accept him/her?"

"If the social worker doesn't think I can be a foster parent, will he/she tell me? Will he/she stop me from doing something stupid?"

"What if I come to really love the child but cannot cope with the demands? That would be like giving up my own child. I don't think I could handle that."

"But what if I don't come to love the child? What if I come to hate the child? God, what a thought! What if I lose control and injure the child?"

It is normal for mature and responsible people to experience ambivalence when faced with a major decision. In fact, one should be a bit concerned about the people who are so sure about a decision that they do not describe a degree of ambivalence or mixed feelings. The person who insists that he/she has no doubts and no fears probably is unfamiliar with the frustrations involved in the care of a foster child (or any child, for that matter) and/or is unable to communicate openly with others. Also, the social worker should be wary of applicants who make snap decisions. In short, prospective foster parents can be expected to struggle for awhile (several days or weeks) before they decide one way or another. The social worker's job is not to keep them from the struggle or from the pain of decision making; rather, he/she should help them struggle productively so they make a decision with which they can live, one that is realistic and workable for all concerned.

What Techniques Can the Social Worker Use to Help the Applicant Make a Decision about Becoming a Foster Parent?

By thinking about the decision-making process, the social worker can come up with a few techniques that help prospective foster parents in their struggle to decide. For example, when the problem before a person is complicated, he or she has a hard time getting hold of it. One feels overwhelmed and helpless. A useful technique is to try to break the big problem-decision into small steps or small decisions. Some social workers call this technique *partialization*. For example, to partialize the big question "Should I become a foster parent?" help the prospective foster parents break it down into smaller, more manageable questions, such as: Should I become a foster parent to this particular child? Should I become a foster parent to a child who cannot walk or to a child who can walk? Should I become a foster parent to a school-aged child or an adolescent? By first making many small or subdecisions, one usually finds it easier to finally make the big decision.

People need useful information to make decisions. As a general rule, the more relevant the information one has, the better his/her decision. Thus, one can help people make decisions by presenting them with objective and relevant information. A multidimensional approach aids the absorption and utilization of such information. In other words, an approach that uses sight, sound, and touch is preferred over one that only uses sound. The best approach to providing information is to give the prospective foster parents actual experience of being with a foster child or other foster parents. Providing respite care for a weekend or sharing a meal with a foster family are examples. A good foster home study process exposes the applicants to other foster parents. In addition, films or written material prepared by foster parents also helps them to have better appreciation for the realities of foster care and to arrive at a decision about becoming a foster parent.

Emotional reactions and feelings affect decision making. One way to deal with the impact of emotions on decision making is to try to identify, label, and verbalize these feelings. The social worker needs to use certain interviewing techniques and apply basic communication skills to help the prospective foster parents put ambivalent feelings and emotional reactions into words. This important and sensitive task requires a high level of interviewing skill, and proper timing is extremely important. When the applicant understands his or her reactions more clearly, he/she can assess his/her strength and decide if he/she is realistic or not.

What Is a Foster Home Study Report?

A foster home study report is a written agency report that summarizes the information gathered during the foster home study and offers conclusions and recommendations as to the appropriateness of using the home. Recommendations regarding the type of child who should be placed in the home are included. There is no standard method for preparing the report. However, a particular agency may have policies and procedures or prefer that a certain format be followed.

A narrative format is still used by some child welfare agencies. Such accounts are guided by a broad outline, enabling inclusion of whatever information and detail the social worker judges to be relevant. A major disadvantage of narrative accounts is that they are time consuming to prepare and review. In addition, their open-ended format does not guarantee the inclusion of all pertinent information or ensure exploration of all important areas.

A semistructured format seems to address the disadvantages of the narrative format, retains some of the desired flexibility, and has the advantage of requiring less time to prepare. A sample semistructured format for the foster home study report is found in Appendix E. It will be noted that checklists are used. Those interested in this format are encouraged to study this model and then design their own according to relevant licensing standards, agency policy, and personal preference.

CHAPTER 9

The Matching Decision

What Is Meant by Matching?

THE TERM *matching* refers to the process of decision making related to the selection of a particular foster home for a particular foster child. *Matching* leaves something to be desired; some writers prefer the term *selection*. Since selection has been applied in this book to the process of screening and preparation of foster parents, matching is used instead. According to guidelines suggested by the APWA (1975), the matching decision should be based on "the extent to which interests, strengths, abilities, and needs of the foster family enable them to relate to the child's age; interests; intelligence; moral, ethnic and spiritual development; cultural background; parental relationships; educational status; social adjustment; individual problems; and plans for his or her future care" (p. 68).

Other factors to be considered include mutual attraction between foster parent and foster child, capacity of foster parents to deal with the child's unique problems and needs, foster parents' ability to deal positively with the child's natural parents, capacity of the foster family to nurture the child's development and modify the effects of previous unhealthy or disruptive parenting and the proximity of the foster home to specialized services needed by the foster child.

How Does the Age of the Foster Child Affect the Matching Decision?

Research conducted by Aldridge, Cautley, and Lichstein (1974) on foster placements of six- to twelve-year-old children yielded a number of relevant findings on the matching decision. In keeping with their research findings, they suggest the following:

a) Place the foster child where he/she will be the youngest in the family group.
b) If the above is not possible, place the foster child in a foster home where there is only one preschool child rather than several.
c) If two foster children are to be placed in the same home, particularly if one is a preschooler, choose a foster family which does not have any preschool children of its own.
d) If the foster child will become the oldest in the family, choose a home where there is a considerable span of years (at least three, preferably five or six) between the foster child and the oldest child of the foster family. [P. 5]

Guidelines developed by the American Public Welfare Association (1975) state:

> Foster parent(s) shall care for one and not more than two infants (under two), including the foster parent(s)' own children. . . . The age range of the children in a foster home shall be similar to that in a "normal" family in order to lessen competition and comparisons. [P. 46]

How Many Foster Children Should Be Placed in a Given Foster Home?

In offering guidelines on this question the American Public Welfare Association (1975) states:

> Foster families shall not have more than a total of six children, including foster children and foster parent(s)' own children, in the foster home. Exceptions shall be made in order to keep siblings together. . . . All placement situations shall consider the effect of having some children in the foster home whose parent(s) visit them and other children whose parent(s) do not. [P. 46]

The normalization principle suggests that the size of a foster family should be similar to ordinary families in the community. Its size may resemble a large family but should not stand out as unusual or extreme.

Should Religion, Race, and Ethnicity Be Considered in Matching?

To the greatest extent possible, efforts should be made to preserve the foster child's religious, racial, and cultural heritage and to prevent discontinuities in values and cultural identity. Whenever the child's developing value system is psychologically normal and socially acceptable within a given racial or ethnic group, that value system should be preserved by placing the child in a foster family that has similar values. The Child Welfare League of America (1975) states:

> Parents have the right to designate the religious affiliation of the child. Consequently, the agency has a responsibility to select a foster home within the broad religious preference of the parents.
>
> If the parents have no religious preference and the child has no meaningful religious identification, the parents should be offered the opportunity to sign a statement giving the agency consent to place the child in the most suitable home without regard for their religious preference. [P. 24]

National standards also recognize the importance of race and ethnicity in the matching process. For example, a recent guideline developed by the American Public Welfare Association (1975) states, "Unusual efforts and support shall be made to find suitable American Indian foster families for all American Indian children in need of services."

To What Extent Should the Opinions and Wishes of the Foster Parents Be Considered in the Matching Decision?

The child welfare literature supports the contention that the feelings and opinions of the foster parents should be given careful consideration in a matching decision. The foster parents are good judges of whether or not a particular child will work out in their home. Even though they may not be able to verbalize the reasons for their beliefs, more often than not they seem to know what will and what will not work. The implication should be clear: To the greatest extent possible, the social worker should use preplacement visits to bring the child and potential foster parents together. If the foster parents and the child seem compatible and/or if the foster parents are of the opinion that it will work, the match is likely to succeed. If, on the other hand, the foster parents are doubtful about the match or express fear of the placement, chances are good that the placement, in fact, would fail.

The past performance of the foster parents with various children is one of the most important factors to consider in matching. If they have done well with a certain type of youngster, they probably will do well with a similar child. If they have had trouble with a certain type of youngster, in all probability they will have problems with a similar youngster.

It is a serious mistake for the social worker to make a matching decision that is contrary to the expectations of the foster family. If, for example, the parents want and expect to provide foster care to a youngster between five and ten years of age, an adolescent should not be placed in the home. Doing so would set the stage for almost certain failure. Foster parents may be able to handle a certain age-group of children with certain types of problems but not others. They often have an intuitive awareness of their own abilities and limitations. To the greatest extent possible, the matching decision should be consistent with the expectations and desires of the foster parents.

As a result of their research findings, Aldridge, Cautley, and Lichstein (1974) provide an important guideline for the social worker. "If at all possible, avoid making a placement in a foster home you do not feel has a good chance of working out well. In general, it seems far preferable to place a child in a temporary home or a receiving home until an appropriate placement can be found" (p. 41).

The old adage about the ounce of prevention being worth a pound of cure certainly applies to the matching decision. If at all possible, it is better to delay a placement than make a bad matching decision that creates frustration for all concerned.

To What Extent Should the Opinions and Wishes of the Child Be Considered in the Matching Decision?

Except in cases involving the placement of a very young child, the wishes and preferences of the child should be considered and —to the greatest extent possible—followed. Usually, time and skillful interviewing are needed to elicit the feelings and views of children. Yet their views, expectations, and preferences about the foster family with whom they will live have much to do with the eventual success or failure of the placement.

How Does the Social Worker Assess a Foster Family's Capacity for Parenting a Particular Foster Child?

Under ideal conditions, a foster family with certain capabilities is sought for a particular child: There is an attempt to find a unique home for a specific foster child with unique needs and problems. That is the ideal situation. In most cases, the social worker must select a foster home from among a small pool of those who have met certain minimum criteria and basic licensing standards.

It is important to realize that some foster families succeed with certain children but not others. If a placement is to succeed, there must be a match between the needs of the child and the capabilities of the foster parents. This always is a complex professional judgment. Experience and training are needed to make good decisions in foster care. Research by Aldridge, Cautley and Lichstein (1974), for example, found that placement decisions made by experienced social workers were more successful than those made by inexperienced workers.

It is not possible to list a set of factors that are important in all cases to the successful foster parenting of a foster child. It is only possible to present a list of questions or issues that are relevant to many election decisions. This list of questions can be thought of as a deck of IBM cards. Given a particular situation, the worker mentally sorts through the cards and continually asks, "Does this apply?" or "To what extent is this factor important in this particular case?" In a sense, the list presented below is a checklist or a set of reminders about what factors may be important in a given situation. It will be noted that the questions are phrased in such a way that a "yes" answer supports a match between a particular foster child and foster home, and a "no" answer may signal a potential mismatch. The reader may wish to add other questions that are pertinent to the selection of foster homes for children of a particular age group, those with certain emotional or behavioral problems or those with certain handicapping conditions.

The Matching Decision in Foster Care: A Checklist

_____ 1. Will the foster parents learn to care for and enjoy the foster child?

_____ 2. Will they be able to give affection to this child without receiving much in return, at least not initially?

—— 3. Will the foster family provide the foster child with a family environment characterized by warmth, trust, and appropriate limits?

—— 4. Will other children in the family (foster parents' own children or other foster children) be able to accept and get along with the foster child?

—— 5. Can the family absorb the foster child into its usual routines and activities without undue disruption to the family system?

—— 6. Is the foster child favorably disposed to this particular foster family?

—— 7. Is the foster family willing and able to relate to the foster child's natural parents?

—— 8. Does the foster family have the flexibility necessary to meet the ever-changing needs of the foster child, e.g. developmental changes from latency to adolescence?

—— 9. Does this foster family have the temperament and skills needed to deal effectively with the special problems of the foster child, e.g. bed-wetting or lying?

—— 10. Is the foster family realistic about what is actually involved in caring for this particular child?

—— 11. Is the foster parents' marriage stable enough to absorb whatever added stress and strain are involved in caring for this particular foster child?

—— 12. Will this particular child find acceptance from the foster family's relatives, e.g. grandparents, and neighbors?

—— 13. Is the foster family's physical location, e.g. community or neighborhood, such that it will allow the foster child to have easy access to needed services, e.g. dental care, medical clinics, or special classes?

—— 14. Will the foster family provide the child with religious and cultural experiences compatible with the child's previous life experience and heritage?

—— 15. Is the foster family willing and able to cooperate with whatever professionals may be involved in working with the foster child, e.g. teacher, psychologist, or physical therapist?

—— 16. Does the family have the time necessary to provide the attention, tutoring, or training needed by the foster child?

—— 17. Does the family have the ability to maintain whatever records may be necessary to specialized treatment plans for the foster child?

—— 18. Do these foster parents have the amount and type of child care experience needed to parent this particular foster child?

—— 19. Are the foster parents resourceful and assertive so that this particular foster child will receive needed services and assistance from various community agencies and professionals?

—— 20. Are these particular foster parents willing and able to accept guidance, direction, and supervision from the social worker and other professionals who may need to design treatment or training programs for this particular foster child?

—— 21. Do these foster parents have an informal network of supports that will help them sustain their motivation and ability to parent this particular foster child and work with the child's natural parents?

—— 22. Is the foster family's physical location (city, community, etc.) such that visits by the natural parent(s) are feasible or, if necessary for this particular child, does the physical location offer protection from violent or unpredictable natural parents?

—— 23. If placed in this particular foster home, will the foster child attend a school that will be accepting of and helpful to him/her?

CHAPTER 10

The Foster Parents

What Is Meant by the Foster Parents' Role Ambiguity?

MANY PROBLEMS in foster care are related to the unclear role definition of the foster parent. Agencies, reflecting the uncertainty of society about substitute care, have not been able to adequately address this problem. The issue of role ambiguity is both longstanding and complex. Pearlman (1968) describes it as follows:

> Part of the long-known but little plumbed difficulties in foster home placements of children lies in the ambiguous role of the foster parent. They are sought out for their capacity to love and nurture and care for children. Yet they are not supposed to care too much nor love too much lest they be unable or unwilling to detach themselves from the child when, for whatever reasons, he must be removed. They are expected not have [sic] financial gain as their motive in taking a child, yet they are expected to bear the stress of tasks and problems with few other kinds of rewards. Are they to be Mr. and Mrs. Doe to the child or "Dad" and "Mom" or "Uncle and Auntie"? Are they to be the agency's staff member, client, supervisee? Are they to be antagonist or aide to the child's true parents? The shifting nature of this role must often lead to inconsistencies and ambivalences towards child, agency, and the role-tasks. [Pp. 158-159]

Kadushin (1974a) also describes role ambiguity:

> The foster parent role presents a number of problems, some of which derive from the crucial differences between foster parenthood and biological parenthood. The foster parents enact the parental role in their day-to-day contact with the child, yet they do not have the full rights of the true parents. Because they are acting for the child's biological parents, not replacing them, and because they receive the child through the agency, they are only partial parents; they share control of the child with both the biological parents and the agency.
>
> The foster parents want a child to board. Yet, in getting a child, they find they get an agency as well. The agency sets limits and

advances directives as to how the foster parents are to behave toward the child—a situation not normally encountered by biological parents. The shared control and responsibility for the child is clearly set forth in the instruction pamphlets issued to foster parents. . . .

Limited control implies limited responsibility as well. The fact that the agency is responsible for the basic cost of maintenance of the child indicates an essential difference between foster parenthood and biological parenthood. Furthermore, the foster parents are responsible for the child for only a limited segment of his life span. And because the duration of their contact with the foster child is indefinite, the foster parents cannot plan for the child's future, nor can they legitimately expect to share in the child's future achievements. [Pp. 432-433]

Given the national organization of foster parents, the expansion of training programs for foster parents and other moves toward professionalization, it is likely that the emerging role of the foster parent will be that of an agency employee having specialized skills and providing a particular type of service.

What Are the Common Concerns and Complaints of Foster Parents?

Foster parents frequently complain that they are not informed about or helped to understand their rights and responsibilities. Many are confused about their role and unsure of exactly what is expected of them. Many foster parents feel used—that the difficulties of their job are not understood nor appreciated by the social worker, the agency, and the public. They feel that they give and give but get little in return.

Many think that their views and opinions are not taken seriously by social workers and other professionals. Because they live with the child twenty-four hours a day, seven days a week, they feel that they know the foster child better than the professionals, yet they seldom are consulted when plans are being made for the child. Foster parents frequently complain that they do not see their social worker on a regular basis or are unable to reach him/ her when necessary. They also complain about the rapid turnover of social work staff. Often they are just getting to know the worker when he or she leaves the agency.

Some foster parents complain that they are not trusted. For

example, they may be told little or nothing about the child being placed in their home. Since the child lives in their home, they believe they have a right to all pertinent information about the child and the natural family. Foster parents often feel ill prepared to deal with certain children or problems, yet they are not given the training or supervision needed to handle difficult situations. They have a sense of being set up to fail. When a social worker, psychologist, or psychiatrist offers assistance, it sometimes is irrelevant to the day-to-day problems with which foster parents are concerned. Many complain that they are not adequately prepared to deal with the natural parents. They say that although they need special help or training in this area they receive little or none.

Foster parents assert that the foster home study was inadequate or rushed. As a result, the agency does not know their abilities and limitations well enough to make appropriate matching decisions. They also complain when they are asked to accept a child who is different from what they expected or requested. For example, they wanted and expected a girl of grade-school age but were encouraged or asked to take an adolescent boy.

A common complaint and concern is that the foster home payments are inadequate to cover the actual costs of caring for the foster child. This forces the foster parents to dip into their own pockets or else deprive the foster child of some basic pleasures, e.g., class rings, recreation, yearbooks, money for dates, or birthday presents. This, they believe, is unfair to foster parents and foster child.

Many foster parents say they have little opportunity to question or modify agency policy and procedures. Moreover, they do not know how to appeal decisions affecting them. They may want to lodge a complaint against the social worker or agency but feel intimidated; they fear that the foster child will be removed from their home, that they will no longer be used as foster parents, or that they will be asked to accept children with whom it is impossible to live.

What Serious Problems Arise within Foster Family Homes?

In addition to all of the frustrations associated with the rearing of children—especially those who have been neglected or abused —and the problems related to the foster parents' role ambiguity, foster parents face a number of other potential problems. The child coming into a foster home tends to repeat past behavior. This is hardly surprising, since all people repeat behavior that has been previously reinforced. In other words, people repeat behavior that helped them cope in the past. However, when the child's behavior patterns have been shaped by intensive family conflict and troubled parents such as those with a mental illness, the foster child may bring to the foster home a pattern that subtly draws the foster parents into behavior that resembles the relationship the child had with his/her natural parents. For example, a child who has been rejected expects to be rejected by the foster parents and often behaves in a way that invites rejection from others. The child who has spent years in a family characterized by psychopathological relationships may elicit highly unusual behavior from the foster parents. Not infrequently, foster parents express surprise at how easily they slipped into behavior they wanted to avoid. When communicating openly and honestly, many foster parents report times when they found themselves feeling and behaving in an unexpected and undesirable manner toward a particular foster child. When foster parents state that the child is "driving them crazy," they often are describing the capacity of some disturbed children to exploit and manipulate human weakness. Cases of child abuse by foster parents may relate to the tendency of some children to elicit a repetition of past experience, and in a sense they prove that the foster parents are no different from their own parents. Foster parents need special training and supervision to care for these children.

In recent years, there has been a growing concern over the number of foster parents who become sexually involved with their foster children. Reported cases most often are those that involve a rape or other exploitation; there are not reliable estimates on the number of unreported cases. This situation is most likely to occur between a foster father and a teenaged foster daughter, but sexual relationships between foster mother and foster child also occur. Heterosexual relations are most common, while homosexual relations are rare.

Sexual attraction is a human reality. Thus, the social worker considering the placement of a teenaged child must be open and forthright in discussing this matter with the prospective foster parents. If the channels of communication can be kept open, the matter of sexual attraction can be dealt with before it leads to overt sexual behavior.

What Is the Code of Ethics for Foster Parents?

In 1975, the National Foster Parent Association adopted an eleven-point code of ethics designed to provide a moral and ethical framework for foster parents. The social worker can use the code as a means of explaining the role of foster parents. By permission of the National Foster Parent Association, the code is presented below.

Code of Ethics for Foster Parents

Preamble

Foster family care for children is based on the theory that no unit in our society, other than the family, has ever been able to provide the special qualities needed to nurture children to their fullest mental, emotional and spiritual development. If, for a certain period, a family ceased to provide these special qualities, substitute care must be used. It is recognized that, ideally, foster care is temporary in nature. Parents who provide foster family care must have commitment, compassion and faith in the dignity and worth of children, recognize and respect the rights of natural parents, and be willing to work with the child placing agency to develop and carry out a plan of care for the child.

Foster care is a public trust that requires that the practitioners be dedicated to service for the welfare of children, that they utilize a recognized body of knowledge about human beings and their interactions, and that they be committed to gaining knowledge of community resources which promote the well-being of all without discrimination.

Each foster parent has an obligation to maintain and improve the practice of fostering, constantly to examine, use and increase the knowledge upon which fostering is based, and to perform the service of fostering with integrity and competence.

Principles

1. I regard as my primary obligation the welfare of the child served.

2. I shall work objectively with the agency in effecting the plan for the child in my care.
3. I hold myself responsible for the quality and extent of the services I perform.
4. I accept the reluctance of the child to discuss his past.
5. I shall keep confidential from the community information pertaining to any child placed in my home.
6. I treat with respect the finding, views and actions of fellow foster parents, and use appropriate channels, such as a foster parent organization, to express my opinions.
7. I shall take advantage of available opportunities for educating and training designed to upgrade my performance as a foster parent.
8. I respect the worth of all individuals regardless of race, religion, sex or national ancestry in my capacity as a foster parent.
9. I accept the responsibility to work toward assuring that ethical standards are adhered to by any individual or organization providing foster care services.
10. I shall distinguish clearly in public between my statements and actions as an individual, and as a representative of a foster parent organization.
11. I accept responsibility for working toward the creation and maintenance of conditions within the field of foster family care which enable foster parents to uphold the principles of this code.

Should Foster Parents Receive Training?

There is general agreement that the complexities of foster parenting require formal training. The training of foster parents is of two general types: preservice and in-service. Preservice training occurs prior to the placement of a child into the foster home. In-service training occurs while the foster parents are actively caring for a foster child.

A number of factors should be considered in designing programs of training for foster parents. Adults learn differently from children. Adult learning is influenced strongly by felt need and real problems. Adults are motivated to learn if the material is related directly to some current need or problem with which they are concerned. Thus, foster parent training must relate to the real and everyday concerns of the foster parent. It is important that foster parents be involved in designing the structure and content of the training.

When the presentation of theoretical material, e.g. stages of child development or reinforcement theory, is necessary, it should be related to specific situations or problems with which foster parents are concerned. Case examples drawn from the common experiences of foster parents are a sort of middle ground between abstract theory and the unique concerns of an individual foster parent in the training group. More than anything else, the training for foster parents should be practical and deal with the real world as they see and experience it.

Adults learn best in an informal environment. Most foster parents appreciate an opportunity to discuss, share, and compare their experiences and perceptions. Training should not be an aimless discussion, however. A certain amount of structure is necessary to maintain focus.

A variety of teaching methods and techniques should be used, because adults are stimulated by variety. Thus, a mix of films, case vignettes, lectures, group discussion, and guest speakers, etc., should be employed. Emphasis on one educational technique causes the foster parents to lose interest. Presentations or discussions led by experienced foster parents are especially well received and are appreciated by inexperienced foster parents.

What Is a Foster Parent-Agency Handbook?

A foster parent-agency handbook is a manual that provides practical information to foster parents. According to Stone and Hunzeker (1974), a handbook has three basic purposes:

1) To provide in one source the policies used in administering the foster family care program
2) To give the information foster parents need to have about their responsibilities to the foster children, the agency, the natural family and the community and
3) To offer in a convenient way informal resources and suggestions on solving some of the daily problems in foster care. [P. 5]

A handbook should be available for all foster parents.

What Should Be Included in a Handbook for Foster Parents?

Those interested in developing a handbook for foster parents will find the booklet by Stone and Hunzeker (1974) helpful. It was prepared after reviewing seventy-six manuals for foster parents. The booklet provides model forms that can be used to record information on the child's development, medical history, and family background and a sample foster parent-agency agreement form. Most state child welfare agencies have developed some type of handbook for foster parents. Format and content vary. Among the topics usually included in a handbook for foster parents are the following:

1. Definitions of foster care
2. National Foster Parents Code of Ethics
3. Rights and responsibilities of foster child
4. Rights, responsibilities, and role of social worker
5. Rights and responsibilities of natural parent
6. Rights, responsibilities, and role of foster parent
7. Information on agency licensing and home study procedures
8. Importance of confidentiality and ethical principles that apply to the foster parents and the social worker
9. Importance of teamwork and cooperation between foster parents and agency
10. Description of educational-training opportunities available to or required of foster parents
11. Explanation of agency policy and provisions related to foster care payments; transportation and clothing for child; personal allowances for child; medical, dental care, and education costs for child; vacations; record keeping; child discipline, etc.
12. Information on and explanation of agency policy related to liability, insurances, taxes, and travel out of state
13. Explanation of legal procedures and basic legal terminology, e.g. custody, guardian *ad litem*, neglect, and abuse
14. Descriptions of foster parent associations
15. Sources of useful information for foster parents
16. Explanation of channels of appeal or complaint that may be used by foster parents
17. Explanation of agency purpose, structure, organization, and funding
18. Importance of keeping natural parents involved with their

child and explanation of how visits by parents can be handled.

Persons wanting to develop a handbook for foster parents should review existing ones for ideas on content and organization. Handbooks should be clear and simply written. Professional jargon should be avoided. Interested foster parents and local and state foster parent organizations should participate in the preparation of a handbook for foster parents.

How Important Is the Foster Father to the Success of a Placement?

The foster father has a key role in the success or failure of a foster home placement. Unfortunately, many social workers spend more time with the foster mother than with the foster father. This is a serious error; if anything, the situation should be reversed. Research suggests that the feelings, views, and motivation of the foster father are more predictive of placement success or failure than are those of the foster mother. Aldridge, Cautley, and Lichstein (1974) state that there is much evidence that the foster father is important to the success of the placement.

> First of all, more of the information obtained from him than from the prospective foster mother in their initial interviews when first applying for foster care was of value in predicting the ultimate success of the placement.
>
> . . . Those fathers who reported being actively involved with the foster child (that is, engaging in an activity just with the foster child) and enjoying this involvement were far more likely to be successful than those fathers who were either not involved or did not report enjoying any involvement which they had. . . .
>
> . . . Those fathers who evidenced skill in their specific interaction with the foster child, as indicated in their description of responding to both "difficult" and "pleasing" behaviors of the foster child, were more successful.
>
> . . . The foster father's active support of his wife, who generally carried the major responsibility for day to day care of the foster child was judged to be an important ingredient of success. . . .
>
> . . . There is evidence that the worker contributed to the success of the foster father by including him in the preparation, as those fathers who were better prepared for the child were considerably more likely later to become more actively involved with the child.

Also, the worker's contacts with the father during the first three months of the placement were significantly related to his overall satisfaction with the placement and with his eventual success.

. . . The foster father provided clearer clues than the foster mother that the placement was "in trouble" and that a request to the agency to remove the child would be forthcoming. . . . There is evidence that the foster father's indication of the overall "morale" in the foster home was a reflection of both his own and his wife's point of view. It came through more clearly in his interview, however. [Pp. 24-25]

Despite the demonstrated importance of the foster father, custom and certain practical problems may limit the father's involvement. Special efforts by the social worker are necessary to overcome these barriers. Aldridge, Cautley, and Lichstein (1974) offer some practical advice on including the foster father.

Make sure the foster father is included in the preparation for the placement, and that he not only is informed regarding agency policy but also is prepared specifically for the foster child. Good preparation of the father in itself increases the chances that the placement will work out.

Make sure you talk with the foster father early in the placement. Since contacts with him most likely will have to be in the evening or on the weekends, plan to suffer this inconvenience early in the placement, as effort exerted then is more valuable than later effort. Once a foundation of carefully planned input with both foster parents has been laid, maintaining the placement should be easier.

Use the telephone. Call the foster home when you believe the foster father will be in. If he answers, don't ask for the foster mother (as is traditional) but talk with him to indicate that you consider him to be an integral part of the placement. If the mother answers and you conduct the telephone interview with her, also ask to speak with the foster father. Ask him specifically if there is any information he feels they need.

And if you plan to make a special trip out to the foster home, call ahead to make clear that you are interested in dealing with *both* of them. [P. 26]

The foster father is every bit as important as the foster mother to the success of the foster placement. In some ways, his attitudes and behavior are of more importance. Thus, the social worker should involve the foster father in all interviews used to monitor the placement.

Are Preplacement Visits Important to the Success of the Placement?

Preplacement visit usually refers to a meeting between the child in need of a home and the licensed foster family ready to accept a foster child. Research on foster care of six to twelve year olds suggested that preplacement visits contribute to the success of placements. There is reason to believe that preplacement visits are of even greater importance for teenaged foster children.

> Further analysis revealed the importance of these visits: the placements where the worker had arranged a preplacement visit [even one short visit] were more likely to be successful than those where the children had not visited the home before the placement. [Aldridge, Cautley, and Lichstein, 1974, p. 7]

The use of preplacement visits is highly recommended. Preplacement visits ease the foster child's adjustment by reducing some of his/her fears and help the foster parents arrive at a proper decision about whether or not a particular child will fit into their family.

In addition to the actual visits between foster child and foster parents, the social worker should spend additional time with the foster parents prior to the placement. Aldridge, Cautley, and Lichstein (1974) suggest the following preplacement sequence:

> a) A casework visit with both foster parents in which the worker would:
> Review the foster parent role in general, the expectations the agency has of them and what the parents may expect of the agency.
> Focus on the specific child to be placed with them, including information about the child's own family member(s). . . .
> Leave a written statement of agency policy
> b) Allow at least a week for the foster parents to discuss and note any further questions they may have. The worker could leave a note pad and a pencil with the parents to emphasize this responsibility to think through just what is involved. This would be the best period to have the child visit the home.
> c) Return at a prearranged time to the foster home, or telephone the foster parents and make an appointment to go over their questions. [P. 8]

It should be noted that the procedure outlined above is designed for new foster parents. The preplacement sequence can be modified for experienced foster parents.

What Information Should Be Given to Foster Parents about to Receive a Child into Their Home?

Foster parents need basic information about the foster child. They have a right to information about matters that will have a significant effect on family members, daily routine, and their responsibilities as substitute parents. The method of imparting this information must be individualized. A list of general items of information is presented below and is based on one developed by Aldridge, Cautley, and Lichstein (1974).

INFORMATION ON THE LENGTH OF PLACEMENT: The foster parents should be told how long the social worker expects the foster care placement to last. They should be informed of any pending decisions or obstacles that may affect or alter the length of the placement, e.g. pending court decisions, situation of natural parents, or plans to move child to special school when opening develops. The foster parents should be informed of any positive or negative consequences related to subsequent movement of the child from a foster home.

INFORMATION ABOUT HEALTH OF CHILD: Foster parents should be informed of and instructed on any special health problems that the foster child may have, e.g. allergy, bed-wetting, seizures, or medication. They also should know where medication can be secured (name of pharmacy, prescription numbers, etc.). Foster parents must be informed of agency policy and procedures related to medical and dental care for the child. Foster parents need to be given names and telephone numbers of doctors or dentists treating the child and/or told which doctors should be used in the future. Foster parents should be informed of legal issues related to the authorization of medical treatment for the foster child. If available, copies of existing authorizations for medical care should be given to foster parents. They should be informed of any medical emergencies that may arise and be helped to understand their responsibilities in such emergencies.

INFORMATION ON HANDICAPPING CONDITIONS OR UNUSUAL BE-HAVIOR PROBLEMS: Foster parents should be told about any handicaps that require their attention including use of any special equipment or appliance needed by the foster child, e.g. wheelchair, ramps, or leg braces. Foster parents should be informed of any exercises, physical therapy, or other treatment in which they are expected to participate. They should be informed of ongoing behavior or training programs designed to correct specific behavior problems.

INFORMATION RELATED TO THE SCHOOL: Foster parents should be given information on where the foster child will attend school and any special problems, if any, related to the child's transfer from one school to another. They should be told whether the foster child's school records have been forwarded to the new school and given information on how the child is to get to school, e.g. walk or bus.

INFORMATION RELATED TO FOSTER CHILD'S NATURAL PARENTS: Foster parents should be told the major reason(s) why foster care is necessary. They should be informed of procedures to be used to facilitate visits between the natural parents and the foster child. Foster parents should be told how to handle unusual problems that may arise as a result of visits by the natural parents.

INFORMATION RELATED TO FINANCIAL ARRANGEMENTS: The entire financial arrangement concerning foster care—including reimbursable expenses, monthly payments, and clothing allowances, etc.—should be reviewed and made explicit.

Can Foster Parents Be Told Too Much about the Foster Child?

Some believe that if foster parents are told about the child's behavior problems, for example, they will become anxious and wait for the problem to occur, and a self-fulfilling prophecy is set in motion. They expect problems, they look for problems; thus, they have problems. Other social workers argue that some foster parents will refuse to accept a child if they know the child has serious behavior or other problems. They believe that giving too much information actually may deprive a child of a home.

Still other social workers argue that the foster parents have a right to know as much as possible about the child coming into their home; foster parents cannot offer much help unless they know what to expect and have relevant background information. Aldridge, Cautley, and Lichstein (1974) provide added insight into this issue:

> Some workers may be concerned that if they describe in detail all of the foster child's problem behaviors, the foster parents will decide they are not up to caring for such a child. The alternative to careful preparation is to let the foster parents discover on their own how difficult the child can be; in our research a frequent result of this was a feeling of dismay and discouragement on the part of the foster parents. [P. 10]

There is reason to believe that what the foster parents are told is of less importance than how they are told. If done properly, a great deal of useful information can be presented to the foster parents without alarming them or causing them to look for problems that may not develop. In addition, it is possible to provide the foster family with useful information without violating the principle of confidentiality. It must be recognized that the proper preparation of foster parents takes time and skill. Discussions of the foster child's behavior must be individualized to the concerns, values, and characteristics of the foster parents. This takes many hours, but it is an investment that actually saves time in the long run. In discussing their research findings on the preplacement preparation of foster parents, Aldridge, Cautley, and Lichstein (1974) state:

> [The] extent of preplacement input with the foster parents is also related to success. Those placements where the worker had talked to both the foster parents at least twice for a total of at least three hours were more likely to work out well than were those in which the workers had only one contact for less than an hour with the foster parents or the few cases in which the worker had no contact with the foster parents. [P. 7]

If the social worker does not invest adequate time in preparing the foster parents, and/or lacks the skill to do it well, the chances of failure are greater. A placement failure, in turn, requires the investment of time. Thus, a little time saved in the beginning of a placement may result eventually in an even greater time expenditure on replacement. Even more important is the fact that replacement is extremely painful for the foster child and demoralizing to the foster parents.

Are There Some Suggestions That Can Be Given to Foster Parents to Help Them Do a Better Job?

Jarrett (1977b) has prepared a list of do's and don'ts for foster parents. An edited and somewhat revised version is presented below. The reader may wish to give the list to foster parents or use this list as a model for the development of another version.

Some Do's and Don'ts for Foster Parents

1. Ask the social worker for a social history and other background information on the child being considered for placement into your home. If, on the basis of this information, you doubt seriously that the placement will work out, don't accept the placement. A placement that blows up or breaks down is traumatic for all concerned, especially the foster child. Replacements, i.e. the movement of the child from one foster home to another, are painful and damaging to the foster child.

2. Ask the social worker to arrange a preplacement visit. Try to have more than one such visit with the child being considered for placement. When the child is in your home, only the immediate family members should be present. Do not dilute this visit by allowing neighbors or friends to be present.

3. Offer food to a visiting child and to the just-placed foster child. Show the child his/her private living quarters right away. Children want to know exactly where their room is and where they will sleep. They want to know the whereabouts of their private space in the home.

4. Allow the foster child to select the name you will be called, e.g. mom, Mrs. Brown, Betty, or John. If the foster child cannot decide on a name, offer some suggestions. Don't insist that the child call you whatever he/she calls his/her biological parents.

5. Obtain information from the social worker as to why the child is in foster care. Many foster children are confused about

why they are being placed in a foster home. From the beginning, try to help the child deal with his/her questions and insecurities.

6. If the child is old enough to use and understand language, speak in a way that can be understood. Don't underestimate the ability of small or mentally handicapped children to understand and express their concerns and worries.

7. Don't be afraid to let the foster child express feelings. Talk straight and don't be afraid to show your feelings. Don't try to hide reality from the child. Chances are he/she knows as much about his/her situation as you do.

8. Don't judge or be critical of the foster child's parents. The child probably loves them regardless of what they may have done or failed to do in the past. It is possible to discuss why the child is in foster care and the negative behavior of the parents without judging or criticizing.

9. Allow the foster child to talk freely and openly about his/her natural family. Permit the child to talk about both the "good" and the "bad." If the child wants to talk about concerns and worries, encourage him/her to do this. Don't push the child; wait until the child is ready. If what the child says bothers you, discuss this with your social worker.

10. Allow the child to grieve for his/her parents. The child separated from his/her parents experiences a great sense of loss regardless of the parents' past behavior or the circumstances that led to foster care placement.

11. Allow your foster child to be upset after he/she visits with his/her natural parents. Such visits often are upsetting. Saying goodbye is difficult. Such realities are hard to take but necessary and important to the child's adjustment. The child must not be shielded from harsh realities. In the end, the child will be better off if he/she faces the painful realities.

12. Don't conclude that it is bad for the foster child to visit with his/her natural family. Even if they are upsetting, there are more advantages than disadvantages to such visits.

13. If outrageous things happen during visits by the natural parents, report this to the social worker. In addition, report any physical abuse. But remember that visits—even emotionally up-

setting visits—facilitate the child's adjustment by helping him/her come to grips with reality.

14. Most foster children feel that they somehow caused the breakup of their family. They may feel as if foster care is a punishment for some real or imagined bad deed. Recognize that such feelings are common to foster children and gently help them to verbalize these feelings and to understand the real reasons for their placement.

15. Never attempt to discipline or punish a foster child by threatening his/her expulsion from the foster home. Given the worries and fears common to foster children, such a tactic can be traumatic and counterproductive. It is likely to create more problems.

16. Don't attempt to discipline or control the foster child by threatening to tell the social worker. That tactic also creates more problems than it solves.

17. Do suggest that the foster child talk to the social worker about problems and concerns, especially those with which you have been unable to help.

18. Don't insist that the foster child tell you what he/she discussed with the social worker, counselor or other professional, e.g. doctor. Everyone needs to have confidential relationships. Don't be threatened by the fact that your foster child may want to exercise this right to privacy.

19. Don't punish the foster child the first time he/she does something wrong in your home. Every family has its own rules and ways of doing things. It takes a while for the foster child to learn what is expected in your home. When the child does something wrong, tell him/her exactly what he/she did wrong and explain why the right way is important in your family. Try to prevent discipline problems by praising and rewarding all good behavior. Compliment the child whenever he/she does well, including ordinary and expected tasks. When punishment is necessary, accompany it with a clear explanation of what the child did wrong. Avoid physical punishment. Instead, withhold a privilege for a specific period. When unusual disciplinary problems arise, consult your social worker.

20. Allow the child to have privacy and his/her personal property. Do not open the child's mail or search his/her room.

21. Do not discuss the foster child's history or circumstances with anyone outside the immediate family. Inform friends and neighbors that the youngster is a foster child but explain that foster parents are expected to maintain confidentiality and respect the child and his/her natural parents' right to privacy.

When Can the Social Worker Make the Greatest Contribution to the Success of the Placement?

Foster care workers describe a honeymoon period common to the first few weeks of a placement. Typically, during this period, things go quite well. Because no big problems arise during this period, the social worker frequently spends his or her time on more pressing matters, usually those placements that are starting to break down. This is an unfortunate situation. Available research indicates that the first weeks of a placement are crucial, and it is this period that should command the worker's attention. On the basis of their research findings, Aldridge, Cautley, and Lichstein (1974) state, "If a worker has to make a choice between giving help to foster parents during the first few months of the placement and then letting them go on their own, or ignoring them for that period of time (letting them 'get used to the child' for example) and planning to see them when the placement has lasted, say, for example, six months, the first alternative seems clearly preferable" (p. 16).

The worker should do everything possible to help the placement get off to a good start. During the first month of placement, the worker should have weekly face-to-face interviews with the foster child and the foster parents. If this is impossible, interviews should be conducted by telephone. The importance of frequent contacts is related directly to the age of the child. It is of less importance if the foster child is an infant and of great importance if the foster child is an adolescent. If the foster parents have children of their own, these youngsters also should be involved in discussions of how things are working out.

It is during the first few weeks of the placement that contact with the natural parents is especially important. This is when a pattern of regular visiting is most easily established. It is also during this period that it is at least difficult to lay the foundation for a good working relationship between the foster parents and the natural parents.

What Can the Social Worker Do to Help the Placement Get Off to a Good Start?

As previously mentioned, research indicates that the first few weeks and months are critical to the success of the placement. Aldridge, Cautley, and Lichstein (1974) offer the following guidance to the social worker:

> Make sure you do your best to provide answers to the questions raised by the foster parents. Quite possibly you will not be able to answer some, for example, about the expected length of the placement or the child's previous experiences. In such instances, it is far preferable for you to be open with the foster parents and explain that you do not have the information. If you share what you know, as well as your uncertainties or lack of knowledge, with the foster parents they will feel much more comfortable than if you do not explain the reasons for this lack of knowledge. In the latter case, a foster family is likely to feel that the agency is reluctant to share information it has.
>
> If questions come up regarding specific problem behaviors of the foster child and you are not sure what kind of handling would be most desirable, offer to "think with" the foster parent about the details of the problem, going over what happened, how the parents had attempted to handle it, what the outcome is, whether other methods have been tried, etc. This can be done over the phone. Sometimes the act of describing the sequence in detail is in itself helpful and the foster parent gains a better understanding of what is going on. And as a "counselor" you will be in a position to make suggestions about difficulties you may see. At the very least you will know enough about the problem to be able to discuss it with your supervisor and talk with the foster parents later. Your expression of concern and interest is helpful in itself. Your use of a "problem-solving" approach is also helpful.
>
> The overall support and encouragement you give to foster parents may make a great difference in their own feelings about their role. New foster parents in particular may develop feelings of uncertainty and unsureness and may need reassurance and encouragement in order to continue working with the foster child.

During the early months of the placement, be alert to opportunities to do the following where possible:

a) Increase the foster parents' understanding of the child.
b) Encourage their use of praise and warmth in responding to pleasing behavior of the foster child, indicating that in general a positive response to desired behavior is a particularly effective way to bring about improvement in the child.

Regard and treat the foster parents as colleagues, as members of a "team," to use an overworked term. Together you are trying to provide the best care possible for the particular child involved. You, as a representative of the agency, have one kind of skill, and the foster parents have another kind of skill. Both are essential. Strengths in one may be used to overcome weaknesses in the other [Pp. 20-21]

What Can a Social Worker Do to Assist the Foster Parents?

The sixty-eight-page book, *Guidelines for Placement Workers,* by Aldridge, Cautley, and Lichstein (1974) is an excellent source of practical guidelines on foster family care. Of significance is the fact that their guidelines are based on research findings. Many of the suggestions presented are drawn from this source.

The social worker must be available, by telephone and in person, to the foster parents, who must feel that they can obtain help from the social worker if and when they need it. Being able to count on the social worker makes their task less frightening and lonely.

Foster parents should be treated with respect and appreciation and viewed as members of the team. Their ideas should be sought. They must be trusted. Foster parents need encouragement and support. If they do not receive reinforcement, they become demoralized, they worry that they are not doing a good job, or feel they are being used.

If the social worker cannot have frequent face-to-face contact with the foster parents, he/she should use the telephone. Even a brief conversation in which inquiries are made about the concerns and needs of the foster parents and foster child can do much to demonstrate that the social worker is available, willing to help, and appreciative of the work being done by the foster parents. Small gestures, such as a birthday card sent to a foster parent, are important.

The social worker should look for opportunities to increase the foster parents' understanding of the foster child and children in general. People are most open to learning and changing when they are trying to solve a problem. Use the concern of the moment as a springboard for introducing knowledge and information that may be helpful to the foster parents.

Foster parents usually need special help in understanding the behavior of natural parents and the importance of keeping the natural parents involved with the child. Not infrequently, foster parents develop feelings of anger toward the natural parents. These feelings should be dealt with in an open and honest manner. Foster parents need to be prepared for problems that may arise with the natural parents. If, for example, the natural parent is alcoholic, the foster parents need to realize that the parent may be drunk when he/she visits. The social worker should help foster parents anticipate problems and learn how to deal with them. Being prepared in advance lessens some of the frustrations.

Foster parents should be helped to understand that there are wide variations in family behavior and life-styles. Thus, the foster child may have different standards of physical hygiene, eating habits, clothing care, and home care, etc. If they can be helped to understand these differences, they are less likely to be bothered by the child's behavior and more likely to give the child time to adjust to the rules and expectations that apply within the foster home.

The social worker should not apply labels to the foster child or the natural parents. For example, terms such as *mentally retarded, emotionally disturbed,* or *hyperactive,* etc., should not be used. Such terms are misunderstood easily and are likely to add to the problem. Rather than use labels or diagnostic terminology, the social worker should help the foster parent identify and describe the specific behaviors that are troublesome.

Research indicates that the anniversary of the placement is a critical time. One year after becoming foster parents to a child, the foster parents typically go through a personal assessment of how they are doing with the youngster and whether or not they are happy in the role. If the foster parents are going to throw in the towel, it is likely to happen about this time. Thus, the worker should be attentive to the concerns of the foster parents, give them appropriate recognition for what they have accomplished, and the support they need to carry on.

Interestingly, some studies suggest that foster children also respond to anniversaries, e.g. when they were separated from their parents or when they were placed in a foster home. On or around these anniversaries, the child may be moody, depressed, or particularly difficult to handle. The foster parents should be informed that children may react to the anniversary of a significant or painful life event.

What Techniques Can Be Used to Monitor a Placement?

Ideally, a foster home should be monitored closely so that problems can be prevented or caught early in their development and to ensure that the child is receiving the type of care needed. Unfortunately, there often are problems in the area of monitoring and supervision. One social worker described it this way, "The foster parents keep saying that everything is working out fine and then bang, there is a big explosion and you suddenly find out that things have not been going fine and that problems have been building for a long time." Certain techniques should be used to detect emerging problems before they become serious.

When the social worker talks with the foster parents about the placement, he/she should be prepared to ask specific questions and should avoid general questions such as, "How are things going?" Many people are conditioned to say fine or all right when asked such general questions. Specific questions such as "Is Johnny still having nightmares?" "Are you still feeling discouraged?" or "Did the foster home payment arrive yet?" are more likely to elicit the real concerns of the foster parents. Also, the social worker should ask the foster parents to jot down between visits their questions and concerns. This ensures that they are not forgotten and actually are discussed when the foster parents and social worker meet again. Problem checklists also can be useful as a means of communicating. Aldridge, Cautley, and Lichstein (1974) have developed a semistructured interview schedule for use with foster parents during the placement. Because its use increases the opportunity for the foster parents to voice concerns and identify problems before they become serious, the use of this schedule is strongly recommended.

Below is a list of questions that might be employed in interviews with foster parents. It is noted that the questions are designed to elicit specific information from the foster parents. Some of these questions were drawn from *An Interview Guide for Workers to Use When Discussing Foster Home Placements with Foster Parents*, which was developed by Aldridge, Cautley, and Lichstein (1974).

1. At this point, how do you feel about being a foster parent?

2. Does being a foster parent to (foster child) seem more or less difficult than you expected?

3. At this point, how does (foster child) feel about living in your home?

4. How would you evaluate (foster child's) progress since . . . ?

5. What changes have you noticed in (foster child)? Do you see this as progress or a step backward?

6. When we talked last you mentioned . . . as being a problem. How has that been going?

7. What specific problems is (foster child) experiencing? How would you like things to be different? What have you done to try to help? Has it worked? What else have you thought about doing?

8. Now that (foster child) is living in your home, how is his/her presence affecting your relationship with your husband/wife?

9. Is (foster child) having an effect on your own children (and/or other foster children)? In what way?

10. Are you experiencing any financial problems because of the foster care arrangement? Are there any questions about agency policy or procedures?

11. We have talked about problems. What about the good side of things? Have you and (foster child) been able to do anything together? Have you enjoyed this? Has (foster child) enjoyed this?

12. When you and (foster child) do get along well and enjoy each other, what happens that makes it a positive experience? Is there anything that can be learned in this? Can you think of any

way of transferring some of that positive experience into some of the problem areas?

13. What does (foster child) really enjoy? What is really important to him/her? Is there any way of using his/her interests and pleasures as a way of rewarding (foster child) for good behavior?

14. Does (foster child) talk much about his/her parents? Brothers and/or sisters? What does he/she say? How do you respond to what he/she says about his/her family?

15. How have the visits by (foster child's) parents worked out? Are there specific problems? Do you have ideas on how the visits could be made less troublesome? At this point, how do you feel about having the parents visit?

16. Does (foster child) seem to understand why he/she is in foster care? What questions does he/she have?

17. Within the past week or so, what was the most difficult problem you have had with (foster child)? Why do you think he/she behaved this way? Have you thought of any ways of handling or preventing this problem?

18. Within the past week or so what was the best thing that happened with (foster child)? Why do you think he/she behaved this way? Have you thought of any ways of increasing the chances that there will be more good experiences?

19. Do you have any additional questions to ask me? Is there some information that would be helpful? Would you like some special help with a particular problem?

20. When is a convenient time for us to meet again?

Questions such as those listed should be reviewed with the foster mother and father. It is a serious mistake to speak only with the mother and neglect the foster father.

How Are Problem Checklists Used in Foster Care?

Good communication between the foster parents and social worker is critical. Heavy case loads, however, limit contact. Because this is prevalent, the social worker must find ways of focusing on the most pressing problems, thereby making the best use of the limited time that can be spent with foster parents. A problem checklist is one such tool. Basically, it lists common problems encountered in foster care. The foster parent is asked to read through the list and check those problems or topics he or she would like to discuss with the social worker. The checklist permits the parent to have input into the planning of time spent with the worker. If the social worker obtains the completed checklist before the session, it permits him/her to plan for the session and secure specific information requested by the foster parents.

The use of problem checklists, like that of similar tools, should be individualized to the situation. Checklists may be helpful to some foster parents but not to others. The social worker should explain the checklist to the foster parents and ask if they would like to use one. Moreover, the social worker should modify the items in the list so they are relevant to the foster parent. For example, specially designed checklists may be needed by a foster parent of an older child, a child with a physical handicap, or for the foster parent working intensively with a natural parent. A sample problem checklist is presented below.

A Problem Checklist for Foster Parents

This problem checklist has been designed for your use. It is a tool to help you communicate with your social worker and make sure that your meetings focus on things that are important to you. It simply lists problems and concerns sometimes mentioned by foster parents.

Go through the list and check (✔) those items that are of concern to you. Give or mail this list to your social worker, who then will have a better idea of your concerns or worries. These topics can be discussed in detail. Space also is provided for you to add items not found on the list.

Concerns/Problems Related Mostly to My Foster Child

——fighting and aggression   ——upset by visits with parents
——argues, will not obey   ——lacks friends or peer group
——poor personal hygiene   ——friends are a bad influence
——eating problems   ——destroys toys or property
——sleep or bedtime problems   ——very sad or depressed
——isolation from others   ——lying

——medical problem
——dental problem
——unusual sexual behavior
——speech problems
——coordination problems
 (balance)
——excessive dependency
——offensive language
——religious conflict
——stays out too late
——temper tantrums
——drug or alcohol abuse

——stealing
——bed-wetting
——soiling
——runs away
——poor school performance
——poor school attendance
——problem with other
 children in home
——problem related to own
 parents
——frequent illness
——talks of suicide
——self-mutilation

Concerns/Problems Related Mostly to My Role as Foster Parent

——not making progress with
 foster child
——not enough money to
 cover expenses
——don't understand agency
 policy or regulations on
 . . . (explain)

_____

——not getting enough help
 from my social worker
——not sure how to handle
 medical and dental care of
 foster child
——have doubts about
 wanting to continue as
 foster parent
——not being treated fairly by
 agency
——don't know how to deal
 with school personnel

——foster care is having
 adverse affect on my
 marriage
——foster care is having
 adverse affect on my
 other children
——not sure how to handle
 visits by biological parents
——not enough time away
 from stress and
 responsibilities
——neighbors and/or relatives
 are creating problems
——things are just not going
 well
——need help in figuring out
 how to deal with child's
 problem
——foster child is very
 different than expected
——don't have enough information about child's
 background

Other Concerns

List here any other topics you want to discuss. Identify any questions you have. _____

_____

_____

_____

_____

_____

What Is the Postcard Technique?

The social worker can maintain an open line of communication with foster parents, the foster child, and the natural parents by employing the simple postcard technique. The social worker gives several postcards to the person with whom he/she wants to keep in touch. The stamped postcards are preaddressed to the social worker. The foster parent, child, or natural parent is asked to write a few lines whenever he/she feels a need to ask a question, request an appointment, or mention a problem. When the social worker receives the postcard, he/she responds by telephone or in person.

While it is true that a telephone call serves the same purpose, some individuals who hesitate to call will write a postcard. In rural areas, this technique may be especially useful because the cost of long-distance telephone calls may hamper communication. In addition, many rural areas have party lines, and people are reluctant to discuss personal concerns over the telephone.

How Can the Foster Parents Build a Working Relationship with the Foster Child's Parents?

Below are examples of what the foster parents can do to help create and maintain a working relationship with their foster child's parents.

1. Give praise and recognition to the natural parents for any behaviors related to positive parenting. Reinforce all such behaviors, regardless of how small or insignificant they may seem.

2. Work with natural parents to construct a scrapbook or photo album containing mementos for the child.

3. Help natural parents construct a family tree or life book so the child can understand his/her roots.

4. Invite natural parents to dinner, picnic, or other outing.

5. Help parents locate and use needed resources for housing, clothing, transportation, and training.

6. Invite natural parents to accompany foster parents to parent education class, adult education classes or other community activities.

7. Give natural parent a birthday or Christmas gift—one from foster parent rather than from child.

How Can Foster Parents Involve the Natural Parents in the Care of the Foster Child?

Below are some activities that may help to keep the natural parents involved in the care of their child.

1. Involve natural parents in school conferences, school functions and PTA meetings.

2. Involve natural parents in decisions about the child's clothing and include them in shopping trips.

3. Involve natural parents in plans aimed at helping child with health, behavior, or school problems.

4. Involve natural parents in holidays special to the child, e.g. include parents in birthday parties, graduations, Christmas celebrations, or Thanksgiving dinner.

5. Involve natural parents in child's visits to the doctor and dentist.

6. Write or telephone natural parents on a regular basis and give them a progress report on how their child is doing.

7. Take photographs of child with parents and give prints to parents and foster child.

How Can the Motivation of Foster Parents Be Sustained?

A simple but useful way of conceptualizing motivation is to view it as a balance between the pull of hope and the push of discomfort. To sustain or increase motivation for foster parenting, it is necessary to elevate the sense of progress and achievement and decrease the impact of those things about foster parenting that cause discomfort or are adversive.

Many foster parents become discouraged because they do not see progress or change in the foster child. They lose hope and become demoralized. Behavioral approaches can help to counteract this loss of hope because they emphasize the use of baseline measurements that permit the measurement of progress. For example, if temper tantrums are a problem, a parent may become discouraged because the tantrum behavior continues after many weeks or months of working with the child. Not infrequently, the behavior is actually changing, but because it changes so slowly or because a baseline was never taken the foster parent is not aware that progress is underway. By keeping accurate records of problem behavior, the foster parent can detect even small changes. Progress, even slow progress, has the effect of raising hope and sustaining motivation. There are many simply written books that describe behavioral approaches to problem behavior (Becker, 1971; Becker and Becker, 1974; Krumboltz and Krumboltz, 1972; and Patterson, 1971).

Foster parents must be reinforced for foster parenting. Unless they find foster parenting reinforcing, they gradually lose interest and are drawn to activities that are more rewarding. It is important to realize that what is reinforcing for one foster parent may not be reinforcing for another. Attempts to reinforce foster parents for the job they are doing must be individualized. A foster care reinforcer is anything that increases or maintains the occurrence of a foster parenting behavior. Possible reinforcers include praise from social worker, happiness expressed by the foster child, warmth expressed by the child, achievement of goals, feelings of progress, money, public recognition, participation in special social events for foster parents, certificates of appreciation, opportunity to secure training, intellectual stimulation, opportunity to attend conferences or workshops, appreciation expressed by friends or relatives, and fulfilling certain religious ideals, etc. To reinforce foster parenting, the social worker should attempt to discover what is important to the foster parent and find ways of securing these reinforcers for the foster parent.

Motivation is tied closely to the concepts of time and expectation. People can and will continue to work on very difficult tasks if they know that the task can be achieved or they can stop working on the task at some designated time. These concepts are used in the task-centered approaches in social work (Reid and Epstein, 1977) and in behavioral contracting. These notions can be applied to foster parenting. For example, a foster mother may be willing to care for a disturbed or problematic child if she knows that it will be only for a specified period. On the other hand, she may be reluctant to take on a difficult task if she does not know whether it will last for one month or one year. To the greatest extent possible, the social worker should help foster parents cope with unusually difficult situations by time structuring the placement. For example, the foster parents may be asked to care for a child for a six-month period with an agreement that a reassessment will be made at the end of that time. If at the end of six months the parents want the placement terminated, it will be done. If, on the other hand, they are willing to continue with the placement, another contract period is established. Limiting difficult tasks to specific blocks of time makes coping easier for most people.

Should Foster Parents Be Allowed to Adopt Their Foster Child?

Sometimes foster parents express an interest in legally adopting their foster child. This situation usually occurs after a long-term placement and after the child has finally been legally freed for adoption through court action. This issue can be troublesome, and court cases involving this question have attracted national attention.

In cases of conflict between the foster parents wishing to adopt and the social agency, the conflict has been precipitated by the agency's decision to remove the child from the foster home and place him/her with an adoptive family. In other words, the agency rejected the foster parents as potential adoptive parents. Such action, of course, results in the child being separated from familiar adults and placed with strangers. A report by the National Association of Attorneys General (1976) states:

> Several reasons have been advanced for discouraging foster parents from attempting to adopt their foster children. . . . The explanation traditionally given is that the rights of foster parents are mini-

mized in order to prevent interference with the natural parents' rights. Another reason advanced by child welfare agency workers is that the motivation of the foster parents for the adoption of the foster child may be suspect. They fear that foster parents may be attempting to adopt their long-term foster child out of feelings of guilt, or they may seek to adopt the child because of subtle agency pressure to do so. This latter situation may result from the agency's belief that it may have difficulty in placing the child elsewhere for adoption. The final explanation for agency refusal to permit adoption by foster parents is that, almost universally, the standards one must meet in order to qualify as an adoptive parent are higher than the standards for a foster parent. Agencies argue that to permit these "lesser qualified" foster parents to adopt their foster children could lead to a misuse of the system and possible danger to the child.

Several commentators have offered suggestions which take into account the prevalence of long-term foster placements, the desire of many foster parents to adopt their foster child, and the wish of child-welfare agencies to protect the child and place him in the best home possible. One suggestion . . . is for periodic review of foster placements with a definite limit on the amount of time a child may be in foster care before his natural parents' rights may be terminated and he is freed for adoption. This suggestion has been incorporated in several states' laws regarding termination of parental rights and adoption. The expansion of the concept of subsidized adoptions negatives much of the concern about pressure from the agency to get hard-to-place children adopted by their foster parents. Finally it has been suggested that foster parents who are selected and licensed should "have the capacity to be good adoptive parents as this is the case for increasing numbers of them." [P. 11]

It is important to note that the different licensing standards for adoptive parents and foster parents are a major cause of this problem. Sometimes agencies are so hard pressed to find foster homes that they license people who lack healthy motivation, emotional and marital stability, and a capacity to parent. In addition, many foster home placements violate the normalization principle by placing a young child with older foster parents. When such foster parents express a desire to adopt their foster child, the agencies understandably are reluctant to agree to this arrangement. This, in turn, raises questions about the relative importance of the existing foster parent-child relationship vis-à-vis the importance of placing a child in a more suitable adoptive home.

In recent years, there has been a trend toward the acceptance of foster parents as adoptive parents. This trend is related to the concept of *psychological parent* and the growing belief that stability, even in a less than desirable situation, is less harmful than the trauma of replacement and change. This does not mean that the foster child should never be removed from his/her foster parents or that the foster parents should always be allowed to adopt their foster child. Rather, it means that a removal decision must be made with great caution and a careful assessment of the relative advantages and disadvantages for the child. This point of view is expressed in selections from an *amicus curiae* filed with the United States Supreme Court and cited in the *Child Rights Report* (1977).

To be a child is to be in a crucial and dependent phase of human growth in which primary relationships cannot be turned off and on again without damage. An erroneous wrenching of the nurturing bonds between the long term foster child and his long term foster family is the kind of damage that is not fully—or even substantially—recompensable even by ordering a resumption of the broken relationships. In terms of irreparable injury, an erroneous breaking up of delicate and complex long term foster family relationships is far more serious than would be such an unthinkable action as, for example, an agency intentionally breaking a child's arm for some therapeutic purpose, recognizing that such a mistake may be "corrected" by resetting the limb which, though scarred, may grow together again as "strong" as it ever was. . . . (U)nlike most private property interests affected by official action—the private liberty interest of child and parent to be secure in their relationship can never be fully restored by retroactive relief. Amici finds it difficult to conceive of any more consequential deprivation than the forced separation of a child from the adult persons upon whom he has grown to rely.

The members of the group do not seek to press upon the Constitution a particular theory of human nature. Rather they seek only to have recognized what is a universal experience of humankind, the familial bond that develops between parents and children in their long term care. The life support system provided children in the form of long term foster parents must not be withdrawn without anything less than careful consideration of the impact of such action upon the child and the adequacy and availability of permanent parents. It is the process for withdrawing such life support systems from the child, not the substantive basis for such action, that is in issue here. The group argues only that before a child and his long term foster parents are separated, the process should provide a full hearing for all concerned parties before an impartial and independent decisionmaker. The group, prompted as much by common sense as by its collective expertise, asks the Court to confirm the unconstitutionality of state action which forcibly breaks familial bonds without a process which can protect against discrimination, whim and caprice. [Pp. 2-3]

The new trend toward adoption by foster parents is reflected in a recent policy statement issued by the City of New York Human Resources Administration (1978).

> In the past, many agencies operated under policies which discouraged or did not permit foster parents to adopt their foster children even when a significant relationship had been established between them. Today, adoption of foster children by foster parents is generally considered to be an excellent way of providing permanence. New York State Law and Regulations encourage such adoptions, which are designed to formalize ties on a permanent basis when the emotional commitment has already been established. For example, the law gives first preference in adoption to foster parents who have continuously cared for a child for 24 months or more. SDSS Regulations indicate that when an agency is in the process of freeing a child, it must notify the foster parents, inform them of the provisions of the subsidy program, and request written acknowledgement of receipt of such information. Because foster parent adoptions will become even more numerous in the future, agencies should be developing internal procedures that address the key issues such adoptions present regarding the adoption study process, subsidy, and post-placement services.
>
> Every agency is obligated to provide to all their foster parents information about adoption and the availability of adoption subsidy. [P. 10]

The adage an ounce of prevention is worth a pound of cure is especially applicable to the problems that surround the request by foster parents to adopt. Many problems could be avoided if the agency and social worker (1) adhere to rigorous standards and procedures for the selection and licensing of foster parents; (2) use written contracts with foster parents that explain relevant policy on this matter; (3) take action toward permanency planning as early as possible, i.e. before the child has spent many years with a foster family; and (4) utilize professionally sound matching criteria for the original foster placement.

How Is Systems Theory Used in Foster Family Care?

Much of what the social worker does within the field of child welfare deals directly with the family system. Thus, a brief discussion of selected systems concepts, as applied to the family, seems indicated. Systems theory helps to explain certain recurring research findings and serves to bridge several types of intervention, e.g. behavioral approaches, crisis intervention, and family therapy.

Before presenting selected systems concepts, it is important for the reader to understand that systems theory is complex. Also, there are several types of systems theory, and concepts are used differently by various disciplines. For example, the systems theory used by engineers and operation analysts is highly mathematical and of little direct relevance to child welfare. The biologist also uses a form of systems theory. For the social worker, the most useful systems concepts are those drawn from social sytems theory and general systems theory. General systems theory pulls together concepts from biological and social sciences and attempts to describe the elements common to all living systems, e.g. the human body or social organization. This integration of the biological and social sciences is best illustrated in the work of Miller (1977).

Various systems concepts have been examined for their relevance to social work theory and practice (Hearn, 1969). These include the concepts of system, environment, boundary, entropy, negentropy, input, processing, output, feedback, equifinality, growth, and development, etc. Bertalanffy (1967, 1968), considered by many to be the founder of general systems theory, has defined systems as "sets of elements standing in interaction" or as a "complex of components in interaction." In essence, a system is an organization of components into systematic relationships. Each of the components is to some degree directly or indirectly influenced by the other components. A system is a whole that is more than the sum of its parts. It is an example of organized complexity, always changing but still maintaining itself as an entity. Buckley (1967) clarifies the nature of system when he states:

> The particular kinds of more or less stable interrelationships of components that become established at any time constitute the particular structure of the system at that time, thus achieving a kind of "whole" with some degree of continuity and boundary. Also, we are mainly interested in systems within which some process is continually going on, including an interchange with an environment across the boundary. It is generally agreed that when we deal with the more open system with a highly flexible structure, the distinction between the boundaries and the environment becomes a more and more arbitrary matter, dependent on the purpose of the observer.
>
> In fact, it is becoming clear that we cannot make a neat division of those things that are not systems; rather, we shall have to recognize varying degrees of "systemness." [Pp. 41-42]

All systems with which the social worker is concerned (individual, family, group, organization, community) are open systems. An open system exchanges materials, energies, or information with its environment. The boundary of an open system is semipermeable, in that it permits a wide range of exchanges and transactions between the system and its environment. Such transactions are essential to the maintenance and growth of the system. A system dies or loses its organization when it cannot adequately interact with its environment. When a system becomes disorganized, its parts are functioning in a random manner, resulting in a loss of wholeness. The disorder, disorganization, or randomness of functioning is known as *entropy*. An open system maintains itself and is capable of progressing to an even higher state of development because it can import matter, energy, and information from its environment.

Basic to the general systems perspective is the view that open systems tend naturally toward higher or more complex levels of organization. If a system does not continue to grow and develop, entropy or the tendency toward disorder causes the system to deteriorate. A particular level of system organization or differentiation is termed a *steady state*. A steady state represents a temporary balance of exchange or transaction between the system and its environment. Because the open system is in transaction with its environment, it always is in a state of change and is only temporarily at any particular level of organization. A given steady state may represent either a higher or lower level of organization than the one that preceded it. Systems vary in regard to their relative stability. Although each steady state represents only a temporary balance of transactions between the system and its environment, a particular steady state may or may not be easily altered. The concept of threshold has been found useful in describing the responsiveness of a system or its resistance to change.

If systems concepts are applied to the family, then the individuals making up that system can be viewed as subsystems; the family's wider environment, e.g. neighborhood or community, makes up its suprasystem. The family is in constant interaction with its environment, and depending on the degree to which its boundary is permeable, it affects and is affected by its environment. It is of considerable interest that Cautley and Lichstein (1974) found that the foster home applicants most likely to be successful foster parents were those who frequently had opened their home to other children. Those homes in which children stayed for weeks or months at a time were more successful than those who had never had children stay for one, two, or three nights. It appears that the most successful foster homes are those that have a highly permeable family boundary. Other individuals can enter and leave these families without disrupting the steady state. In contrast, the families that tend to be closed to the outside environment are less successful with foster children.

In keeping with the systems perspective, the family is more than the sum of its parts. Each family system develops its own unique values, internal structure, communication patterns, rules for decision making, and methods for handling stress and problems. In a sense, each family—like each individual—has a unique personality, its own ways of coping with life.

Each individual in the family system affects and is affected by all others. Whenever the behavior of one is altered, it affects the behavior of others in the family. It is for this reason that all family members—adults and children—should be involved in the foster home study and in all monitoring activities subsequent to the placement of a foster child into the family. All are affected by the foster care experience and all contribute to its success or failure.

It is important for the social worker to examine the actual composition of the foster family system. In many cases, the family consists of the husband, wife, and children, all living in the household. Many times, however, additional individuals are part of the family system. There may be grandparents, aunts and uncles, and other relatives who are part of the system. This is especially true among those ethnic or cultural groups characterized by an extended family structure, e.g. Native American. Since all individuals in the system may affect and be affected by foster care, all need to be involved in the home study, placement decisions, and follow-along activities. Too often, these significant others are overlooked until problems arise in the placement, and it is discovered that someone outside the immediate household is having an important impact on the placement.

As previously indicated, each family develops a unique structure and style. Obvious examples are the seating arrangement at the dinner table, favorite foods, and bedtimes, etc. Much more complex and subtle examples include alignments and splits among family members, patterns of double binding, and a definite communication hierarchy. However one views this phenomenon conceptually, the important point is that such patterns exist in a steady state and are resistant to change. The addition of a foster child to a family may put stress on these patterns. In attempting to describe this reality, Wilkes (1974) states:

> Families develop an equilibrium in their functioning so that there are familiar patterns of activity, relationship, decision making and problem solving. Stress of any type tends to disrupt the equilibrium and by and large, the greater the stress the greater the disruption. An additional child in the home is a significant stress and always causes disruption in the existing transactional patterns. [Pp. 373-374]

It also is important to recognize that the foster child comes from a unique family whose values, patterns, and rules, etc., were undoubtedly different from those of the foster family. For the child who must enter the life of strange family, a form of cultural shock is involved. Since the placement of a foster child places stresses on or upsets the steady state of the foster family and disrupts the child's usual way of life, the first few weeks of a placement are a time of rapid change and readjustment. The foundation for a successful or unsuccessful placement is laid very early in the placement. It is a formative period. Within a matter of weeks, a new pattern of interaction and mutual expectation emerges and soon solidifies into a steady state. The importance of the early weeks of the placement has been confirmed by research conducted by Aldridge, Cautley, and Lichstein (1974).

> There is strong evidence that the pattern of interaction with the foster child is established early in the placement—that is, the expectations the foster parents have of the child, the kinds of discipline they use, etc. . . .
> The quality of the interaction revealed in the first [research] interview with the foster mother (when the child had been in the home just four weeks) and with the foster father (when the child had been in the home three months) was significantly related to the eventual success of the foster parents. [Pp. 17-18]

These findings relative to the critical importance of the first few weeks of an adjustment process are compatible with crisis theory, clinical observations, and research findings related to crisis intervention. It is noted frequently, for example, that the nature of an individual's experiences during the first four to six weeks following the death of a loved one has a significant effect on subsequent life adjustment. Williams (1973) reported on work with the bereaved and observed that "those who receive intervention counseling during the first few weeks after a significant loss show less morbidity or maladjustment than those who receive assistance at a later time" (p. 151).

Parenthetically, it should be noted that many social workers have discussed elements of the foster child's adjustment in terms of a mourning process and observed reactions in children similar to those observed in bereaved persons. To be separated from his or her parents and familiar surroundings may be similar to an experience with death of a loved one.

Consistent with notions of crisis theory and intervention, research in foster care indicates that early intervention is of great importance. What is done during the first few weeks of a placement is of more importance than assistance provided at a later time.

> [Research] . . . findings suggest that attempts to help the parents develop optimum patterns of such interaction need to be made early —before the parents have settled into their own way of doing things, and we do have evidence that workers can indeed help foster parents to understand the child, which in turn affects the way parents interact with the child. Early in the placement foster parents are especially open to information about the foster child, want to understand him better and frequently question whether they are helping the child as much as possible.
>
> If these questions can be asked at the time they arise, the foster parents will not only feel much more comfortable about what they are doing but will learn more rapidly, as generally information is more quickly assimilated and retained when a specific need is felt for it. [Aldridge, Cautley, and Lichstein, 1974, p. 18]

The child welfare literature refers to the honeymoon period sometimes observed at the beginning of a placement. It is a period usually several weeks long, characterized by the absence of expected problems and related usually to the shock of separation. A more detailed explanation of the honeymoon period has been presented in Chapter 6. It should be noted that the honeymoon period occurs during the time when system or steady-state adjustments are taking place. The existence of a period when things seem to be going well should not distract the social worker from investing as much effort as possible in the first few weeks of the placement.

Concepts of steady state and internal family organization also help to explain another recurring research finding—one showing that the longer a child remains away from his or her natural home, the less likely he/she is to be reunited with the natural family. Once a child leaves the family system, the natural family establishes a new steady state, a new pattern of functioning that no longer includes the child. Once that new pattern of adjustment is firmly established, the natural family resists a disruption of this steady state and hesitates to bring the child back into the family. This is why it is important to keep the natural parent actively involved with his or her child during foster care placement. Keeping parent and child mutually involved tends to preserve the system of reinforcements that maintains parenting behavior and, in a sense, keeps the parent-child relationship from dying.

General systems theory postulates that a system in trouble, one starting to breakdown, may attempt to preserve a steady state by adding or discarding components. Many social workers refer to this phenomenon as *repeopling*. A troubled family may attempt to cope by pushing one family member out of the system, thereby eliminating a source of stress or causing a realignment in its internal organization. Requests by parents for help in removing a family member are common to social service agencies, e.g. nursing home placements, institutional placements, or foster care. These families are attempting to solve system problems by repeopling. On the other extreme, some families may attempt to preserve a steady state or deal with an internal problem by adding members to the family system. Adding subsystems forces modifications of families' internal organization and can be viewed as a problem-solving effort. For example, the couple who wants to become an adoptive home or foster home is attempting to achieve a different level of functioning by adding people to their family system. This is why the social worker making a foster home or adoptive home study must examine carefully the motivation behind a request for an action that will have a substantial impact on the family system. There can be healthy and unhealthy motives for repeopling or rearranging a system. An attempt to preserve a shaky marriage, for example, is an understandable but an unacceptable reason for wanting to become a foster family.

How Can the Concept of Basic Human Needs Be Used to Help Foster Parents Understand Children?

The social worker in the field of child welfare deals with complex human behavior, both normal and abnormal. Many social workers utilize the concept of basic human need as one way of understanding and explaining behavior. Because the concept is relatively simple, it can be used with foster parents as a framework for understanding the behavior of foster children and natural parents. It also can be used to help foster parents understand their reactions to foster care. The value of understanding behavior is that it helps people to be more tolerant and accepting of behavior different from their own.

Central to this conceptual framework is the assumption that all individuals are alike insofar as they have certain basic human needs or desires. While these needs are expressed differently in various societies, cultures, and ethnic groups, they are essentially the same for all human beings. When one recognizes that there are certain common needs and that people are more alike than different, it is possible to understand much human behavior, even behavior that seems illogical, strange, or sick. Among the basic human needs are the following:

1. Food, water, and shelter from the cold and adverse weather
2. Physical safety and security
3. Respect and acceptance by persons respected and valued
4. Feeling worthwhile, useful, and therefore valuable to those we value
5. Achieving a degree of intimacy with others (to know and be known in a personal way by another person)
6. Giving and receiving affection (including both physical and nonphysical affection)
7. Having one's life experience and perceptions validated, i.e. be assured that one is not alone in how he or she experiences life and know that others have had similar thoughts and experiences
8. A sense of meaning and purpose in life
9. Playing, trying out new experiences, and experimenting with novelty

As growth and development occur, various behaviors that meet these needs are learned. Culture, family beliefs, and many other factors encourage or reinforce certain need-meeting behaviors and discourage others. In a sense, each unique personality is the sum of an individual's particular approach to meeting these basic human needs. Much need-meeting behavior is habitual and unconsciously employed. Seldom is a deliberate choice made about how to behave. Instead of thinking about or choosing their actions, people rely on habitual patterns that have developed over time. When, for one reason or another, usual habitual need-meeting behaviors are not working, discomfort and even emotional pain are experienced. As a reaction, an attempt is made to correct the situation. A person may try out some new behavior or go through a period of testing or trial-and-error behavior until discomfort is lessened: Various behaviors are tried until one is found that seems to work or lessens discomfort. One commonly sees this approach in children who have just entered foster care. They do not know what is expected by the foster parents or how to act. Thus, they try different behaviors until a certain pattern of reward and punishment is established. In some instances, if the discomfort is great and a way cannot be found to meet a need, people may try to deny or suppress the need. For example, the child who has difficulty making and keeping friends may reach a point where he or she says that no one else is needed, that he/she has no desire for friends. If a child repeatedly has been hurt physically or emotionally, i.e. denied the need for security and safety, he/she may withdraw and avoid others and in effect suppress the need for affection and intimacy. When the real world is harsh and punishing, fantasy and extensive daydreaming may be used as an attempt to meet needs.

An attempt to meet needs also may include manipulating others or somehow forcing them to do what is wanted. The person who is a manipulator usually is offensive to others; if manipulation works and is thereby reinforced, it will continue. The point to be made here is that even offensive behavior, e.g. manipulation, lying, stealing, or hurting others, can be understood in terms of learned need-meeting behavior. That does not make it any more desirable, but it does make it understandable.

The concept of need-meeting behavior also can help explain certain behaviors that foster parents find particularly troublesome. A good example is the natural parent who visits his or her child in foster care and makes promises that cannot be kept. To many foster parents, it seems as if the natural parent is lying to the child.

If one views this behavior as an attempt to counteract feelings of inadequacy or as a way of securing needed affection and admiration from the child, the parent's behavior is understandable.

The idea of need-meeting behavior can be used to explain the patterns and organization that develop within a family system and even why an individual is attracted to some people but not others. One of the ways needs are met is to seek out and enter into satisfying human relationships. An individual is attracted to those people who meet his/her needs in a way that complements or is compatible with the way he/she usually behaves. This may explain why two people marry. The marriage is stable as long as each is having his or her needs met and, at the same time, is meeting the needs of the other.

What Are Some Books Specifically for Foster Parents?

Below is a list of several inexpensive and simply written books that are designed especially for foster parents. The ones by Reistroffer are popular with foster parents.

Mary Reistroffer, *What You Always Wanted to Discuss about Foster Care But Didn't Have the Time or the Chance to Bring Up* (1971, 41 pp.).

Mary Reistroffer, *What's So Special About Teenagers?* (1972, 42 pp.).

Mary Reistroffer, *Foster Parents and Social Workers on the Job Together* (1974b, 55 pp.).

Florence McGuire and Mary Reistroffer, *Thank Goodness Foster Parents Are Hooked on Helping* (1975, 35 pp.).

Mary Reistroffer, *Foster Family Care: A Collection of Papers and Abstracts* (1974a, 70 pp.).

Marie O'Connell, *Helping the Child to Use Foster Family Care* (1953, 39 pp.).

Irwin Sarason, Karen Linder, and Keith Crnic, *A Guide for Foster Parents* (1976, 37 pp.).

Evelyn Felker, *Foster Parenting Young Children: Guidelines from a Foster Parent* (1974, 96 pp.).

Robert L. Geiser, *The Illusion of Caring: Children in Foster Care* (1973).

Evelyn H. Felker, *Foster Parenting Young Children, Guidelines from a Foster Parent* (1974).

What Are Some General Books about Parenting, Child Rearing and Parent-Child Problems That May Be Helpful to Foster Parents?

Raymond Corsini and Genevieve Painter, *The Practical Parent: ABC's of Child Discipline* (1975).

Wesley Becker and Janis Becker, *Successful Parenthood* (1974).

Gerald Patterson, *Families: Applications of Social Learning to Family Life* (1971).

Wesley Becker, *Parents Are Teachers: A Child Management Program* (1971).

Thomas Creer and Walter Christian, *Chronically Ill and Handicapped Children* (1976).

Nathan Arzin and Richard Foxx, *Toilet Training in Less Than a Day* (1974).

Herbert Birch, Stella Chess, and Alexander Thomas, *Your Child Is a Person* (1971).

Fitzhugh Dodson, *How to Parent* (1971).

Rudolph Dreikurs, *Children: The Challenge* (1964).

Haim Ginott, *Between Parent and Child* (1965).

Thomas Gordon, *Parent Effectiveness Training* (1970).

Rudolph Dreikurs, Shirley Gould, and Raymond Corsini, *Family Council* (1974).

Gerald Patterson and M. Elizabeth Gullion, *Living With Children*, revised edition (1968).

Don Dinkmeyer and Gary McKay, *Parents Handbook* (1976).

Virginia Satir, *Peoplemaking* (1972).

Haim G. Ginott, *Between Parent and Teenager* (1969).

Leontine Young, *Life Among the Giants, A Child's Eye View of the Grown Up World* (1971).

Victor Baldwin, H. D. Fredricks, and Gerry Brodsky, *Isn't It Time He Outgrew This or A Training Program for Parents of Retarded Children* (1973).

Gabriel Della-Piana, *How to Talk With Children (and Other People)* (1973).

CHAPTER 11

Legal Concepts in Foster Care

What Is Meant by Periodic Review in Foster Care?

B ASICALLY, TWO TYPES of periodic review are discussed in child welfare literature: periodic administrative review and periodic court review. The administrative review is an internal agency procedure. In contrast, the court or judicial review is external to the agency and involves a court hearing. Both procedures have a similar goal: to review on a regular basis each foster care case to determine whether or not a child should be continued in foster care, returned to his/her natural parents, freed for adoption or, if legally free for adoption, placed in an adoptive home. Reviews are intended to prevent drift in foster care. Most states are establishing some form of administrative review. Several states have enacted laws requiring periodic court reviews. For example, California requires a semiannual review; New York requires a review every eighteen months.

There are pros and cons to each type of review procedure. Some claim that the judicial procedure is costly, time consuming, and unnecessary. Others argue that administrative review conducted by agency staff does not provide for an adequate or objective review of agency practice and decisions.

The current trend is toward the use of judicial reviews. Wald (1976) proffers several arguments for the judicial review.

> When parents are not receiving adequate services [from the agency] court hearings provide a forum in which they and their child through her attorney can challenge the agency's inaction. A court review is superior to lodging a complaint with the agency, since parents likely will assume that the high authorities within the agency will support the caseworker. Moreover the presence of counsel at a court hearing may make it easier for parents to raise complaints about the agency.
>
> Second, the hearing provides a mechanism for reviewing parental performance so that it can be determined whether they have shown an interest in resuming custody. At each hearing both the supervis-

ing agency and the child's attorney can document the parents' failure, if any, to work toward resuming custody. It is essential that parental non-cooperation be documented as quickly as possible. Otherwise it will be difficult to obtain termination when necessary. In a number of cases, courts have refused to order termination because the judge sympathized with the claim that the agency had not provided services, had discouraged visitation, or had made return difficult. [Pp. 681-682]

Festinger (1976) provides research data indicating that periodic court review procedures do, in fact, facilitate the movement of children out of foster care. However, there have been reports indicating that some court reviews are rendered useless because the cases are handled in a routine and superficial manner. A serious effort to prevent drift in foster care must make use of both court and administrative reviews.

What Should Happen in a Periodic Court Review Hearing?

Too often, periodic court reviews of children in foster care turn into mere formalities. Wald (1976), for example, made the following observations:

I recently conducted a study of review hearings, held annually, in one California county. Over 100 hearings were observed. In most cases neither the parents nor the social worker was present and the hearing lasted only seconds. Even when parents were present, the hearings averaged less than five minutes. No planning was done; the need for continued placement was not explored. [P. 683]

A review hearing that does not take a serious look at the placement and the need for continuing the placement violates the purpose of periodic review. Wald (1976) suggests that the court should make findings on at least the following issues:

1) What services have been offered and provided to the parents to facilitate reunion;
2) Whether the parents are satisfied with the services;
3) The extent to which the parents have visited the child and any reasons why visitation has not occurred or has been infrequent;
4) Whether the agency is satisfied with the cooperation received from the parents;
5) Whether additional services are needed to facilitate the return of the minor to her parents; and
6) When return of the child can be expected. [P. 683]

Under ideal conditions, the social worker should be prepared to provide the court with data that would help answer these questions. If needed services are unavailable, the social worker should make this point clear, so that there is documentation of the community's or agency's inability to provide needed services. While this documentation may be of little direct help to the individual foster child or his/her parents before the court, it eventually may prod the community to create needed services.

What Is Meant by the "Best Interest" Standard as It Is Applied to Placement Decisions?

This legal concept directs courts to order the disposition that promotes a child's best interests. For example, the best interest standard is used to decide whether a neglected or abused child remains with his/her parents or is placed in a foster home. In recent years the best interest test has come under much criticism. Mnookin (1973) argues that

> what is wrong with the existing legal standards is that they call for individualized determinations based on discretionary assessments of best interests of the child and these determinations cannot be made consistently and fairly. [P. 602]

In their book, *Beyond the Best Interests of the Child*, Goldstein, Freud, and Solnit (1973) also conclude that the best interest standard is unworkable. They argue for a substitute standard called the *least detrimental alternative*. In discussing the best interest and the least detrimental principles, the United States Department of Health, Education and Welfare's National Center on Child Abuse and Neglect (1978) explains:

> Usually it is assumed that it is in the child's best interest and least detrimental if the child remains in the home, provided that the parents can respond to treatment. However, this response may be difficult to assess and it may not be known whether the necessary resources are available. A few authorities believe that except where the child's life is in danger, it is always in the child's best interest to remain in the home. This view reflects the position that in evaluating the least detrimental alternative and the child's best interest, the child's psychological as well as physical well-being must be considered. . . . Whereas "best interest of the child" suggests that some

placement may be justified, "least detrimental alternative" is stronger in suggesting that any placement or alternative should be monitored. [P. 5]

Wald (1976) has observed that the best interest standard leaves much to be desired. He states that the standard

is deficient in a number of respects. First, no state statute identifies specific factors a court should consider in determining the child's best interests. Obviously, this term can take on many different meanings. Should a court be concerned with the child's physical well-being, intellectual development, material comforts, emotional stability? What weight should be placed on each of these? Should a court determine whether the child is more likely to become delinquent, go to college, have close, warm relationships with an adult, or grow up "happy" in her own home or in some other placement? Should courts consider the likely impact of foster placement on each of these variables, or on any other variables, and compare the home to each possible placement to see which one has the most pluses? Are they to determine the child's best interest in the short run or the long run?

In the absence of legislative definition, decisions merely reflect each judge's own "folk psychology." As a result this standard promotes excessive and often discriminatory, removal. It also permits judicial decisions to be based on value judgments not commonly held by society or approved by the legislature. [Pp. 649-650]

Given the problems with the best interest standard, Wald (1976) proposes a test he describes as protection from "specific harm." He argues that, instead of trying to decide whether removal would promote the child's best interest, the court should decide whether removal is the only means of protecting the child from specific harm(s). Placement out of the home would be justified only when no other means of protection is available. Wald believes the specific harm test would provide a clear focus and a clearly identified reason(s) for state intervention into the parent-child relationship, lessen the impact of value judgments and bias in judicial decisions, and minimize the possibility of unwarranted removal.

Wald also suggests an outline for the social report to be submitted to the court. The social report is to be prepared by an interdisciplinary team (social worker, psychologist, teacher, physician, etc.). Given the proposed specific harm standard, Wald (1976) states that the social report "should focus squarely on the need for removal and the availability of alternative placements if removal is ordered." His suggested outline is as follows:

(1) A statement of the specific harm(s) to the child, as defined by statute, that intervention is designed to alleviate.

(2) A description of the specific programs, for both the parents and the child, that are needed in order to prevent further harm to the child; the reasons why such programs are likely to be useful; the availability of any proposed services; and the agency's overall plan for ensuring that the services will be delivered.

(3) A statement of the measures, e.g., specific changes in parental behavior, that will be used to determine that placement is no longer necessary.

(4) If removal is recommended, a full description of the reasons why the child cannot be protected adequately in the home, including a description of any previous efforts to work with the parents and the child in the home; the in-home treatment programs, e.g., homemakers, which have been considered and rejected; and the parents' attitude toward placement of the child.

(5) A statement of the likely harms the child will suffer as a result of removal. This section should include an exploration of the nature of the parent-child attachment and the meaning of separation and loss to both the parents and the child.

(6) A description of the steps that will be taken to minimize the harm to the child that may result if separation occurs. [Pp. 659-660]

It is interesting to note that the emphasis on specifying the problem and alternatives is consistent with another trend in child welfare: the use of behavioral contracting. Contracting is discussed in Chapter 4.

It is noteworthy that while acknowledging the problems associated with the best interest concept, Kadushin (1974b) provides an expansion on the realities of placement decisions and calls attention to the fact that this debate may be more semantic than substantive.

Social workers, while having the "best interest of the child" in mind, have always operated in terms of the "least detrimental available alternative." They rarely have the luxury of providing the deprived child with a choice of "good, better, best," but more often have to decide among "bad, worse, worst." The "best interest of the child" has often been served by providing the "least detrimental available alternative" of a bad home as against a worse home. [P. 509]

The popular and influential book, *Beyond the Best Interests of the Child* (Goldstein, Freud, and Skolnit, 1973), has been faulted for ignoring or being unaware of current social work research and practice in the field of child welfare, underscoring the need for greater exchange of information between the professions of social work and law.

What Legal Terms and Concepts Are Most Often Encountered in Foster Family Care?

A recent book, *Interdisciplinary Glossary on Child Abuse and Neglect: Legal, Medical, Social Work Terms*, published by the National Center on Child Abuse and Neglect of the U. S. Department of Health, Education and Welfare (1978), provides simplified definitions and explanations of many legal terms and concepts associated with child welfare. Selected definitions drawn from the book are presented below.

Abandonment—Act of a parent or caretaker leaving a child without adequate supervision or provision for his/her needs for an excessive period of time. State laws vary in defining adequacy of supervision and the length of time a child may be left alone or in the care of another before abandonment is determined. The age of the child also is an important factor. In legal terminology, "abandonment cases" are suits calling for the termination of parental rights.

Affidavit—Written statement signed in the presence of a Notary Public who "swears in" the signer. The contents of the affidavit are stated under penalty of perjury. Affidavits are frequently used in the initiation of juvenile court cases and are, at times, presented to the court as evidence.

Allegation—Charge or complaint which is proven true or false at a hearing or trial. In a child abuse or neglect case, the allegation is a petition or statement containing charges of specific acts of cruelty or improper care which the petitioner hopes to prove at a trial.

Burden of Proof—The duty, usually falling on the state as petitioner, of proving allegations against a parent in a trial. It is up to the state to prove the case; neither the child nor the parents have the duty to explain unproven allegations.

Children's Rights—Rights of children as individuals to the protections provided in the Constitution as well as to the care and protection necessary for normal growth and development. Children's rights are actually exercised through adult representatives and advocates. The extent to which children's rights are protected varies according to the individual state laws providing for the identification and treatment of child abuse and neglect. An unresolved issue is the conflict between children's rights and parents' rights or rights to privacy.

Complaint—

1) An oral statement, usually made to the police, charging criminal, abusive, or neglectful conduct

2) A district attorney's document which starts a criminal prosecution

3) A petitioner's document which starts a civil proceeding. In juvenile or family court, the complaint is usually called a petition

4) In some states, term used for a report of suspected abuse or neglect

Courts—Places where judicial proceedings occur. There is an array of courts involved with child abuse and neglect cases, partly because different states divide responsibility for certain proceedings among different courts, and also because tradition has established a variety of names for courts which perform similar functions. Child abuse reports can result in proceedings in any of the following courts:

Criminal Court—Usually divided into superior court, which handles felony cases, and municipal court, which handles misdemeanors and the beginning stages of most felony cases.

Domestic Relations Court—A civil court in which divorces and divorce custory hearings are held.

Family Court—A civil court which, in some states, combines the functions of domestic relations, juvenile, and probate courts. Establishment of family courts is often urged to reform the presently wasteful and poorly-coordinated civil court system. Under some proposals, family courts would also deal with criminal cases involving family relations, thus improving coordination in child abuse litigation.

Court of Conciliation—A branch of domestic relations courts in some states, usually staffed by counselors and social workers rather than by lawyers or judges, and designed to explore and promote reconciliation in divorce cases.

Juvenile Court—Juvenile court, which has jurisdiction over minors, usually handles cases of suspected delinquency as well as cases of suspected abuse or neglect. In many states, terminations of parental rights occur in juvenile court proceedings, but that is generally the limit of juvenile court's power over adults.

Probate Court—Probate court may handle cases of guardianship and adoption in addition to estates of deceased persons.

Custody—The right to care and control of a child and the duty to provide food, clothing, shelter, ordinary medical care, education, and discipline for a child. Permanent legal custody may be taken from a parent or given up by a parent by court action. . . . Temporary custody of a child may be granted for a limited time only, usually pending further action or review by the court. Temporary custody may be granted for a period of months or, in the case of protective or emergency custody, for a period of hours or several days.

Custody Hearing—Hearing, usually held in children's court, to determine who has the rights of legal custody of a minor. It may involve one parent against the other or the parents vs. a social service agency.

Delinquency—Behavior of a minor which would, in the case of an adult, constitute criminal conduct. In some states, delinquency also includes "waywardness" or disobedient behavior on the part of the child. In contrast to dependency cases, where the parent(s) rather than the minor is assumed responsible, delinquency cases assume that the minor has some responsibility for his/her behavior.

Dependency—A child's need for care and supervision from a parent or caretaker. Often a legal term referring to cases of children whose natural parent(s) cannot or will not properly care for them or supervise them so that the state must assume this responsibility. Many states distinguish findings of dependency, for which the juvenile is assumed to have little or no responsibility, from findings of delinquency, in which the juvenile is deemed to be at least partially responsible for his/her behavior.

Detention—The temporary confinement of a person by a public authority. In a case of child abuse or neglect, a child may be detained pending a trial when a detention hearing indicates that it is unsafe for the child to remain in his/her own home. This is often called protective custody or emergency custody. The child may be detained in a foster home, group home, hospital, or other facility.

Detention Hearing—A court hearing held to determine whether a child should be kept away from his/her parents until a full trial of neglect, abuse, or delinquency allegations can take place. Detention hearings must usually be held within 24 hours of the filing of a detention request.

Detention Request—A document filed by a probation officer, social worker, or prosecutor with the clerk of a juvenile or family court, asking that a detention hearing be held, and that a child be detained until the detention hearing has taken place. Detention requests must usually be filed within 48 hours of the time protective custody of the child begins.

Disposition—The order of a juvenile or family court issued at a dispositional hearing which determines whether a minor, already found to be a dependent or delinquent child, should continue in or return to the parental home, and under what kind of supervision, or whether the minor should be placed out-of-home, and in what kind of setting: a relative's home, foster home, or institution. Disposition in a civil case parallels sentencing in a criminal case.

Due Process—The rights of persons involved in legal proceedings to be treated with fairness. These rights include the right to adequate notice in advance of hearings, the right to notice of allegations of misconduct, the right to assistance of a lawyer, the right to confront and cross-examine witnesses, and the right to refuse to give self-incriminating testimony. In child abuse or neglect cases, courts are granting more and more due process to parents in recognition of the fact that loss of parental rights, temporarily or permanently, is as serious as loss of liberty. However, jury trials and presumptions of innocence are still afforded in very few juvenile or family court cases.

Evidence—Any sort of proof submitted to the court for the purpose of influencing the court's decision. Some special kinds of evidence are:

> *Circumstantial*—Proof of circumstances which may imply another fact. For example, proof that a parent kept a broken appliance cord may connect the parent to infliction of unique marks on a child's body.

> *Direct*—Generally consisting of testimony of the type such as a neighbor stating that he/she saw the parent strike the child with an appliance cord.

> *Hearsay*—Second-hand evidence, generally consisting of testimony of the type such as "I heard him say. . . ." Except in certain cases, such evidence is usually excluded because it is considered unreliable and because the person making the original statement cannot be cross-examined.

> *Opinion*—Although witnesses are ordinarily not permitted to testify to their beliefs or opinions, being restricted instead

to reporting what they actually saw or heard, when a witness can be qualified as an expert on a given subject, he/she can report his/her conclusions, for example, "Based upon these marks, it is my opinion as a doctor that the child must have been struck with a flexible instrument very much like this appliance cord." Lawyers are sometimes allowed to ask qualified experts "hypothetical questions," in which the witness is asked to assume the truth of certain facts and to express an opinion based on those "facts."

Physical—Any tangible piece of proof such as a document, X-ray, photograph, or weapon used to inflict an injury. Physical evidence must usually be authenticated by a witness who testifies to the connection of the evidence (also called an exhibit) with other facts in the case.

Evidentiary Standards—Guidelines used when examining evidence presented in order to determine if that evidence is factual and legally proves the case being tried. Various standards of proof are:

Beyond a Reasonable Doubt—(criminal court standard) The evidence presented fully satisfies the court as being factual.

Clear and Convincing Evidence—Evidence which is fully convincing; equivalent to beyond a reasonable doubt.

Preponderance of Evidence—(civil court standard) Evidence which leaves the court with the strongest impression of credibility and is determined to be fact.

Expert Testimony—Witnesses with various types of expertise may testify in child abuse or neglect cases; usually these expert witnesses are physicians or radiologists. Experts are usually questioned in court about their education or experience which qualifies them to give professional opinions about the matter in question. Only after the hearing officer determines that the witness is, in fact, sufficiently expert in the subject matter may that witness proceed to state his/her opinions.

Expungement—Destruction of records. Expungement may be ordered by the court after a specified number of years or when the juvenile, parent, or defendent applies for expungement and shows that his/her conduct has improved. Expungement also applies to the removal of an unverified report of abuse or neglect that has been made to a central registry.

Fifth Amendment—The Fifth Amendment to the U.S. Constitution guarantees a defendant that he/she cannot be compelled to present self-incriminating testimony.

Guardian—Adult charged lawfully with the responsibility for a child. A guardian has almost all the rights and powers of a natural parent, but the relationship is subject to termination or change. A guardian may or may not also have custody and therefore actual care and supervision of the child.

Guardian Ad Litem—Adult appointed by the court to represent the child in a judicial proceeding. The *guardian ad litem* may be, but is not necessarily, an attorney. Under the Child Abuse Prevention and Treatment Act, a state cannot qualify for federal assistance unless it provides by statute "that in every case involving an abused or neglected child which results in a judicial proceeding a *guardian ad litem* shall be appointed to represent the child in such proceedings." Some states have begun to allow a GAL for children in divorce cases.

Hearing—Judicial proceeding where issues of fact or law are tried and in which both parties have a right to be heard. A hearing is synonymous with a trial.

Hearing Officer—A judge or other individual who presides at a judicial proceeding. The role of judge is performed in some juvenile court hearings by referees or commissioners, whose orders are issued in the name of the supervising judge. Acts of a referee or commissioner may be undone after the supervising judge has conducted a rehearing in the case.

Immunity, Legal—Legal protection from civil or criminal liability

1) Child abuse and neglect reporting statutes often confer immunity upon persons mandated to report, giving them an absolute defense to libel, slander, invasion of privacy, false arrest, and other lawsuits which the person accused of the act might file. Some grants of immunity are limited only to those persons who report in good faith and without malicious intent.

2) Immunity from criminal liability is sometimes conferred upon a witness in order to obtain vital testimony. Thereafter, the witness cannot be prosecuted with the use of information he/she disclosed in his/her testimony. If an immunized witness refuses to testify, he/she can be imprisoned for contempt of court.

In Local Parentis—"In the place of a parent." Refers to actions of a guardian or other non-parental custodian.

Jurisdiction—The power of a particular court to hear cases involving certain categories of persons or allegations. Jurisdiction may also depend upon geographical factors such as the county of a person's residence.

Legal Rights of Persons Identified in Reports—Standards for legal rights stress the need for all persons concerned with child abuse and neglect to be aware of the legal rights of individuals identified in reports and to be committed to any action necessary to enforce these rights. According to the National Center on Child

Abuse and Neglect *Revision to Federal Standards on the Prevention and Treatment of Child Abuse and Neglect (Draft),* these rights include the following:

1) Any person identified in a report as being suspected of having abused or neglected a child should be informed of his/her legal rights

2) The person responsible for the child's welfare should receive written notice and be advised of his/her legal rights when protective custody authority is exercised

3) A child who is alleged to be abused or neglected should have independent legal representation in a child protection proceeding

4) The parent or other person responsible for a child's welfare who is alleged to have abused or neglected a child should be entitled to legal representation in a civil or criminal proceeding

5) The local child protective services unit should have the assistance of legal counsel in all child protective proceedings

6) Each party should have the right to appeal protective case determinations

7) Any person identified in a child abuse or neglect report should be protected from unauthorized disclosure of personal information contained in the report

Miranda Rule—Legal provision that a confession is inadmissible in any court proceeding if the suspect was not forewarned of his/her right to remain silent before the confession was disclosed.

Misdemeanor—A crime for which the punishment can be no more than imprisonment for a year and/or a fine of $1,000. A misdemeanor is distinguished from a felony, which is more serious, and an infraction, which is less serious.

Negligence—Failure to act. May apply to a parent, as in child neglect, or to a person who by state statute is mandated to report child abuse and neglect but who fails to do so. Negligence lawsuits arising from failure to report are increasing, and any failure to obey the statutes proves negligence. Lawsuits claiming damages for negligence are civil proceedings.

Parens Patriae—"The power of the sovereign." Refers to the state's power to act for or on behalf of persons who cannot act in their own behalf; such as minors, incompetents, or some developmentally disabled.

Parents' Rights—Besides the rights protected by the Constitution for all adults, society accords parents the right to custody and supervision of their own children, including, among others, parents' rights to make decisions about their children's health care. This plus parents' rights to privacy may complicate investigations of suspected child abuse and neglect and treatment of confirmed cases. Parents' rights may be cited in court in order to prevent the state from taking custody of a child who is in danger in his/her own home.

Perjury—Intentionally inaccurate testimony. Perjury is usually punishable as a felony, but only if the inaccuracy of the testimony and the witness's knowledge of the inaccuracy can be proven.

Petition—Document filed in juvenile or family court at the beginning of a neglect, abuse, and/or delinquency case. The petition states the allegations which, if true, form the basis for court intervention.

Petitioner—Person who files a petition. In juvenile and family court practice, a petitioner may be a probation officer, social worker, or prosecutor, as variously defined by state laws.

Plea Bargaining—Settlement of a criminal prosecution, usually by the reduction of the charge and/or the penalty, in return for a plea of guilty. Plea bargains are sometimes justified by congested court calendars. They are attacked as devices which weaken the intended effect of penal statutes and which reduce the dignity of the criminal justice system. Far more than half of all criminal prosecutions in this country are resolved by plea bargains.

Pre-Trial Diversion—Decision of the district attorney not to issue charges in a criminal case where those charges would be provable. The decision is usually made on the condition that the defendant agrees to participate in rehabilitative services. In child abuse cases, this usually involves cooperation with child protective services and/or voluntary treatment, such as Parents Anonymous.

Prima Facie—"On its face." A prima facie case is one which has been proven sufficiently to sustain the charges, unless the defendant or parent can produce strong evidence in rebuttal.

Privileged Communications—Confidential communications which are protected by statutes and need not or cannot be disclosed in court over the objections of the holder of the privilege. Lawyers are almost always able to refuse or disclose what a client has told them in confidence. Priests are similarly covered. Doctors and psychotherapists have generally lesser privileges, and their testimony can be compelled in many cases involving child abuse or neglect. Some social workers are covered by such statutes, but the law and practice vary widely from state to state.

Probable Cause—Legal standard indicating a reasonable ground for belief in the existence of facts supporting a complaint that has been made.

Probation—Allowing a convicted criminal defendant or a juvenile found to be delinquent to remain at liberty, under a suspended sentence of imprisonment, generally under the supervision of a probation officer and under certain conditions. Violation of a condition is grounds for revocation of the probation. In a case of child abuse or neglect, a parent or caretaker who is convicted of the offense may be required, as part of his/her probation, to make certain promises to undergo treatment and/or to improve the home situation. These promises are made as a condition of the probation in which the child is returned home and are enforced with the threat of revocation of parental rights.

Public Defender—Person paid with public funds to plead the cause of an indigent defendant.

Reporting Laws—Laws which require specified categories of persons, such as professionals involved with children, and allow other persons, to notify public authorities of cases of suspected child abuse and, sometimes, neglect. All 50 states now have reporting statutes, but they differ widely with respect to types of instances which must be reported, persons who must report, time limits for reporting, manner of reporting (written, oral, or both), agencies to which reports must be made, and the degree of immunity conferred upon reporters.

Res Ipsa Loquitor—Latin expression meaning "the thing speaks for itself." It is a doctrine of law which, when applied to criminal law, means that evidence can be admitted which is acceptable despite the fact that no one actually saw what occurred, only the results. An example in criminal law would be admitting into evidence in a child abuse case the medical reports of the injured child victim which reflect multiple broken bones and the doctor's opinion that said injuries could not have been caused by an accident. The court using the *res ipsa loquitor* doctrine can convict the person having had exclusive custody of the child without any direct testimony as to how, when, where or why the injuries were inflicted.

Sentencing—The last stage of criminal prosecution in which a convicted defendant is ordered imprisoned, fined, or granted probation. This is equivalent in a criminal case to the disposition in a juvenile court case.

Stipulation—A statement, either oral or written, between lawyers on both sides of a particular court case which establishes certain facts about the case that are agreed upon by both sides. The facts delineated usually involve such issues as the addresses of the persons involved in the case, their relationships to one another, etc.

Subpoena—A document issue by a court clerk, usually delivered by a process server or police officer to the person subpoenaed, requiring that person to appear at a certain court at a certain day and time to give testimony in a specified case. Failure to obey a subpoena is punishable as contempt of court.

Subpoena Duces Tecum—A subpoena requiring the person subpoenaed to bring specified records to court.

Summons—A document issued by a court clerk, usually delivered by a process server or police officer to the person summoned, notifying that person of the filing of a lawsuit against him/her and notifying that person of the deadline for answering the suit. A summons does not require the attendance at court of any person.

Termination of Parental Rights—A legal proceeding freeing a child from his/her parents' claims so that the child can be adopted by others without the parents' written consent. The legal bases for termination differ from state to state, but most statutes include abandonment as a ground for TPR.

Warrant—Document issued by a judge, authorizing the arrest or detention of a person or the search of a place and seizure of specified items in that place. Although a judge need not hold a hearing before issuing a warrant and although the party to be arrested or whose property will be seized need not be notified, the judge must still be given "reasonable cause to believe" that a crime has occurred and that the warrant is necessary in the apprehension and conviction of the criminal.

Willful—Done with understanding of the act and the intention that the act and its natural consequences should occur. Some conduct becomes unlawful or negligent only when it is done willfully.

Witness—
1) A person who has seen or heard something.
2) A person who is called upon to testify in a court hearing.

What Are Some Useful Sources of Legal Information Needed by the Social Worker?

Donald Brieland and John Lemmon, *Social Work and the Law* (1977) (West Publishing Company, 50 West Kellogg Blvd., P.O. Box 3526, St. Paul, MN 55165).

National Association of Attorneys General, *Legal Issues in Foster Care* (1976) (Committee on the Office of Attorney General, 3901 Barrett Drive, Raleigh, NC 27609).

Cynthia Bell and Wallace J. Mlyniec, "Preparing for a Neglect Proceeding: A Guide or the Social Worker," *Public Welfare* (Fall, 1974), pp. 26-37.

Stephen Liebo, *The Social Worker as Expert Witness in the Courtroom* (1971) (Minnesota Resource Center for Social Work Education, 731 21st Ave. South, Minneapolis, MN 55454), 35 pp.

Law and Social Work: Statements Prepared by the National Conference of Lawyers and Social Workers (1973) (National Association of Social Workers, 1425 H Street N.W., Washington, DC 20005), 64 pp.

Joseph Findling, *Legal Aspects of Fostering and Preparing for the Court Hearing* (1977) (Foster Parent Training Project, Eastern Michigan University, Ypsilanti, MI 48197).

Stanford Katz, "The Changing Legal Status of Foster Parents," *Children Today*, Vol. 15, No. 6 (Nov.-Dec., 1976).

Glen Downs and John Volkman, *A Concise Legal Study of Foster Care in the United States* (1977) (Regional Research Institute for Human Services, Portland State University, Portland, Oregon).

Cynthia Bell, "Legal Consultation for Child Welfare Workers," *Public Welfare* (Summer, 1975).

Michael S. Wald, "State Intervention on Behalf of Neglected Children: Standards for Removal of Children From Their Homes, Monitoring the Status of Children in Foster Care and Termination of Parental Rights," *Stanford Law Review*, Vol. 28, No. 4 (Apr., 1976), pp. 623-706.

Janis Selbo and Ann Lynaugh, *Legal Training for Child Welfare Workers* (1975) (Center for Social Service, University of Wisconsin-Extension, Madison, Wisconsin).

U. S. Department of Health, Education and Welfare, National Center on Child Abuse and Neglect, *Interdisciplinary Glossary on Child Abuse and Neglect: Legal, Medical, Social Work Terms* (1978) (U. S. Government Printing Office, DHEW Publication No. (OHDS) 78-30137).

Robert Mnookin, "Foster Care—In Whose Best Interest," *Harvard Educational Review*, Vol. 43, No. 4, Nov., 1973, pp. 599-638.

CHAPTER 12

Issues in Foster Care for American Indian Children

What Are the Unique Concerns Related to the Utilization of Foster Family Care for American Indian Children?

IN RECENT YEARS, increasing attention has been given to ethnicity in the design and delivery of child welfare services. Heightened awareness of the subtleties of racism has caused administrators, professionals, and concerned citizens to reexamine existing policies and programs. For example, recent articles by Edwards and Edwards (1977), Greeley (1977), Longres (1977), Murase (1977), Sotomayor (1977), Street (1977), and Tidwell (1977) review current developments in the human services as they relate to minorities in America, especially American Indians, Asian Americans, blacks, Chicanos, Puerto Ricans, and white ethnics. Increasingly, mainstream social work and child welfare journals contain articles on ethnicity. Social work education programs are giving added attention to issues of ethnic diversity. Standard-setting organizations, such as the Child Welfare League of America, the American Public Welfare Association, the National Association of Social Workers, and the Council on Social Work Education, have called attention to the importance of ethnicity in the human services and provided guidance to those attempting to respond to critical issues. Despite these positive efforts in recent years, many problems remain, especially within the field of child welfare, where agency policies and professional procedures touch directly on such sensitive areas as family values, religious beliefs, and child-rearing practices.

Nowhere is the complexity and importance of ethnicity more apparent than in the field of Indian child welfare. A recent report, *Indian Child Welfare*, issued by the United States Department of Health, Education and Welfare (1977b), states:

Among minority groups in the United States, Indian tribes are unique in two respects. First, the Constitution, federal legislation, and numerous court decisions all affirm that federally recognized Indian tribes possess substantial powers of self-government and that Indians on reservations shall look to tribal governments for the exercise of many of the functions which are provided elsewhere by state governments. Except where Congress has acted to limit tribal powers and to permit states to assert their jurisdiction and authority, . . . states have little or no authority to enforce their laws on Indian reservations. Recent federal policy has explicitly sought to strengthen tribal governments in the name of Indian self-determination.

Second, the Indian Health Service and the Bureau of Indian Affairs have a specific mandate to provide certain services to federally recognized Indian tribes, including Alaska Natives. Indian reservation lands are held in trust for tribes by the federal government and thus are exempt from state and local property taxes, and management of these lands is the responsibility of the BIA. The legal and historical facts of tribal self-government and federal trust responsibility are unique to federally recognized Indian tribes and have a pervasive influence on the delivery of social services, as well as on many other matters involving Indians. [Pp. 3-4]

The report outlines numerous legal and administrative problems and issues related to Indian child welfare, including tribal participation in service programs of the Social Security Act, the power of tribal court orders, the power of state governments to enforce the licensing standards needed to obtain federal reimbursement for certain types of foster and day care, and whether tribes must pay the 25 percent local match necessary to earn the 75 percent federal share for services under Title XX of the Social Security Act. Until these and other complex jurisdictional problems are resolved, confusion regarding who can and should provide child welfare services for American Indian children living on and off the reservation will continue.

Of particular concern to child welfare experts is the large number of Indian children placed in non-Indian foster family and adoptive homes. A bulletin published by the Association on American Indian Affairs (AAIA) (1974) states:

An analysis of recent statistics gathered by the AAIA demonstrates that a minimum of 25 per cent of all Indian children are either in adoptive homes, foster homes, or boarding schools. In Minnesota, for example, one out of every four Indian children born today will be removed from the home of its natural parents to be put in adoptive or foster care. The number of Indian children taken from their parents is grossly disproportionate to their percentage of the population. In Montana, Indian children are taken out of their homes and placed in foster care at a rate thirteen times that for non-Indian children; in South Dakota, the rate is sixteen times higher; and in the State of Washington, nineteen times higher. In Wisconsin, it is sixteen times more likely for an Indian child to be removed from its family than for a non-Indian child. A survey done by the AAIA in 1969 reveals that 85 percent of the Indian children in foster care are in non-Indian homes. [P. 1]

These alarming statistics reflect a situation that has arisen from a lack of understanding and appreciation of cultural difference and overt discrimination against Indian families. In the process of introducing a bill known as the Indian Child Welfare Act of 1977, the following statement by Senator Abourezk was entered in the April 1, 1977, *Congressional Record.*

many Americans and the Congress are becoming more aware of the difficulties Indian communities face in a broad range of areas: Health, education, land, and water rights, economic development, and others. But there are few who are aware of the difficulties American Indians face in a matter of vital concern to them; namely the welfare of their children and their families.

It appears that for decades Indian parents and their children have been at the mercy of arbitrary or abusive action of local, State, Federal, and private agency officials. Unwarranted removal of children from their homes is common in Indian communities. Recent statistics show, for example, that a minimum of 25 percent of all Indian children are either in foster homes, adoptive homes, and/or boarding schools, against the best interest of families and Indian communities. Whereas most non-Indian communities can expect to have children out of their natural homes in foster or adoptive homes at a rate of 1 for every 51 children, Indian communities know that their children will be removed at rates varying from 5 to 25 times higher than that.

Because of poverty and discrimination Indian families face many difficulties, but there is no reason or justification for believing that these problems make Indian parents unfit to raise their children; nor is there any reason to believe that the Indian community itself cannot, within its own confines, deal with problems of child neglect when they do arise.

Up to now, however, public and private welfare agencies seem to have operated on the premise that most Indian children would really be better off growing up non-Indian. The result of such policies has been unchecked: Abusive child removal practices, the lack of viable, practical rehabilitation and prevention programs for Indian families facing severe problems, and a practice of ignoring the all-important demands of Indian tribes to have a say in how their children and families are dealt with.

Obviously, drastic reforms are needed in the area of Indian child welfare.

How Do Tribal Cultures Differ from the Majority Anglo Culture?

Approximately one-third of United States American Indians live on 280 reservations, while another one-third are permanent urban residents. The remainder migrate between rural reservations and urban areas. Indian traditions are strongest on the reservations, but many Indian ways are evident among urban Indians.

> In spite of the massive changes which have occurred in the subsistence bases of North American Indian tribes, and in spite of two hundred years of federal policies aimed at assimilation, writers in the field agree that the traditional cultures of Indian peoples have proved amazingly strong and resilient. Although it is not true for all tribes, and certainly not for all individuals, a number of basic cultural traits relevant to child welfare have survived. [Slaughter, 1976, p. 35]

Cultural differences are subtle and complex. Because each person grows up within a particular sociocultural context, it often is difficult to understand those who have been shaped by a different set of values, customs, and beliefs. Red Horse (1977) comments:

> Culture represents a variable which many human service professionals prefer to ignore. Professional reluctance to consider cultural differentials often results from a lack of understanding cultural complexities. In the field of human relations, culture has no doubt assumed mystical proportions. To knowledgeable participants and observers, however, culture is not simply an array of mysterious clut-

ter. Beliefs and value systems remain as behavior imperatives to those individuals who are of a culture other than mainstream society. [P. 11]

A detailed discussion of cultural and tribal difference is beyond the scope of this book. However, a sampling of observations by current writers in the field provides an opportunity to appreciate Indian culture as a critical factor in the foster family services.

In presenting a review of tribal cultures, Edwards and Edwards (1977) state:

> Indian culture and life-styles are difficult to define. Each tribal group was unique, and its social structure, religious beliefs, and economic systems were intricately interwoven. Distinctive of most Indian tribes, however, were the serenity of the life-style and the balance achieved in their economic, social, religious and recreational activities. Equally impressive was their regard for all living things and the Supreme Being or Creator who made it all possible. [P. 946]

Religion is very important to the Indian, yet, his/her spiritual beliefs and values are difficult for the Anglo to grasp because American Indian religion is interrelated and interwoven with all of life. In Anglo society, religion frequently is compartmentalized. This is evident in magazines such as *Time* and *Newsweek*, which contain separate sections on economics, medicine, entertainment, and religion, etc. The Indian does not separate the parts from the whole; the emphasis is on wholeness.

Red Horse (1977) emphasizes the importance of the extended family in Native American culture.

> Native American extended families differ from their European counterparts which define an extended unit as three generations within the same household. Rather, Native American extended families assume a distinct village-type network construct. This, of course, has significant impact upon behavior patterns. During early childhood socialization and for general orientation to living, individual transactions occur within a community milieu characterized by several incorporated households. Second, extended family structure facilitates transmission of cultural attributes which conserve family patterns and contribute to individual identity. Third, family serves as a major instrument of accountability. It sets standards and expectations which maintain the wholeness of the group through enforcement of values. [P. 12]

Social workers and other human service professionals must be cautious when drawing conclusions about the behavior of Indian clients and the functioning of Indian families. Red Horse (1977) illustrates the importance of understanding the extended family with a case example.

> A young probationer had strict court orders to remain under the supervision of responsible adults. His counselor became concerned because the youth appeared to ignore this order. The boy was constantly moving around and staying overnight with several different girls. Suspicions were that the boy was a pimp or a pusher. The girls appeared to know each other and enjoyed each other's company. Moreover, they were not ashamed to be seen together in public with the boy. Violation proceedings were being prepared.
>
> I came upon the case quite by accident during lunch with an acquaintance who was curious about Native American behavior patterns. I knew the boy's family well and requested a delay in court proceedings to investigate the matter more thoroughly. It turned out that the girls were all first cousins of the youth. He had not been "staying overnight with them"; he had been staying with different units of his family. Each unit had what the family consider a responsible adult to supervise and care for the boy.
>
> A revocation order in this case would have caused irreparable alienation between the family and human service professionals. The casework decision would have inappropriately punished the youth for normal family behavior. Moreover, its impact would affect people far beyond the presenting client. The young man had a family network consisting of over 200 people. [P. 12]

Within the Indian family, many adults in addition to the biological parents share the tasks of child rearing. Grandparents are especially important. Red Horse (1977) states:

> Single parents are also often misjudged by professionals. Single parent households obviously exist, but within the Native American network, there is no such unit as a single parent family. Human service providers experience difficulty looking beyond nuclear family situations. They are consequently reluctant to see grandparents, aunts, uncles, or cousins as alternative support service caregivers. . . .
>
> Grandparents retain official and symbolic leadership in family communities. Both are active processes sanctioned by children. Official leadership is characterized by a close proximity of grandparents to family. It is witnessed through behavior of children who actively

seek daily contact with grandparents. In this milieu, grandparents have an official voice in child rearing methods, and parents seldom overrule their elders. Symbolic leadership is characterized by an incorporation of unrelated elders into the family. This prevails during an absence of a natural grandparent, but it is not necessarily dependent upon such an absence. Often children and parents select, and virtually adopt, a grandparent. They seek social acceptance from another older member of the community. [P. 12]

As can be seen, there usually are one or more adults willing and available to care for an Indian child if the child's biological parents are unable or unwilling to assume a parenting role. Compared wtih Anglo families, the presence and active involvement of biological parents are of less importance in the Indian family. According to the U. S. Department of Health, Education and Welfare report *Indian Child Welfare* (1977),

Non-Indian social service providers often find it difficult to identify who is responsible for an Indian child and are frustrated by the mobility of a child, who may be the responsibility of different adults at different times. One respondent noted that within one tribal family system the children have a sense of family even if their parents are not present. However, if social workers fail to understand this system or insist on enforcing middle-class Anglo standards, they may intervene when Indians feel there is no reason for intervention. [P. 16]

As a general rule, an Indian child will need substitute care only when the extended family breaks down. It is the breakdown of the extended rather than the nuclear family that may precipitate a crisis and need for formal resources such as the basic child welfare services.

The "extended family" is a trait common to most Indian tribes, although its strength may vary from tribe to tribe or even within reservation communities. In some tribes, clans are strong, while in others they are nonexistent. Some reservation communities are very tightly knit and provide a support system for parents in the raising of children, and in many tribes grandparents have a major role in child raising. However, in other cases the extended family system has broken down to the point where grandparents have child-raising responsibilities with much less support than used to be provided by biological parents and other members of the extended family. [U. S. Department of Health, Education and Welfare, 1977, p. 15]

Reporting on the experiences of an Arizona-based Indian adoption program, Goodluck (1977) states:

> Traditionally, illegitimacy has been accepted among Indian families and additional children have been readily absorbed into the extended family group, but with few exceptions the families of the [Indian Adoption Program] IAP clients have been unable to absorb their newborns into the family group. Extended family breakdown rather than social disapproval appears to be the primary reason for adoptive placement of American Indian children, in marked contrast to the American White community. [P. 8]

As the above statement indicates, illegitimacy is of little consequence in most tribes. It is an Anglo legal concept foreign to Indian culture.

> In most tribes, no stigma is attached to illegitimacy. Children of unwed parents may be cared for by their parents or by the extended family, and often no distinction is made between children born in wedlock and out of wedlock. Thus, family planning programs and counseling services which assume that premarital pregnancies are problem situations may be wrong and may create as many problems as they solve. [U. S. Department of Health, Education and Welfare, 1977, p. 16]

Many writers have discussed the fact that normal Indian child-rearing practices differ significantly from those commonly observed in Anglo families.

> Indian children are rarely told that they cannot do anything, but are told instead of the consequences. To the non-Indian, the Indian child may appear to be "spoiled." Indeed, he is doted on by all older members in the family. . . .
> The Indian child does not ask permission to do ordinary things of normal daily living. He eats when he is hungry and sleeps when he is tired; there is no rigid schedule for these activities. . . . Children are encouraged to be independent, to live and learn by their decisions. Children are taught self-care and caring for others, especially family members. [Primeaux, 1977, p. 93]

The emphasis placed on independence and experiential learning also is noted in *Indian Child Welfare* (1977):

> Non-Indian social workers may expect mothers and fathers to be in control of their children and may become concerned if they feel that Indians have no control over their children. . . . However, many

> Indian families feel that children are competent to care for them-
> selves at earlier ages than non-Indian families, and for this reason
> children are expected to make decisions about their own lives. Thus,
> older children are often left to care for younger children, which
> conflicts with the law in some states (Colorado) where no child
> under age twelve can be left unsupervised. If this type of behavior
> were reported by a social worker who was either ignorant of tribal
> culture or who felt forced to act by the codes of the system,
> then an Indian child could be regarded officially as being "neglect-
> ed."

Anglo social workers, judges, and health care personnel organize their daily activity according to a clock. As implied in the old
adage, time is money: Time, schedules, and efficiency are highly
valued in Anglo society. In contrast, the precise measurement
and use of time is of less importance to Native Americans. Discussing the complexity of providing modern medical care to the
Indian, Primeaux notes:

> The Anglo health worker, so regulated by clocks and time-con-
> sciousness, can have difficulty with Indian time. Time is on a con-
> tinuum with no beginning and no end. In many Indian homes, there
> are no clocks; Indian time is casual and is relative to what needs to
> be accomplished. The Indian may eat two meals today and three
> meals tomorrow, or perhaps four. If medications are timed with
> meals, this becomes a crucial factor for the Anglo nurse to under-
> stand and adapt to. [P. 93]

Familiarity with the concept of Indian time may help Anglo
professionals understand why many Native Americans pay little
attention to appointments set up by health care or social service
providers.

The description by Good Tracks (1973) of the Native American
tradition of noninterference was one of the first to appear in the
professional literature and has done much to help Anglo human
service and health care personnel understand the behavior of
Indian clients and patients. According to Good Tracks:

> Anglos say they prize freedom, minding one's own business, and
> the right of each person to decide for himself, yet they think it right
> to be their brother's keeper, to give advice and take action in their
> brother's best interest—as interpreted by the Anglo, in and by the
> Anglo social context.

In native Indian society, however, no interference or meddling of any kind is allowed or tolerated, even when it is to keep the other person from doing something foolish or dangerous. When an Anglo is moved to be his brother's keeper and that brother is an Indian, therefore, almost everything he says or does seems rude, ill mannered, or hostile. Perhaps it is the Anglo's arrogant righteousness that prevents him from grasping the nature of his conduct. But if the Indian told the Anglo that he was being intrusive, the Indian would himself be interfering with the Anglo's freedom to act as he sees fit. [P. 30]

Anglo society does value and sanction interference. Public health and child abuse and neglect laws, in addition to the use of techniques such as crisis intervention and behavior modification, rest on the assumption that it is acceptable for one human being to influence another.

Several authors have argued that the concept of social work intervention is itself antithetical to the Indian value of noninterference. Others state that techniques such as confrontation, which facilitates the display of emotions, or nondirective techniques are inconsistent with Indian cultural patterns and may be ineffective or counterproductive in dealing with Indian problems. [U. S. Department of Health, Education and Welfare, 1977, p. 16]

This brief overview of Native American culture only scratches the surface of a complex area. However, the important point is that cultural differences are significant. To the greatest extent possible, Native Americans should be involved in the design and delivery of services used by Native Americans. In situations where Native Americans must use services designed by and for the majority culture, Native American professionals should be available to help the clients bridge the two cultures.

Where Can the Social Worker Obtain Information about Indian Child Welfare?

Several excellent reports on Indian child welfare present detailed descriptions and analyses of the complex legal, administrative, and policy issues. Three such reports have been prepared under contract for the U. S. Department of Health, Education and Welfare by the Center for Social Research and Development at the University of Denver. They are as follows:

Ellen Slaughter, *Indian Child Welfare: A Review of the Literature* (Denver, Colorado: Center for Social Research and Development, University of Denver Research Institute, Jan., 1976), 111 pp.

Center for Social Research and Development, *Legal and Jurisdictional Problems in the Delivery of SRS Child Welfare Services on Indian Reservations* (Denver, Colorado: University of Denver Research Institute, Oct., 1975), 102 pp.

Center for Social Research and Development, *Indian Child Welfare: A State of the Field Study* (Denver, Colorado: University of Denver Research Institute, July, 1976), 421 pp.

It is noteworthy that the U. S. Department of Health, Education and Welfare has issued a summary of the above-mentioned 421-page report, *Indian Child Welfare: A State of the Field Study Summary of Findings and Discussion of Policy Implications* (1977). This 49-page booklet is DHEW Publication No. (OHD) 77-30096.

A less technical booklet and one more oriented to the issue of cultural difference is *Supportive Care, Custody, Placement and Adoption of American Indian Children* (American Academy of Child Psychiatry, 1977). This ninety-three-page booklet summarizes the proceedings of the Battle Hollow Conference. The reader interested in obtaining general information on Native American culture will find useful works by Bahr, Chadwick, and Day (1972); Farris and Farris (1976); Good Tracks (1973); Lewis and Ho (1975); Locklear (1972); and Unger (1977).

In What Way Is the Factor of Tribal Enrollment Important to Foster Care?

Approximately one million American Indians live in the United States. They represent more than four hundred tribes. About one-half of all Indians belong to nine major tribes, of which the Navajo, Cherokee, Sioux, and Chippewa are the largest.

Whenever a social worker learns of an Indian child in foster care and/or is involved in the placement of an Indian child into foster care, he or she should verify the child's tribal enrollment. If the child is eligible but has not been enrolled, the social worker should facilitate official tribal enrollment. Unless a child is enrolled, he or she is not eligible for certain benefits and income generated from Indian land. Children can be enrolled as infants, but occasionally parents fail to engage in the necessary paperwork, procrastinate, or simply forget. If an unenrolled Indian child is placed in foster care—especially if the child subsequently is placed in an adoptive home—there is a danger that the child and his or her offspring will be deprived of rightful benefits and income. Tribal enrollment also helps to preserve cultural identity.

As indicated previously, there is much controversy over the practice of placing Indian children with non-Indian families. Increasingly, tribes and child welfare experts are protesting this practice because it destroys the child's cultural heritage and sense of identity. The current move to return to the tribes greater responsibility and authority for child welfare is an effort to prevent further destruction of tribal cultures and encourage the development of programs relevant to the needs and unique values of the American Indian.

CHAPTER 13

The Social Worker

What Are the Major Staffing Problems in Child Welfare?

SERIOUS CHILD WELFARE staffing problems have been identified in recent studies. These problems are having an effect on the quality of service available to foster children, natural parents, and foster parents. Some of these staffing problems were described in a recent report, *Child Welfare in 25 States: An Overview* (1976), prepared by the U. S. Department of Health, Education and Welfare.

> In theory, the combination of child and family services brought about by federal mandate is sound and, in the long term, may prove to be beneficial to service delivery. However, the merger has in many states resulted in merged caseloads and generalized assignments for all social services workers. This has diffused the time of experienced and trained child welfare staff which, unfortunately, has not been replaced by others with equivalent background or training.
>
> Educational and experiential criteria for child welfare personnel have been reduced or eliminated. Special civil service classifications for child welfare are now infrequent. Minimally trained personnel enter the system and are rarely provided with appropriate inservice training or staff development. Frustration and low morale, born of inability to meet the demands of difficult and complicated tasks, contribute to high personnel turnover. Program specialists, consultation, and skilled and appropriate supervision have been reduced. As a result, available resources and proven techniques of helping children and their families are poorly utilized.
>
> A serious gap identified by the survey is the almost total absence of training programs specifically directed toward workers serving children and their families. Most available training is focused on generic social services or on implementation of policies and procedures. [Pp. xi-xii]

Many of the problems mentioned above grew out of attempts to reduce or hold down program costs.

Staff turnover is a major problem. For example, in summarizing results drawn from five studies, Vasaly (1976) noted that in some districts of Arizona workers remained on the job for an average of only nine months; in Massachusetts the public welfare worker attrition was 29 percent per year.

> The qualifications and training of social workers varies widely in the states studied and within some states. Most of the workers are college graduates although some states do not require a degree or that the worker's degree be in social work, child welfare or a related field. Most states do not require or provide programs of training for the workers either prior to, or during employment. [P. 86]

Given the high case loads, staff turnover, lack of experienced and well-trained staff, and complexity of practice, it is not surprising that major problems exist within child welfare programs.

In Terms of Case Load, What Is a Reasonable Workload for the Child Welfare Worker?

"To provide effective [foster family] services to the child, his natural parents and foster parents during the period the child is in care a full-time practitioner should be expected to provide service to no more than 20 to 30 children" (Child Welfare League of America, 1975b, p. 91).

The CWLA *Standards for Child Protective Services* (1973, p. 60) states: "If effective [protective] service is to be provided, a full time practitioner is needed for every 20 families, assuming the rate of intake is not more than one new case for every six open cases."

For direct services social work staff, the *Standards for Foster Family Services Systems* developed by the APWA (1975, p. 40) suggests that "the average workload for the agency, including uncovered cases and other responsibilities, shall be no more than that represented by an average of forty-five foster children and their families."

It should be noted that case loads in the majority of public agencies exceed these standards. Frequently, the case loads are three to five times the recommended number. Excessive case loads contribute to staff burnout, high staff turnover, and a crisis-oriented approach rather than a planned approach geared to preventing problems. Worst of all, these negative effects contribute, in turn, to inappropriate placement of children, high turnover of foster parents, high replacement rates, and insufficient attention to needs of the foster child and the natural parents.

What Is Meant by Burnout among Child Welfare Workers?

In general, *burnout* refers to a shift from empathy, a desire to help, and a genuine concern with human problems to an attitude of cynicism, negativism, and self-centeredness. Burnout is caused in part by the stress and emotional demands on those who are continually and intimately involved with troubled people. By permission of *Human Behavior Magazine,* quotations from an article on burnout by Maslach (1976) are presented below.

> Hour after hour day after day health and social service "professionals" are intimately involved with troubled human beings. What happens to people who work intensely with others, learning about their psychological, social or physical problems? Ideally, the helpers retain objectivity and distance from the situation without losing concern for the person they are working with. Instead our research indicates, they are often unable to cope with this continual emotional stress and burnout occurs. They lose all concern, all emotional feeling, for the persons they work with and come to treat them in detached or even dehumanized ways. . . .
>
> There is little doubt that burnout plays a major role in the poor delivery of health and welfare services to people in need of them. They wait longer to receive less attention and less care. It is also a key factor in low worker morale, absenteeism and high job turnover (for a common response to burnout is to quit and get out). [P. 16]

The report by Maslach makes several references to burnout among social workers.

> For the social welfare workers, one of the major signs of burnout was the transformation of a person with original thought and creativity on the job into a mechanical, petty bureaucrat. . . .
>
> Social welfare workers said the high ratio of clients to staff was one of the major factors forcing a dehumanized view of clients. "There are just so many, you cannot afford to sympathize with them all," explained a social worker. "If I had only 50 clients, I might be able to help them individually." . . .

In many of the institutions we studied, there was a clear split in job responsibilities—either the professional worked directly with clients or patients, or they worked administration. . . . We were initially surprised to discover how many social workers were returning to school to get advanced training of this kind of higher level "non client" work. . . . As one social worker said, "We can all point to people who have burned out—who are cold, unsympathetic, callous and detached. And each of us knows that we have the potential to fit that role as well, if we haven't already. And that's why we're going back to school to become administrators or teachers or whatever—so that our client contact will be limited, and we won't be forced to become callous in order to stay sane." [Pp. 18-21]

There is reason to believe that burnout is manifested in physical and medical problems, resulting in frequent use of sick leave. Burnout often occurs after about one and one-half years on the job. While there are data supporting the relationship of burnout to direct client contact and high case loads, it is reasonable to assume that burnout also occurs among administrative and middle-management personnel who want to facilitate the delivery of human services but are frustrated by bureaucratic problems, lack of funds, etc. Burnout and the high rate of staff turnover have a negative effect on children in foster care and child welfare services in general. For example, in Massachusetts there was a 29 percent worker turnover, and 66 percent of the children in foster care had seen the same worker for less than one year. The constant turnover of staff creates frustration for the foster child, foster parents, and natural parents.

What Social Work Skills Are Especially Important in the Area of Foster Family Services?

One of the most extensive and detailed studies of social work skill was conducted by Shulman (1977). Given the fact that the data were drawn from child welfare settings and social work practice with foster parents, natural parents, adolescents in foster care, adopting parents, and young unmarried parents, the findings are especially relevant to those involved in foster family services. Making extensive use of videotapes of actual social work interviews, follow-up interviews with consumers of service, and several other sources of data, Shulman employed a computer analysis to sort out worker behaviors and skills associated with effectiveness and client satisfaction.

It is impossible to provide an adequate summary of this significant research (Shulman's report is 580 pages long). A presentation of selected research findings, however, will give the reader some indication of the type of skills that were associated with building the helping relationship and being of help to the client. Much of Shulman's research focused on twenty-seven worker behaviors. They appear below with parenthetical comments illustrating how the behavior might be perceived by the client.

1. *Clarifying Purpose* (e.g., In our first meetings my worker explained the kinds of concerns we might be discussing.)
2. *Clarifying Role* (e.g., My worker explained how we would work together, describing the kind of help a social worker could give.)
3. *Encouraging Client Feedback on Purpose* (e.g., During our first meeting, my worker asked me for my ideas on specific subjects we would discuss together.)
4. *Displaying Worker's Belief in the Potential of the Work* (e.g., During our first meetings my worker told me she really believed I could get help from this agency with my concerns.)
5. *Holding to Focus* (e.g., When we began to discuss a particular concern the worker kept me on the topic.)
6. *Direct Contact with Systems People* (e.g., When I had trouble talking to someone the worker would meet with them to make it easier for me to speak to them.)
7. *Viewing Systems People in New Ways* (e.g., The worker helped me to understand the behavior of other people in new ways.)
8. *Moving From the General to the Specific* (e.g., When I raised a general concern the worker asked me for examples.)
9. *Connecting Feelings to Work* (e.g., My worker helped me to see how my feelings affected how I acted.)
10. *Reaching for Between Session Data* (e.g., The worker began our visit by asking if anything had happened between visits that I wanted to talk about.)
11. *Pointing out the Illusion of Work* (e.g., When the worker thought I was not working hard in our discussions she let me know.)
12. *Reaching Inside of Silences* (e.g., When I was unusually silent during our visits, the worker tried to find out why.)
13. *Supporting Client in Taboo Areas* (e.g., The worker helped me talk about subjects which were not easy to talk about.)

14. *Sharing Personal Thoughts and Feelings* (e.g., The worker shared her personal thoughts and feelings which helped me to get to know her better as a person.)
15. *Understanding Client Feelings* (e.g., When I told my worker how I felt, she understood.)
16. *Dealing with the Authority Theme* (e.g., When I was upset about something my worker did or said, she encouraged me to talk about it.)
17. *Checking for Artificial Consensus* (e.g., When I agreed with an idea too quickly the worker asked me if I really meant it.)
18. *Putting the Client's Feelings Into Words* (e.g., The worker seemed to understand how I felt without my having to put it into words.)
19. *Partializing Client's Concerns* (e.g., The worker helped me look at my concerns one at a time.)
20. *Supporting Client's Strength* (e.g., The worker believed I could handle the situations we discussed.)
21. *Identifying Affective Obstacles to Work* (e.g., The worker would point out when my feelings about something made it hard for me to talk during our visits.)
22. *Providing Data* (e.g., The worker shared her suggestions about the subjects we discussed for my consideration.)
23. *Worker Displaying Feelings Openly* (e.g., The worker let me know her feelings about the situations we discussed.)
24. *Pointing Out Endings Early* (e.g., Sometime before our last visit the worker explained that our visits would be ending soon.)
25. *Sharing Worker's Ending Feelings* (e.g., The worker let me know how she felt about our finishing.)
26. *Asking for a Review of Learning* (e.g., The worker asked me what I got out of our visits together.)
27. *Reaching for Ending Feelings* (e.g., The worker asked how I felt about ending our visits). [Pp. 169-171]

Analysis attempted to determine what behaviors were statistically related (0.05) with relationship building and helpfulness as perceived by the client. Some behaviors were related to relationship but not to helpfulness, some were related to both, and some were related to neither. A few of the twenty-seven behaviors were found to be negatively correlated to both relationship building or helpfulness. Making matters even more complex are findings that some behaviors were of more importance with some client groups, e.g. foster or natural parents, than other client groups. This not only reveals the complexity of the helping process but also points to the need for individualizing the client, i.e. adapting approach and technique to the particular characteristics and needs of the client.

In an attempt to summarize the practice implications of the research findings on worker behaviors, Shulman (1977) provides the following guidance to social workers:

> The results of the analysis thus far can be summarized in the form of a model of a helping process. The model is described with three levels of findings. The first are those with correlations high enough to offer encouraging evidence of the importance of the behaviors. The second level includes those which yielded correlations significant at the .05 level but not large enough to contribute substantial evidence of their importance. The final level includes behaviors with interesting changes in correlations but at levels so low that they can serve only as highly speculative clues. . . .
>
> There is good evidence in the data that as the worker begins with the client he needs to be conscious of the importance of *sharing his personal thoughts and feelings* related to the work. The client needs access to the worker as a real person so that trust can develop. As the worker listens to the client he must use his tuning in, his past experiences and immediate reactions to *put the client's feelings into words* just slightly before the client articulates them. This behavior sends an important signal to the client that the worker can understand and accept the client's feelings without the client having to risk the expression before he trusts the worker. The worker needs to be conscious that the client may have some difficulty in sharing those thoughts and feelings that are experienced as taboo. The worker needs to watch for clues and offer assistance *to ease the client's efforts to deal with taboo subjects.*
>
> The worker *will avoid pointing out to the client that his feelings seem to block him* as that may be experienced as a criticism. This can have a negative impact on the work when a good relationship does not exist. As the work proceeds, the worker needs to systematically and genuinely *demonstrate empathy with the client's expressed feelings.* This will help to clarify those feelings thus assisting the client in dealing with their impact. The worker needs *feedback from the client,* early in the work, on the concerns about which the client feels some urgency. This form of contracting will help to keep the work relevant for the client.
>
> The data yields less convincing support for the importance of the following set of behaviors. The worker needs to *clarify his role for the client,* early in the relationship so the client has a clear sense of what the worker can offer. This boundary on the work helps to

free the client from his fear of the authority and allows him to invest more of himself in the relationship. The worker will *provide relevant data,* early in the contact, so that the client experiences him as a giving person. The data is shared in a way that leaves the client open to reject it. At the start of each session the worker needs to demonstrate his belief in the importance of the client's sense of urgency by *checking for the client's agenda.* When global problems are shared, the worker partializes them thus making the work more manageable and demonstrating that the client's tasks are the focus of the work. The worker consistently demonstrates his *ability to understand the behavior of others in new ways,* opening up alternative views for the client, and refusing to simply mirror the client's perceptions.

Throughout the development of the working relationship the worker consistently *demonstrates an openness about his own feelings related to the work* so that the client begins to trust what the worker says is what he really feels. It will be important, after a relationship develops, that the worker *support the client's strength* by clearly demonstrating his belief in the client's strength to tackle difficult problems. The worker will pay some attention to the need to *discuss the authority theme,* how he and the client get along with each other. He needs to be sure, however, that a positive relationship has been developed. If not, attempts to discuss the relationship when it is going badly, without any prior development of trust, may be experienced negatively. Finally, the skills of *moving from the general to the specific* and *clarifying purpose* show some tentative indications that they may contribute to helpfulness. These findings, however, remain in a speculative realm. [Pp. 231-234]

Among the behaviors that did not have correlations with either helpfulness or relationship building were the following: (1) holding to focus, (2) direct contact with systems people, (3) connecting feelings to work, (4) pointing out the illusion of work, (5) reaching inside silences, and (6) checking for artificial consensus. Shulman (1978) reports that there are limitations to his research, and his findings should be considered tentative and exploratory. Additional research will be needed to confirm and further clarify these findings.

Added perspectives on the skills needed by social workers in the area of foster family services can be drawn from the extensive research effort known as the *Florida Human Service Task Bank* (State University System of Florida, 1975). This task analysis was conducted within public human service agencies that included child welfare and protective services programs. Of special interest are the five functions (linkage, mobilization, counseling, treatment, and administration) and eleven roles of human service work (brokering, client advocating, activating, systems advocating, counseling, consulting, rehabilitation, care giving, client programming, systems researching, and administrating). By permission of the State University System of Florida, the five functions and eleven roles are presented below:

FIVE FUNCTIONS AND ELEVEN ROLES OF HUMAN SERVICE WORK

1. *LINKAGE*

Helping potential consumers attain appropriate human services. The primary objective of linkage is a confluence between the consumer and an appropriate source of help for the problems indicated. Linkage may take the form of simple communication via advertising or a formal information and referral source; enabling people to utilize human service resources by helping them negotiate the system; or advocating the rights of the potential consumer who is being denied service.

A. *BROKERING*

The major thrust of brokering is facilitating the actual physical connection between the individual or individuals with a problem and services which have the potential for resolving or reducing the problem. It is the ability to help the potential consumer of services to finesse the service delivery system which may be relatively unaccommodating at times. Some manipulation may be involved in preparing the potential consumer and/or the potential provider for a positive contact. The relationship assumes a standard procedure or a negotiable situation and may include some discussing or bargaining to reach agreement.

B. *CLIENT (CONSUMER) ADVOCATING*

The major thrust of client advocating is the successful linking of a rejected consumer with appropriate services. The "client advocate" literally stands in the place of a consumer to bring about a change in the stance of the rejecting organization in favor of the person involved. This is a confronting relationship; and usually, a formal appeal based on legal or human rights is presented to accountable authorities.

2. *MOBILIZATION*

Working to fill the gaps within the service delivery system by developing or creating resources, i.e., programs, services, organizations. The primary objective of mobilization is the adaption of services to meet current needs. Mobilization includes humanizing services for existing consumers; bringing services to potential consumer groups or classes by changing inequitable or discriminatory practices, regulations, policies, and/or laws; or creating new human service resources, services or programs.

A. ACTIVATING

The major thrust of activating is the development of new human service resources to meet changing social needs. Activating may involve working to define and communicate specific community needs to providing the catalyst for the formation of self-help fellowships. Definition of problem, motivation of interest groups, and consensus of opinion which lead to organized solutions of community problems are objectives of the activator.

B. SYSTEMS ADVOCATING

The major thrust of systems advocacy is changing or adjusting the framework of the service delivery system to accommodate individuals who would otherwise be rejected or denied. Systems advocating may involve making a case or proposal, rebuttal is expected, and preconceived change in practices, rules, regulations, policies or laws is the desired outcome. Prevention and treatment as well as rehabilitative measures are the turf of systems advocating.

3. COUNSELING

Short-term coaching, counseling, teaching, consulting in a problem focused framework. The primary objectives are to convey and impart information or knowledge and develop various kinds of skills either to the individual or group. Counseling includes both direct service and consultive activities.

A. COUNSELING

The major thrust of the counseling is to teach, counsel, coach or support consumers in a short-term problem-focused situation. The counselor/counselee relationship is usually therapeutic in nature and improved understanding, improved skills, or increased skill levels is expected. A consensus concerning the problem and desired outcome in these situations is usually agreed upon in the initial stages of contact. Although contact is usually initiated by the counselee, it is not uncommon for the counselor to initiate the contact.

B. CONSULTING

The major thrust of consulting is in the colleague or organizational setting. Consulting may involve case conferences to receive or supply relevant information, or consultation may be utilized as an instructive technique. Usually, problems regarding knowledge deficiencies are determined or expressed, and the consultant offers instruction, discussion or alternatives which the consultee(s) is free to accept or reject; however, it is not unusual for consultants to reach into the communal domain of the consultee to offer new or previously unused information, materials or methods.

4. TREATMENT

Longer term, disability focused support, therapy or control on an ongoing basis. The primary objectives are increased status of functioning or humane care. Treatment includes consideration for physically, mentally or socially handicapped individuals.

A. REHABILITATING

The major thrust of rehabilitating is to provide extended disability-focused therapy to dysfunctioning human service consumers. Rehabilitation may involve a variety of therapeutic methodologies. The objectives of rehabilitation are increasing functional levels, and the goal of treatment is independence and the expectation of continued independence.

B. CARE GIVING

The major thrust of care giving is to extend maintenance and/or control to handicapped or maladapted individuals. Care giving involves a consideration for the consumers which will, at the very least, do the individual no physical or emotional harm. These physically, mentally and/or socially deprived persons are usually controlled or maintained with a reasonable expectation of therapeutic episodes or treatment developments being implemented to decrease their dependency.

5. ADMINISTRATION

The collection of data and the processing of the information leading to decision making or monitoring at either the consumer or system levels. The primary objective is data generated as the foundation for reasonable decisions. Administration includes information management for both monitoring and planning purposes.

A. CLIENT (CONSUMER) PROGRAMMING

The major thrust is to plan for client services. Client programming involves data collecting and processing for the purpose of making decisions regarding case disposition. It ranges from simple case data gathering and individual program planning to follow-up.

B. SYSTEMS RESEARCHING

The major thrust is to collect and process data relevant to particular areas of programmatical or organizational concern. Systems researching involves research for the purpose of making decisions and taking action. It ranges from gathering information and preparing statistical reports of program activity to program evaluation and sophisticated research.

C. *ADMINISTRATING*

The major thrust is decision making at all organizational levels and in all organizational contexts. Administrating involves decisions concerning program management, personnel supervision, budgeting, fiscal operations, and facilities management. Also, policy development, program implementation and organizational decision making are involved in the administrating context. [Pp. 25-28]

Descriptions of functions and roles such as those listed are especially helpful to persons attempting to conceptualize the training needs of child welfare personnel and/or prepare job descriptions. Also identified in the *Florida Human Service Task Bank* are fifty knowledge categories and seventy skill categories. These, too, are of assistance to those preparing job descriptions and describing prerequisite knowledge and skill for effective work in child welfare. This material is presented in Appendix D. An additional listing of social work knowledge and skill categories has been presented by Cummins (1976).

What Journals Are of Importance to the Social Worker in Child Welfare?

A variety of professional journals contain information directly or indirectly related to practice issues and concerns in the field of child welfare. Clearly, *Child Welfare* is one of the most widely read journals in the field. Useful articles can be found in many other journals. For purposes here, two groups are identified: (1) journals that frequently contain articles related to child welfare and (2) journals that occasionally contain articles relevant to child welfare.

Journals that Frequently Contain Articles Relevant to Child Welfare

American Journal of Orthopsychiatry
Australian Social Work
British Journal of Social Work

Canadian Welfare
Carnets de l'enfance/Assignment Children
Child Care Quarterly
Child Welfare
Child Development
Children Today
Clinical Journal of Social Work
Family Involvement
The Forum for Residential Therapy
International Social Work
International Child Welfare
Journal of Sociology and Social Welfare
Journal of Social Service Research
Journal of Social Welfare
Journal of Applied Social Sciences
Practice Digest
Public Welfare
Smith College Studies in Social Work
Social Casework
Social Service Review
Social Work
Social Work in Education
Social Work Research and Abstracts
Social Work Today
Social Work/Travailleur Social
Social Work With Groups

Journals that Occasionally Contain Articles
Relevant to Child Welfare

Administration in Social Work
Behavior Research and Therapy
Canada's Mental Health
Child Psychiatry and Human Development
Community Mental Health Journal
Crime and Delinquency
Family Coordinator
Family Law Quarterly

Family Process
Federal Probation
Health and Social Work
Journal of the American Academy of Child Psychiatry
Journal of Applied Behavioral Analysis
Journal of Clinical Psychology
Journal of Consulting and Clinical Psychology
Journal of Education for Social Work
Journal of Family Law
Journal of Marriage and Family Counseling
Journal of Experimental and Child Psychology

What Can the Social Worker Do When There is Not Time to Do All That Needs to Be Done?

A common complaint among social workers, especially those in the complex and fast-moving field of child welfare, is that they do not have enough time. Frequently, this is due to a real staff shortage and can be corrected only by the addition of more staff. Some, however, can make better use of limited time by adhering to principles of time management. Simple ideas such as those suggested by Bliss (1976) may help.

Plan each day—Start each day by making a schedule or list of tasks to be accomplished. Place particular emphasis on two or three major goals for the day.

Anticipate future tasks and deadlines—in making a daily schedule, anticipate those jobs that must be started now in order to accomplish goals or meet deadlines weeks or even months away.

Concentrate on your work—The amount of time available usually is less critical than whether or not it is uninterrupted time that concentrates energy on the task at hand.

Reward yourself—Find ways of rewarding yourself for small accomplishments. It may be as simple as putting a line through an item on your list of things to do or giving yourself a piece of gum. These little actions underscore the accomplishment and give one a feeling that progress has been made.

Take breaks from your periods of intense work—Briefly switching to a different type of activity counteracts boredom. If you were sitting, take a brief walk; if you were reading, do something with your hands; if you were writing, read something unrelated to your work, etc.

Avoid clutter in your work space—Clean your desk on a regular basis. Get rid of things that can be discarded. Try to start each day with a clean desk.

Organize your paperwork and set your priorities—Go through the paperwork to be completed and divide it into categories such as (1) high priority, (2) low priority, (3) pending, and (4) read. Put your papers in separate piles and attack the high-priority pile first.

Avoid being a perfectionist—Do a good job but do not spend valuable time and energy trying to make it perfect and consequently fall behind on other tasks.

Say no when necessary—Do not be afraid to say no to requests for your time. Decline those requests not related to your professional role. If you do not attempt to control the demands on your time, you will become overloaded, overwhelmed and dissatisfied with your performance. To obtain job satisfaction, you must accomplish goals and experience success.

Delegate tasks to others—Do not be afraid to ask others to take on work that falls within their job description. Delegating work does not mean asking others to do work that you should be doing.

Separate your work from other parts of your life—Do not let your work interfere with your family and social life, and do not let your personal life interfere with the time spent at work. Try to keep them separate; allow one to provide a break from the other so each day has variety.

Use appointments—To the greatest extent possible, use scheduled appointments for interviews with clients and collateral contracts, etc. Reduce the travel time involved in home visits by scheduling all those in a given locality for the same day.

Schedule time for emergencies—Schedule at least one hour of unplanned time each day so that time is available to deal with unanticipated tasks.

Keep track of your time expenditures—Keep track of how you spend each day. Once you have these raw data, analyze them;

identify those areas that need special attention and those areas in which you can make time-saving changes.

Secure needed training—If a lack of skill or knowledge is slowing you down or causing you to make mistakes that take additional time to correct, request additional training or consultation.

Develop a workable recording and note-taking system—Ask experienced workers to help you develop an effective and efficient system of keeping work notes and records.

Maintain a personal filing system—A great deal of time can be lost trying to locate work-related information (memos or policy statements, etc.) and recall the names of people who may be valuable resources in particular situations. Since social workers deal with a large number of persons other than clients, e.g. doctors, lawyers, other social workers, some type of name-reminder file is highly useful. As you learn about and/or meet other human service personnel, be sure to place their names, addresses, phone numbers and other relevant data in a file for future reference.

Those who have serious problems making the behavioral changes necessary to time management may find well-researched self-help books useful (for example, Watson and Tharp, 1972).

What Principles Should Guide Case Recording and Report Writing?

Social workers spend many hours each week recording cases and writing reports. Adherence to certain principles of writing may shorten the time spent on these tasks while increasing the usefulness of records and reports. A useful book by Harris (1976), *Support Skills for Direct Service Workers: Managing Your Job,* presents several principles that should guide written communications.

1. *Shortness:* Say no more than need be said and use just enough words to say it.
2. *Simplicity:* Select the least complicated words and phrases. Organize the material carefully.
3. *Accuracy and precision:* Select the proper words to express the thought exactly. Beware of value-laden words and connotative meanings, for example, "women's libber," "heavy drinker," "the client admits he doesn't attend church," "he claims to have

completed high school." Label opinions and personal judgments as such. Be sure to support these statements with objective examples written in concrete, behaviorally specific terms.

4. *Usefulness:* Keep in mind the purpose of the report. Ask yourself who will read it and what they will need to know. Be sure to censor yourself from including information merely because it is sensational rather than specifically useful and relevant.

5. *Confidentiality:* Be sure what is written complies with agency accountability guidelines. Be sure the client knows what you are including in the report or letter. [Pp. 48-49]

Harris offers many other suggestions:

Attempt to simplify and shorten reports. Wordiness lessens the impact of the message and increases the likelihood that the reader will merely skim the report. . . .

Sentences should be short, generally less than twenty words. The subject-verb-object sentence is usually the most effective arrangement. Use active verbs whenever possible. The passive voice adds extra words in the sentence and is usually ambiguous. John was hit by Don says no more than Don hit John; however, it uses 66 percent more words. . . .

Because any one word may have a number of different meanings in different contexts, the writer must be certain that the word chosen is appropriate to convey exactly the intended meaning. . . .

Be cautious in the use of slang. It is usually vague and has different meanings for different readers. . . .

Behavior should be described in terms of the context in which it occurs. No value judgments or labels should be used unless they are supported by more than one relevant documented behavior. Labels should not become a working part of the case records until specific behaviors common to that label have been repeatedly verified. . . .

Avoid cliches because they often pad the report without contributing to clarity. . . .

Be careful not to use "weasel words" in which the writer wriggles out of a position of accountability for an observation, inference, or statement. Examples of "weasel phrases" include:

It would be difficult to estimate. . . .

It is too early to say whether. . . .

In summary, the importance of on-going recording and carefully written reports is a crucial variable in maximally effective client service. Reports should be kept short, simple, precise, accurate, and useful. [Pp. 49-50]

Are There Other Ways of Reducing Time
Spent on Records and Reports?

Because personal style and individual differences have much to do with work performance and efficiency, a technique that saves time for one person may create added problems for another. A person seeking time-saving procedures should experiment with new approaches until he or she discovers those that are most compatible with personal style and preferences. Listed below are a few guidelines helpful to most people.

1. Spend some time each day on record keeping and report writing. Do not let this work pile up.

2. Maintain a filing system for the quick retrieval of information and raw data needed to compile a report or complete a case recording.

3. Develop a workable procedure for note taking and a system for keeping related notes together. A good set of notes shortens the time required to organize and prepare reports and records. A procedure for keeping notes is presented elsewhere in this chapter.

4. Develop workable outlines, forms, or form letters for routine reports.

5. Adhere to principles of effective written communication.

6. Learn to use electronic aids, such as dictaphones.

The last suggestion, using a dictaphone, is especially important because it can cut recording and report writing time by 50 percent. Harris (1976) has outlined several principles for the effective use of dictating equipment.

1. Select a good location for dictating, one that has a comfortable chair, table large enough to spread out materials, and a convenient location for the dictating apparatus. Request interruptions be kept to a minimum.

2. Arrange all the information and background materials in the order in which they will be needed.

3. Make a rough outline in writing.

4. Dictate in a natural tone of voice, being careful to enunciate clearly.

5. Talk at a steady pace, at a slightly slower rate than usual.

6. Spell any words which sound similar to other words, as well as

any uncommon or confusing names. Dictate figures by digits, i.e., refer to the figure 11,065 as "one, one, zero, six, five."

7. Dictate only periods, paragraphs, and unusual punctuation; the transcriber will take care of normal punctuation.
8. Play back the tape to be sure it reflects your intended message.
9. Remember that the initial dictation is only a rough draft. Once the ideas are down in writing, it's easier to revise and fill in the gaps. Between one and three rewrites are required for a polished report or letter. In editing, be sure to clarify and tighten up the ideas expressed.
10. Read all dictated material carefully before signing it. Errors in final copies reflect the professional's carelessness in proofreading before signing rather than the secretary's negligence. [P. 50]

What Is a Simple Method for Maintaining a Set of Case Notes?

Two steps usually are involved in the creation of an official agency record. First, the social worker creates a set of handwritten working notes. Such notes record the many and varied day-to-day or hour-by-hour actions and activities related to a specific case, e.g. "Mr. Smith, Johnny B's teacher called to say. . . ." Notes help the worker keep track of what is happening. Some of these hand-written notes are self-messages or written reminders that a specific task should be undertaken, e.g. contact Mrs. Jones's attorney before next Friday and request. . . . Many of these notes have meaning only to the person who wrote them. Because it is impractical to include all of the working notes in an official record, most social workers periodically dictate a summary of the case activity and include this typed version in the official case record. Given this two-step process, it is important that the social worker establish a workable system of note taking that (a) keeps all case notes in one place so this information is always at hand, (b) maintains a chronological record of activities, and (c) facilitates summarization.

One such method is to utilize a loose-leaf notebook filled with sheets of paper specifically designed for brief handwritten and chronological entries. Moreover, each sheet can be constructed to facilitate the recording of statistics kept by the agency, e.g., number of office interviews, number of out-of-office interviews, and type of contact. Below is a sample sheet with several typical entries. This method maintains all the notes in one place and allows for a quick review and update of what has happened and what should be done. Such a method is especially important when the worker has, for example, fifty cases. Without a good note-keeping system, it is impossible to remember the details of a situation. All of the note sheets are kept in one place and used as a basis for the preparation of a periodic summary, e.g. once a month or bimonthly.

Client **JOHN SMITH**   Case Number **1234**   Cross Reference **JONES FOSTER FAMILY**

Type of Contract										Date	To Do	Time Spent	Notes
client (child)	client (adult)	foster parent	collateral	other	office	out-of-office	telephone	letter	other				
		✓					✓			4/6/78			Mrs. Jones called to say John ran away. He left about 8 AM. She will check with his friends. I will talk to his P.O.
		✓					✓			4/7/78			I called Mrs. Jones. No word on John.
							✓			4/7/78			Learned from Officer Smith that John was picked up. No charge at Police Station.
				✓		✓				4/7/78			John returned to Jones foster home. He says he is having trouble in school, especially with math teacher (Mr. Brown). (Need to set up appt with math teacher & counselor — is tutor a possibility?)
✓		✓				✓				4/8/78	✓		talked with John & Mrs. Jones. Agreed to meet at school on 4/10/78, 4PM, Room 104
✓					✓					4/9/78			Spent hr. with John. Angry with math teacher. Feels he is not treated fair. much has always been unfair. "Idea of tutor is OK. Also upset because his mother forgot his birthday." "She is probably drunk again, I'll always forget." I tried to get to talk about his mother. He doesn't hear last Thursday when she drinks. He wants to visit his sister, Mary. "Mary loves me, understands mom." (arrange meeting between John & Mary)
✓											✓		

Figure 1. Sample Case Notes.

CWLA Intake Interview Guide*

Instructions

This Guide is designed to make the intake process more consistent by assuring the collection of basic data found to be of importance to the decision-making process.

The form is to be employed during the first in-person interview with either the mother, father, or guardian of the child-(ren) in need of service. A child is defined as in need of service even if services are to be given only to the parents on the child's behalf. In presenting the form the interviewer may wish to use the analogy of a hospital intake in explaining why the range of data, some of which may not seem directly relevant to their situation, is being collected.

Pages 2-11 have been designed so that the interviewer can follow closely the questions if he/she desires in conducting the interview. The interviewer is however free to modify the wording or order of questions so long as he/she makes sure to cover each item on the form. The interviewer is encouraged to pursue in greater detail any item on the form on which he needs further information.

At the end of the interview the worker is to complete the Worker Evaluation, starting on page 12, and to indicate the plan for the child. The worker should indicate if the plan for the child is not "ideal" but mandated by lack of resources, parental resistance, etc.

In some instances the worker will not be able to make even a tentative decision about appropriate planning after the first in-person contact. In such a case the worker may defer briefly completion of the Worker Evaluation section until he/she collects the additional data needed from the other parent or collaterals.

On most pages of the questionnaire a space has been left for notations of important information gathered from collaterals. This would include information indicating that what the client reports is incorrect or other significant information that will permit greater understanding of the client's response. Data from collaterals need not be noted unless differences between collaterals and the client are expressed or verification of a parental statement is important. The space should also be used to record additional information from the parent.

---

* Reproduced by permission of the Child Welfare League of America, 67 Irving Place, New York, N. Y. 10003.

August 1972

Name of client_____ Case #_____
        (please print or write legibly)
Address (and additional_____
information re location_____
of house/apartment) _____ Phone #_____

Worker's name_____ Unit_____ District Office___

Referral Information

Date of referral_____
Source of referral:
_____Mother
_____Father
_____Both parents
_____Relatives (specify)
_____Friend, neighbor (specify)_____
_____School (specify)_____
_____Voluntary agency (specify)_____
_____Public welfare agency (including other department, same agency)
_____Other (specify)_____

Problem as described by referral source (including recommendation
if appropriate):_____
_____
_____
_____

Worker notations on previous record material:_____
_____
_____

Other agencies involved:_____
_____

Disposition of referral:
_____Accepted for study
_____Not accepted for study

Client Contact

Contact between client and agency was:
_____Voluntary
_____Involuntary

Date(s) of attempted contact(s):_____
Date of initial in-person contact:_____
Person(s) seen during initial contact:_____
Where initial contact took place:_____

In Protective Cases. Please describe what you told client about
reason for contact and agency role:_____
_____
_____

1. What's the problem? (What do you see   COLLATERAL INFORMATION
    as the reason for our contact with
    you?)_____
    _____
    _____
    _____

2. How long has this problem been
    troubling you? (Worker appraisal of
    response)
    _____New problem
    _____Chronic problem--little recent
         change
    _____Chronic problem--intensified
         or reactivated

3. What would you like us to do for you?
    (If client is not clear what agency
    can offer, worker may wish to review
    available services.)
    _____Nothing--involuntary referral
    _____Day Care
    _____Placement
    _____Homemaker Service
    _____Counseling
    _____Financial Assistance
    _____Other (specify)_____

4. Before (coming to us) (we got in
    touch with you), what did you try to
    do about the problem?_____
    _____
    _____
    _____

5. Did you talk to: <u>COLLATERAL INFORMATION</u>
   ____Friends
   ____Neighbors
   ____Relatives
   ____Doctor, lawyer, clergyman
   ____Other agencies (specify)_____
   ____Other (specify)_____

6. What were they able to do for you?___
   _____
   _____
   _____
   _____

7. Have you ever had contact with this
   agency before?
   ____No
   ____Yes (Why was that?)_____
       _____
       _____

<u>Decision on Case</u>

____Referral appropriate (CONTINUE INTERVIEW)
____Referral inappropriate, refer and close (STOP USE OF FORM)
____Referral inappropriate, no further action (STOP USE OF FORM)

8. Family data and usual household composition. (Be sure to fill
   in all data on this face sheet including the names of all
   members of the household. It is best to begin with information about the respondent. Even if natural father/mother is
   not part of the household, request information about him/her.
   Do not press for data on whereabouts of missing parent until
   end of interview if respondent is reluctant to give such
   information. Be sure to inquire if there is anyone else who
   is usually part of the household but temporarily away (less
   than 90 days) and if there are any children who are permanently away from the home.)

	Last Name	First Name	Relation-ship to Male/Fa.	Relation-ship to Fem./Mo.	Sex	Birth Date	Race	Religion
Male in HH								
Natural Father 1								
Natural Father 2								

	Last Name	First Name	Relation-ship to Male/Fa.	Relation-ship to Fem./Mo.	Sex	Birth Date	Race	Religion
Female in HH								
Natural Mother 1								
Natural Mother 2								
Child #1								
Child #2								
Child #3								
Child #4								
Child #5								
Child #6								
Child #7								
Child #8								
Child #9								
Child #10								
Other Members of House-hold								

Occupation/ Kind of Work	Name and Address of Employer	Hours of Work	Whereabouts/ Address if Not Presently in Household	When Left	Will Return When

Kind of Work/ School Grade	Name and Loca- tion of School or Employer	Hours of Work	Whereabouts/ Address if Not Presently in Household	When Left	Will Return When

COLLATERAL INFORMATION

9. Have any of your children ever been in placement 90 days or more?
   _____ No
   _____ Yes

   (IF YES, ENTER CHILD'S NAME AND CHECK ALL TYPES OF PLACEMENT THAT APPLY.)

   Child's name_____

   Yes, foster home, group home or institution for dependent children___
   _____

   Yes, institution for mentally retarded or emotionally disturbed____
   _____

   Yes, correctional institution_____
   _____

   Yes, other (specify)_____
   _____

10. Who assumes the major responsibility for the care of children in your household?
    _____ Mother or stepmother
    _____ Father or stepfather
    _____ Female relative
    _____ Male relative
    _____ Other (specify)_____

COLLATERAL INFORMATION

11. Are you presently:
    _____Married; Date of present
        marriage:_____
    _____Single
    _____Widowed
    _____Divorced; Date of divorce:_____
    _____Separated; Date of separation__

12. Have you had any previous marriages?
    _____No
    _____Yes: Date married_____
    Date separated/divorced_____

13. Has the father/mother of the
children been married before?
    _____No
    _____Yes: Date married_____
    Date separated/divorced_____

14. What is the total weekly income of
your family from employment after
deductions (take home pay)? $_____

15. Other than employment and welfare
how much do you get weekly (child
support, social security, etc.)?
$_____

16. Are you receiving welfare?
    _____No
    _____Yes: For how long have you
        been getting assistance?_____

    How much do you receive
    monthly?_____

17. IF EITHER PARENT WORKS ASK: Who
takes care of your children while
you (and your husband/wife) are
working?
    _____Not relevant, neither working
    _____Spouse
    _____Take care of selves
    _____Paid baby sitter
    _____Day care
    _____Relative
    _____Neighbor or friend
    _____Other (specify)

18. If you had to go out and leave your   <u>COLLATERAL INFORMATION</u>
children, is there anyone you could
leave them with?
_____No
_____Yes: Who is that?_____

19. Do either you or your husband have
any relatives with whom you are in
contact?
_____No (SKIP TO Q. 20)
_____Yes: Who is that?_____
_____
_____

Do you think they might be able to
help you with this problem?
_____No
_____Yes: In what way?_____
_____
_____
_____

20. Do either of you have any friends
who might be able to help you with
this problem?
_____No
_____Yes: Who? In what way?_____
_____

21. When you find it necessary to
discipline your child, what methods
do you use? (CHECK ALL THAT APPLY)
_____Physical punishment such as
spanking
_____Taking away some privilege
like being able to watch TV
_____Financial penalty like
reducing allowance, refusing
money for other things
_____Confining to room or keeping
home after school, etc.
_____Giving extra work or chores
around the house
_____Just a good scolding
_____Other (specify)

22. Do your children help you around the
house?
_____No
_____Yes: In what way?_____
_____

23. In order to understand what we can do for you and the children, we have found it best to get a picture of each of the children in the family. For each characteristic I read, please tell me if the description is true of any of your children. Let's start with your oldest child, does (NAME) or any of your other children have. . . ? (IT IS BEST TO REVIEW ALL CHILDREN IN HOME ON EACH CHARACTERISTIC BEFORE GOING ON TO THE NEXT CHARACTERISTIC.)

T = True; F = False; NR = Not Relevant

Characteristic	Child's Name T F NR	Child's Name T F NR	Child's Name T F NR
a. A physical disability that limits his functioning			
SPECIFY WHAT IT IS:			
b. Difficulties in school work			
c. Behavior is said to be a problem at school			
d. Cuts classes and some-times skips school			
e. Is hard to handle and does not listen			
f. Fights a lot with brothers or sisters			
g. Refuses to help around the house			
h. Steals from parents			
i. Has run away from home			
j. Has few or no friends own age			
k. Is aggressive, gets in many fights			
l. Gets in trouble because of sexual behavior			
m. Is withdrawn			
n. Has temper tantrums			
o. Lies a lot			
p. Is easily influenced by others			
q. Is immature for age			
u. Demands a lot of attention			
r. Does not get along with other children			
s. Other significant characteristic			
SPECIFY:			

Other comments:_____

_____
_____
_____
_____
_____

COLLATERAL INFORMATION

Now I'd like to ask you a few questions about you
and your husband.

COLLATERAL
INFORMATION

MOTHER (Mother surrogate)　　FATHER (Father surrogate)

24. How is your health? Your husband's (wife's)?
　　　　　　_____ Good
　　　　　　_____ Fair
　　　　　　　　　　 Has disability or illness
　　　*_____ that hampers functioning _____ *
　　　*_____ Is hospitalized _____ *
　　　*_____ Needs hospitalization _____ *

　　　*Specify nature of difficulty:_____

25. Have you or your husband (wife) ever been treated
　　　for a mental illness or a nervous disorder?
　　　　　　_____ No
　　　　　　　　　　 Yes, out-patient treat-
　　　*_____ ment _____ *
　　　*_____ Yes, hospitalized _____ *

　　　*Specify nature of difficulty and dates of
　　　treatment:_____

26. Do you or your husband (wife) currently have such
　　　a problem?
　　　　　　_____ No
　　　　　　_____ Yes _____

27. Have you or your husband (wife) ever had a
　　　problem with drinking? Do you now?
　　　　　　_____ No, never _____
　　　*_____ Yes, past, not now _____
　　　*_____ Yes, now _____ *

28. Have you or your husband (wife) ever used drugs? COLLATERAL
    Do you now?   INFORMATION
    _____ No, never
    _____ Yes, past, not now   _____
    * _____ Yes, now   _____ *

    *What kind of drug is that?_____

29. Do you or your husband (wife) often do things on
    the spur of the moment without thinking?
    _____ No
    _____ Yes   _____

30. Do you or your husband (wife) have any trouble
    managing the money you have?
    _____ No
    _____ Yes   _____

31. Do you or your husband (wife) have any difficulty
    holding a job?
    _____ No
    _____ Yes   _____

32. (ASK ONLY WHERE LIVING WITH SPOUSE--WHETHER RELA-
    TIONSHIP IS LEGAL OR COMMON-LAW) Now I'd like to
    ask you about your marriage. Taking all things
    together, how would you describe your marriage
    (relationship with _____)? Which of these
    terms fits best:
    _____Very happy
    _____Fairly happy
    _____So-so
    _____Fairly unhappy
    _____Very unhappy
    _____No response or don't know

33. I have been asking you mostly about areas in
    which people have difficulty. Tell me about
    some of the good things about your family,
    some of the things that are going well for you
    and your family._____
    _____
    _____
    _____

PLEASE REVIEW FORM, MAKING SURE THAT INFORMATION FROM
COLLATERALS, WHEN DIFFERENT FROM PARENTS' REPORT, HAS
BEEN NOTED.

Sources of Information

Indicate how long contact was with each of the following and where it took place. (If no contact, indicate "none.")

	Number of Minutes	Location
Mother	_____	_____
Father	_____	_____
Children	_____	_____
Other:_____ (specify)	_____	_____
Other:_____ (specify)	_____	_____

Resources Available To Help This Family

	Name of contact	Phone
School	_____	_____
Clinic	_____	_____
Social Agency	_____	_____
Relative/friend	_____	_____
Other	_____	_____

Worker Evaluation

What is the primary reason for the request for service? Check one only.
_____Abuse or neglect of child
_____Parental unwillingness to care for child (including desertion)
_____Marital conflict of parents
_____Emotional or behavioral problem of caretaking parent
_____Physical illness or death of caretaking parent
_____Parent-child conflict
_____Child's emotional or behavioral problem
_____Employment of caretaking parent
_____Financial need, or inadequate housing
_____Other (specify):_____

T = True; F = False; U = Unknown

Child's Name:

Child's situation:	T F U	T F U	T F U
a. Child appears to have little concern about problem			
b. Child wishes to leave household			
c. Child appears to have little capacity for change			
d. Child appears to have poor relationship with parent(s)			

All in all, how would you evaluate child's emotional state?
(Check one item for each child in the same order as listed above.)

Normal			
Somewhat disturbed			
Markedly disturbed but not psychotic			
Severely disturbed, psychotic			
Insufficient data			

What is your estimate of the child's intelligence? (Check one item for each child in the same order as listed above.)

Above average			
Average			
Somewhat below average			
Well below average			
Unknown			

	Mother		Father	
Parent's relationship with child:	True	Not True	True	Not True
a. Shows little concern for children				
b. Does not recognize individual needs and differences between children				
c. Punishments of children are overly severe				
d. Does not set limits for children				
e. Is erratic in handling of children				
f. Is not warm and affectionate with children				
g. Places excessive responsibility on children				
h. Is extremely lax in discipline of children				

For each area of current child care functioning, check whether the family functioning is adequate, somewhat inadequate or grossly inadequate. Functioning is to be considered inadequate if there is a deficiency in an area with all or any one of the children.

Area of child care functioning:	Adequate	Somewhat Inadequate	Grossly Inadequate
a. Protection from physical abuse, exploitation or exposure to dangerous situations			
b. Supervision or guidance			
c. Warmth and affection			
d. Concern regarding schooling			

What is your assessment of the cohesiveness of the family?
____Exceptionally close, warm family relations
____Closely knit, cooperative
____Fair cohesiveness with minor problems
____Considerable tension or lack of warmth
____Severe conflict or absence of affectional ties
____Unknown--insufficient data available

Appearance of the home:
____Not applicable--home not visited
____Fastidiously clean and orderly
____Fairly clean and orderly
____Clean but not too orderly
____Not clean but orderly
____Not clean and not orderly

Parental evaluation: Indicate whether or not each of these descriptions accurately fits this parent.

	Mother		Father	
	True	Not True	True	Not True
a. Exhibits grossly deviant social attitudes				
b. Has unwarranted feeling of being picked on by community				
c. Is suspicious or distrustful or others				
d. Appears withdrawn or depressed				
e. Appears emotionally disturbed				
f. Has diagnosed mental illness				
SPECIFY:				

For each of the following items check the degree to which it characterizes the parent.

High = High degree; Mod. = Moderate degree; Low = Low Degree

	Mother				Father			
	High	Mod.	Low	None	High	Mod.	Low	None
a. Ability to verbalize feelings								
b. Recognition of own part in problem								
c. Desire for change								
d. Capacity for change								
e. Responsiveness to worker suggestions								
f. Concern about problem								
g. Agreement with worker's proposed plan of service								

Please describe anything noteworthy in the appearance of mother, father, or children: _____

_____

_____

_____

_____

Additional comments: (Indicate other significant material not already listed on the form.) _____

_____

_____

_____

Plan of Service

Specify the type of service to be given to each child in need of service.

Child's name   Plan for child _____

_____   _____

_____   _____

_____   _____

_____   _____

_____   _____

Assessment of Social Functioning

Instructions

This outline can be used in two ways. First, it may be used for the preparation of narrative type of social assessment reports. When used for that purpose, the items and categories presented will serve as a reminder of factors that may need to be included and as a way of organizing the report. Secondly, this outline can be used as a rating and recording sheet for the assessment of family functioning. The user is urged not to use this outline in a rigid manner. Preferably, he or she will use this outline as a starting point for the design of an outline especially relevant to his or her professional needs.

The outline items are stated positively. Thus, the outline can aid in the identification of family strengths. A focus on strengths helps to counteract the tendency of problems or deficits to overshadow assets. Since effective intervention must build on existing strengths, the items can be used as a starting point for the development of intervention goals and objectives.

The user may wish to create his or her own code or set of abbreviations for the rating of each item in the outline. A simple code is presented. For example, an item may be descriptive of the family (+), partially descriptive (+−), or not descriptive of the family (−). Some items may not apply to a particular family. In such cases, the item should be checked not applicable (NA). If the user does not have enough data on which to form a judgment about a particular item, it should be marked insufficient data (ID). Space is provided in the outline for comments and additional descriptions of family functioning.

It should be noted that a degree of subjectivity and value judgment is involved in all assessments of complex social behavior. Moreover, different communities, ethnic, religious and cultural groupings have somewhat different norms for family behavior. The user must consider each item within the cultural context that applies to the family. As used in the outline, the term *family* refers to two or more persons related by blood, marriage, or mutual agreement, who interact and provide one another with mutual physical, emotional, social and/or economic care and support. This definition of family is meant to apply to all people in a household and the members of an extended family.

A. IDENTIFYING DATA

Case # _____
Date _____

Name _____
Address _____
Telephone (home) _____ (work) _____

Family composition:

	Name	Sex	Date of birth	Education (highest level achieved)	Occupation	Living at home (yes/no)
Husband						
Wife						
Child						
Child						
Child						
Child						
Child						
Child						
Other						
Other						

Describe unusual or complex relationships among parents, children or relatives (e.g., adoption, foster child, child by another marriage, extended family, kinship structure, etc.). _____
_____
_____
_____
_____

Total number of adults in household _____
Total number of children (below age 18) in household _____
Date/place of current marriage _____
Age at time of marriage: husband _____ wife _____
Previous marriage(s): husband _____
                      wife _____
Date/place of divorce or legal separations _____

Describe unusual or complex legal or informal agreements affecting family (e.g., custody of children, visitation rights by persons outside the family, etc.)_____

_____
_____
_____

Description of family's racial/ethnic/cultural background_____

_____
_____
_____
_____
_____

Description of family's religious affiliations, beliefs and values

_____
_____

B. BASIS OF CONCERN

Describe presenting problem and/or problem(s) of social functioning that led to family's involvement with social worker or agency._____

_____
_____
_____
_____

Source of Referral_____

Family members' perceptions of problem/situation (e.g., How does each family member perceive the problem/situation? Is there agreement or disagreement on nature of problem? Are family members hopeful or pessimistic about resolving problem/situation? Acceptance or denial of problem?)_____

_____
_____
_____

Solutions/suggestions offered by family members on how to resolve problem/situation_____

_____
_____

Codes for Rating

Descriptive of family (+)
Partially descriptive (+-)
Not descriptive of family (-)
Not applicable to family (NA)
Insufficient data on which to make judgment (ID)

C. FAMILY RELATIONSHIPS AND UNITY

Marital or couple's relationship:

		Rating	Comments
1.	Couple lives together		
2.	Couple derives satisfaction from their relationship and shared experiences.		
3.	There is a positive emotional tie between partners; both can express need for the other's help and respond appropriately when the other requires help or support.		
4.	Consistent effort to limit the scope and duration of conflict.		
5.	Consistent effort to keep communication open for resolution of conflicts which arise.		

Relationship between parents and children:

1.	Affection is shown between parents and children.		
2.	Parents usually are consistent and realistic in treatment and expectations of children.		
3.	Children have sense of belonging and emotional security within family.		
4.	Children and parents show respect and concern for each other.		
5.	Parent-child conflict is minimized by open communication and desire for harmony.		
6.	Parents derive satisfaction from caring for children and assume major role in their care.		

Sibling relationships:

	Rating	Comments
1. There are positive emotional ties and mutual identification among children.		
2. Depending on age, children often play together and share playthings.		
3. Siblings are loyal to each other, enjoy other's company and take pride in achievements of siblings.		
4. Disputes and bickering among children are not out of line for age group.		

Family solidarity:

	Rating	Comments
1. Warmth and affection are shown among family members, giving them a sense of belonging and emotional security.		
2. Conflict within family system is dealt with appropriately and in a manner acceptable to all family members.		
3. There is evidence of cohesiveness; for example, members often do things together; eat together.		
4. Family plans and works toward some common goals.		
5. There is feeling of collective responsibility within family unit.		
6. Although family solidarity, individual differences are recognized and respected.		
7. Family members pull together in times of stress.		
8. Family members find considerable satisfaction in family living.		
9. Adults (e.g., parents, grandparents, relatives, boarders, etc.) in household group treat each other with consideration and mutual concern.		
10. Adults in household group do not show favoritism or marked preference for some child(ren) over others.		
11. Adults do not mind the presence of children in household.		

General family functioning:

		Rating	Comments
1.	Family functioning and behavior are in line with wider community expectations and standards.		
2.	Family behavior is in line with reference group norms and expectations (e.g., ethnic group).		
3.	Special needs of handicapped or aged family members are being met.		
4.	Family socialization process stresses positive preparation for present and future roles and the acquisition of social skills.		
5.	Appropriate outside assistance and supports are sought beyond resources of family.		
6.	Family problems are faced and dealt with appropriately.		
7.	Family is free of serious problems (e.g., alcoholism, sexual abuse, violence, mental illness, etc.).		
8.	Family's involvement in community provides necessary and wholesome socialization experiences for children.		
9.	Some family members are active in groups that lend support to community betterment.		

Additional description of family functioning, parent-child interaction, marital relationship, etc._____

_____
_____
_____
_____
_____
_____
_____
_____
_____
_____
_____
_____
_____

D. BEHAVIOR AND SOCIAL ADJUSTMENT OF EACH ADULT(S) IN FAMILY

Instructions:

Each parent, adult parental figure and other adults should be considered individually. Thus, additional pages from this section need to be added for each adult in the family. The family as a whole and the interaction among family members are considered elsewhere.

		Rating	Comments
1.	Law violations are limited to slight infractions (e.g., minor traffic violations).		
2.	Has good range of social skills, relates comfortably to most people.		
3.	Has positive self image, values self.		
4.	Is generally satisfied with his situation and role (e.g., husband, parent, breadwinner, homemaker, etc.).		
5.	If dissatisfied with present situation; is attempting to make appropriate changes.		
6.	Is able to cope satisfactorily in most aspects of living.		
7.	If necessary, receives appropriate treatment for health problems.		
8.	Functioning hampered only slightly if at all by physical handicaps or continuing health problems.		
9.	Disagreements with spouse or partner are satisfactorily resolved or well tolerated.		
10.	As a parent, has positive relationship with children.		
11.	Provides appropriate physical and emotional care to children.		
12.	Has meaningful ties with friends, relatives, neighbors, etc.		
13.	Belongs to some social groups or organizations, which provide satisfactions.		
14.	Has positive attitude toward neighborhood and community.		
15.	When necessary and desired, makes good use of community facilities and resources.		

Additional descriptions of individual behavior and social adjustment (e.g., role performance, physical and mental health, etc.).

_____
_____
_____
_____
_____
_____

E. BEHAVIOR AND SOCIAL ADJUSTMENT OF EACH CHILD IN FAMILY

Instructions:

Each child in the family should be assessed individually. Thus, additional pages from this section need to be added for each child. The family as a whole and the interaction among the children and between adults and children are considered elsewhere.

	Rating	Comments
1. Child's acting out behavior is normal for age (e.g., pranks, mischievousness, fights, etc. are not of serious nature).		
2. Child has positive self-image, values self.		
3. Child enjoys age appropriate activities.		
4. Child is generally satisfied with life situation.		
5. If present, child's diseases or physical handicaps are receiving appropriate care.		
6. If diseases or physical handicaps are present, child is making favorable adjustment.		
7. Child participates in household duties and family life.		
8. If student, child attends school regularly.		
9. If student, child's school performance approximates intellectual and physical ability.		
10. If student, child has positive attitude toward school and enjoys learning.		
11. Child relates well to adults.		
12. Child has friends and is liked by others.		
13. Child participates satisfactorily in peer groups.		

Additional descriptions of child's behavior and social adjustment (e.g., relationship to parents, peers, school performance, health, etc.)._____

_____

_____

_____

_____

_____

F. CARE AND TRAINING OF CHILDREN WITHIN FAMILY

	Rating	Comments
1. Children have adequate food, both in quality and quantity.	_____	_____
2. Children have clothing suitable for weather conditions.	_____	_____
3. Children have safe and adequate sleeping space.	_____	_____
4. Children are kept clean.	_____	_____
5. Children's health needs (preventive and remedial) are looked after promptly and appropriately.	_____	_____
6. Children have access to privacy.	_____	_____
7. Children live within atmosphere of emotional warmth and concern.	_____	_____
8. Children are allowed to pursue interests and develop talents.	_____	_____
9. Children have wholesome attitude toward sex and their bodies.	_____	_____
10. Children are not subjected to physical or sexual abuse.	_____	_____
11. Children are not subjected to intimidation or emotional abuse.	_____	_____
12. Parents' beliefs of how children should behave are generally those acceptable to the community and/or reference group (e.g., ethnic group).	_____	_____
13. Children allowed to take the normal risks associated with learning.	_____	_____
14. Expectations of children and standards of behavior are appropriate to child's age level.	_____	_____
15. Approval of child's good conduct is often shown by parent.	_____	_____
16. Parents are fairly consistent in setting limits and exercising discipline.	_____	_____
17. Discipline methods are usually appropriate to misbehavior.	_____	_____

	Rating	Comments
18. Parents are in basic agreement about exercising discipline and rearing of children.		
19. Parents share in job of training children.		
20. Parents value education for their children.		
21. Parents facilitate regular school attendance.		
22. Parents are cooperative with school personnel when joint planning is indicated.		

Comments _____

_____

_____

_____

G. FAMILY'S ECONOMIC SITUATION

	Rating	Comments
1. Family income is sufficient to cover basic expenses and at least afford a few luxuries and/or permit savings.		
2. Income is derived from work of family members, or from sources such as pensions, insurances, rent, support payments, etc.		
3. Breadwinner works regularly at full-time job.		
4. Breadwinner seeks improvement if not fully satisfied with job situation or earnings.		
5. Breadwinner(s) changes jobs only when it is unavoidable due to economic or other circumstances, or for improvement.		
6. Nature of breadwinner's job is consistent with capabilities, training and talents.		
7. Worker maintains harmonious relations with employer and co-workers.		
8. Money is spent on the basis of agreement between members of family.		
9. Money management is carried out with realistic regard to basic necessities.		
10. Debts are manageable and planned for in budget.		

Additional description of family's economic situation, money management and employment._____

_____
_____
_____
_____
_____

H. <u>HOME CHARACTERISTICS AND HOUSEKEEPING PRACTICES</u>

		Rating	Comments
1.	Property is kept in safe condition.		
2.	Property is free of rats and pests.		
3.	There is sufficient space for family members.		
4.	Necessary household equipment is available and in working order.		
5.	Family members are satisfied and pleased with their home.		
6.	Roads, streets and sidewalks near home are in good condition.		
7.	Neighborhood and/or streets are safe both day and night.		
8.	Home is free of architectural barriers impeding mobility of family members.		
9.	Play and recreational areas for children are available within short walking distance.		
10.	Neighborhood consists mainly of residential dwelling units in good state of repair and upkeep.		
11.	Care of home meets community expectations and is acceptable to neighbors.		
12.	Home is located near transportation, health care and other community resources.		

Additional description of home, household and housekeeping practices and standards._____

_____
_____
_____
_____

I. HEALTH CONDITIONS AND PRACTICES

		Rating	Comments
1.	Meals are served on regular basis and family's diet is well balanced and nutritious.		
2.	Physical health of family members is such that they are able to function satisfactorily in their various roles.		
3.	Appropriate concern is shown about ill health or handicaps and, when needed, health care is promptly sought.		
4.	Medical advice is followed.		
5.	Health care appointments are kept.		
6.	Disease prevention and dental hygiene practices are observed (e.g., immunizations).		

Additional description of family's health condition, problems and practices _____
_____
_____
_____
_____

J. FAMILY'S UTILIZATION OF COMMUNITY RESOURCES

		Rating	Comments
1.	Family is aware of resources and opportunities that are available in community.		
2.	Parents facilitate children's use of community resources.		
3.	Family has positive attitude toward utilization of health agencies and resources.		
4.	Family has positive attitude toward utilization of social agencies and social services.		
5.	Family has positive attitude toward utilization of educational resources and school programs.		
6.	Family has positive attitude toward utilization of religious, spiritual or cultural opportunities and resources.		

		Rating	Comments
7.	If drawn to a particular religious group or body, family feels accepted and welcomed by that group.		
8.	Family utilizes agencies appropriately for improvement of family life or for meeting needs of individual members.		
9.	Family has access to transportation needed for shopping and use of community resources.		
10.	Family members, particularly children, make use of available recreational resources according to age and interest.		
11.	Family members make their views known about needed resources and need for changes in existing community resources.		

Additional description of family's utilization of available community resources._____

_____

_____

_____

K.   <u>FINAL COMMENTS/OBSERVATIONS ON FAMILY'S SOCIAL FUNCTIONING</u>

_____

_____

_____

_____

_____

_____

_____

_____

_____

_____

_____

_____

_____

_____

_____

_____

_____

_____

_____

Questionnaire for Use in the Study of Foster Homes

Introduction

Dear Prospective Foster Parent:

Being a foster parent to a developmentally disabled or handicapped child is a rewarding but demanding task. You are to be commended for taking some first steps in exploring the question of whether or not being a foster parent is for you. In order for you to make a good decision about whether or not to become a foster parent you need to have as much information as possible. In order for us to help you make a good decision, we need to learn about your questions and concerns.

This questionnaire is designed to gather information that will help us focus our visits on important issues and help you to secure the information you need and want. *This is not a test.* Is is simply a tool that will help you learn a bit more about foster parenting and help us learn more about your concerns and questions.

Each handicapped child is different. Like all people, each child has different needs, interests, and problems. In addition, each family has different interests and capabilities. By gathering certain information and finding out about your concerns and interests, we will be in a better position to make decisions that will result in the best arrangement for both foster parents and foster child.

Do your best to answer each question in a way that most accurately expresses your thoughts and feelings. Please note that some of the questions are rather personal. This is not because we want to pry into your personal life. Rather, we must ask such questions because of placement of a child into a foster home is a very serious matter and it is important that we learn of factors that may affect the placement or influence the decision to place a particular child in your specific family situation.

QUESTIONS ARE TO BE ANSWERED INDIVIDUALLY BY THE PROSPECTIVE FOSTER
FATHER AND BY THE PROSPECTIVE FOSTER MOTHER (Each prospective foster
parent is to complete a separate questionnaire.)

Full name_____

Date of birth_____ _____ 19_____ Age in years_____
            month   day   year

Social Security Number_____

Home address (street/route)_____

            (city)_____

Home telephone_____

(If you live on a farm or ranch or your home is somewhat difficult
to find, please give directions to your home.)_____

_____

_____

Work address_____

Work telephone_____

Current marital status (check one)____ married   ____ divorced
                                  ____ separated   ____ widowed
                                  ____ single

----------------------MARRIAGE AND FAMILY-----------------------

Marriage history (check one or explain)

____ I have never been married   ____ now in second marriage
____ now in first marriage   ____ now in third marriage
____ other (explain)_____
     _____

Name of (wife) (husband)_____

If you have been divorced or separated, please describe any
circumstances surrounding your relationship with your former spouse
that might have an effect on a foster child placed in your home
(e.g., visitation of children, physical threats, unpredictable or
unusual behavior, etc.)_____

_____

Below list names and birth dates of all your children (both living and deceased). Use back of page if you do not have enough room for your answer.

name_____ birth date_____

name_____ birth date_____

name_____ birth date_____

name_____ birth date_____

name_____ birth date_____

Which of the above named children are now living with you?_____

_____

Please list the name(s) of those children who have died. Also give cause of and age at death._____

_____

Below list all other persons now living in your home (e.g., grand-parents, relatives, boarders, hired help, etc.). Use back of page if you do not have enough room for your answer.

name_____ birth date or age_____ relationship_____

name_____ birth date or age_____ relationship_____

name_____ birth date or age_____ relationship_____

--------------------EDUCATION AND OCCUPATION--------------------

Education (check highest level attained)

_____grade school   _____some college
_____some high school   _____college degree
_____high school graduate   _____graduate/professional degree
_____other (explain)_____

_____

What is your present occupation?_____

Give name/address of employer or place of business_____

_____

Which applies to your employment status:

_____unemployed, looking for work   _____employed part time
_____homemaker (not employed)   _____unemployed because
_____employed full time   of disability
                                         _____other (explain)___

_____

If employed outside the home, approximately how many hours do you
work each week? _____hours

Please list dates and nature of significant jobs you have held
during past ten years. Use back of page if you do not have enough
room for your answers.

job_____ dates_____ employer_____

job_____ dates_____ employer_____

job_____ dates_____ employer_____

job_____ dates_____ employer_____

If you were to become a foster parent, do you plan to quit a job?
(check one)

_____yes   _____not sure

_____no   _____does not apply; I am not employed

If you were to quit a job as a result of becoming a foster parent,
how much income would you lose?

$_____per week $_____per month   _____question does not apply

Do you drive a car?   _____yes   _____no

Does your job require you to be away from home some nights?

_____yes   _____no   explain_____

-----------------------------HEALTH----------------------------

Please describe any illness, handicap or medical problem that you
have. Explain how it would or would not affect your ability
to care for a foster child._____

_____

_____

Names and addresses of your physicians:

Dr._____ address_____

Dr._____ address_____

Dr._____ address_____

------------------RELIGIOUS/SPIRITUAL BELIEFS------------------

If you belong to a church or formal religious group, please describe or name the denomination._____

_____

How would you describe your religious beliefs? (check one or describe)

_____very strong   _____relatively weak
_____moderately strong   _____have no formal religious beliefs
_____(or explain)_____

_____

If you have reason to believe that your particular religious beliefs and/or personal values and beliefs will have a significant relationship to the type of care, training or discipline you will give a foster child, please explain. In other words, how might your beliefs affect the foster child that comes into your home?_____

_____

_____

_____

--------------------HOBBIES, INTERESTS, ETC.--------------------

Please describe any special interests, hobbies, talent, etc. that you have (e.g., music, hunting, ham radio, sewing, woodworking, etc.).

_____

_____

_____

If you had an extra hundred dollars or some spare time, what would you do with it? In other words, more than anything else, what do you really like to do when you don't have to do something else?

_____

_____

Please list any professional, social, religious or other organizations or groups to which you belong and/or that are important to you._____

_____

In one or two sentences, try to describe the most important reason(s) you are interested in becoming a foster parent to a developmentally disabled child._____

_____

_____

In one or two sentences, describe the main reason(s) why you might be reluctant or fearful about becoming a foster parent to a developmentally disabled child._____

_____

_____

_____

One of the rewarding features of being a foster parent for a handicapped child is that it provides an opportunity for you to acquire new knowledge and skills. This can be stimulating. In the beginning, however, the new ideas and terms can be a bit confusing. Below is a list of terms common to the field of developmental disabilities and foster care. Place a check by those that you do not understand and/or would like explained to you.

____home training of child

____respite care

____seizure disorders (epilepsy)

____speech & language training

____cerebral palsy

____individualized

____habilitation plan (IHP)

____normalization

____special education

____foster home payment

____foster parent training

____hyperactive

____adaptive equipment

____medicaid

____mental retardation

____developmental disabilities

____deinstitutionalization

____behavior modification

____physical therapy

____individual program plan (IPP)

____case manager

____architectural barriers

____foster home license

____foster home study

____others (please specify)____

Individuals who have an interest in becoming a foster parent to a child with handicaps face a big decision and one that deserves a lot of serious thought and discussion. It is not unusual for people to have a mixture of feelings as they struggle with big decisions. Below are some feelings described by foster parents who previously faced the same decision. Place a check by those statements that come close to the feelings you have experienced as you thought about becoming a foster parent.

_____ Basically I feel uncertain. One minute I say yes and the next minute I say no.

_____ I wonder if I will be happier or more satisfied as a foster parent than I am now. Maybe I should leave well enough alone.

_____ What if I try and fail? What will others think of me? I want to do a good job as a foster parent; I don't know if I can.

_____ Will other members of my family (my spouse, my children, etc.) be happier or more satisfied if we become a foster family or will it create problems for them?

_____ I wonder and worry a bit that becoming a foster parent may have a bad affect on my marriage.

_____ Will my friends, in-laws or neighbors accept a foster child--especially if the youngster has problems and handicaps?

_____ The money I will receive for being a foster parent is not much. I wonder if I can afford to become a foster parent.

_____ What if I come to really love the child but find that I just cannot cope with the demands? That would be just like giving up your own child! I don't think I could handle that.

_____ But what if it turns out that I don't or cannot love the child? What if I actually come to hate the child? God, what a thought! What if I lose control and injure the child?

_____ I am aware that there is staff turnover within various agencies and programs. What if I cannot get along with the staff people? That would be a mess!

Please describe any other thoughts or feelings you have had about foster care of handicapped children and perhaps would like to talk or ask about. _____

QUESTIONS MAY BE ANSWERED BY EITHER PROSPECTIVE FOSTER FATHER OR
PROSPECTIVE FOSTER MOTHER (A couple needs to complete only one form.)

What is your current family income (including income from both
husband and wife)?

_____ choose not to answer this   _____ between $10,000 and $14,999
_____ below $3,000 per year   _____ between $15,000 and $19,999
_____ between $3,000 and $4,999   _____ between $20,000 and $24,999
_____ between $4,000 and $9,999   _____ over $25,000

With regard to your current home are you:

_____renting   _____buying   _____other (explain)_____

_____

Do you plan a move within the next year?

_____yes   _____no   _____(or explain)_____

_____

Do you have 24-hour access to a car or transportation?

_____yes   _____no   _____(or explain)_____

_____

In miles and/or minutes, how far is your home from the nearest
general hospital?_____

In miles and/or minutes how far are you from the nearest:

      grade school_____ name of school_____

      high school_____ name of school_____

--------------------PHYSICAL FEATURES OF HOME--------------------

How would you describe your home?   (check one or explain)

_____a single-family dwelling   _____an apartment house
_____a duplex or triplex   _____other (explain)_____
_____mobile home

Please describe any stairways or other physical barriers such as
narrow doorways in or near your home that might affect a child who
cannot walk or has difficulty moving about._____

_____

As they apply to your home, check "yes" or "no" on each of the following descriptions. If necessary, provide further explanation or description.

	yes	no	explain
stairway to basement.			
stairway to second story.			
"child proof" storage for medicines			
"child proof" storage for household chemicals			
unfenced backyard or play area.			
fenced backyard or play area.			
bathtub			
shower.			
only one door to outside.			
two or more doors to outside.			
fireplace built in wall			
free standing fireplace			
indoor bathroom			
bathroom near child's sleeping room			
kitchen			
living room			
separate dining room.			
only one bedroom.			
two bedrooms.			
three bedrooms.			
four or more bedrooms			
attached garage			
wood or coal heating system			
smoke detector.			
fire extinguishers.			
telephone			
separate bed for foster child			
busy street nearby (traffic).			
accumulations of papers or other fire hazards			
sanitary water supply			

Please describe any other physical features in or near your home that may present either a danger or a learning opportunity to a handicapped child (e.g., open ditches, exposed electrical wiring, open water, chemicals, machinery, slippery floors, playgrounds, animals, pets, etc.)_____

_____

_____

_____

_____

Describe where in your home the foster child would have his or her sleeping room.

_____ basement   _____ second floor
_____ first or main floor   _____ other (explain)_____

_____

Describe sleeping arrangement for the foster child. (check one)

_____ will share sleeping room with child of same sex (explain)_____

_____

_____ will share sleeping room with child of opposite sex (explain)_

_____

_____ will share sleeping room with foster parents (explain)_____

_____

_____ will have private sleeping room

_____ other arrangement (explain)_____

_____

Describe any business activity, production or manufacturing conducted within or very near your home._____

_____

Describe any room door locks which, if locked from either the inside or outside, could prevent or slow entrance or exit from the room (e.g., locks on bathrooms, bedrooms, etc.)_____

_____

Below are some of the concerns reported by foster parents caring for developmentally disabled children. Of the following, which would be of greatest concern. Place #1 by the one that concerns you most, #2 by your second choice and #3 by your third choice. Place an X by the one that would concern you least.

_____public misunderstandings about handicapped children and lack of community acceptance of child

_____inadequacies of local school programs for handicapped children

_____lack of needed services and programs in community

_____child's behavior problems

_____frustration with child's slow progress

_____lack of adequate medical or dental care in community

_____problems or conflicts with child's natural parents

_____conflicts with agency staff supervising the foster home placement

_____my inability to meet child's needs

Which four (4) of the following do you think are of greatest importance in being a foster parent to a developmentally disabled or handicapped child? Place #1 by your first choice, #2 by the second most important factor, #3 by your third choice and #4 by your fourth choice. Put an X by the two (2) you believe would be least important in caring for a handicapped child.

_____lots of love and attention

_____guidance and discipline

_____freedom for self expression

_____systematic training and teaching

_____protection from physical danger

_____protection from criticism and teasing

_____religious training

_____good neighborhood

_____encouragement to try new and different things (even if risk is involved)

_____sympathy for handicaps

_____interaction with normal children

_____opportunity to interact with other handicapped children

_____good nutrition

_____wholesome recreation

If there are other factors that you think are important but not found in the list above, please describe here._____

All of us have different capacities and attitudes. We can handle some situations but not others. We may have emotional difficulty dealing with certain problems or handicapping conditions but not others. Please place a check by those problems or handicaps that would be very difficult for you to handle.

_____ child is blind
_____ child is deaf
_____ child cannot walk
_____ child cannot dress self

_____ child cannot wash or bathe self
_____ child lacks bladder control during day

_____ child lacks bowel control (soils)
_____ child wets bed at night
_____ child masturbates or touches sexual parts of body

_____ child is messy at table (spills, uses fingers)
_____ child puts inedibles in mouth and swallows them

_____ child breaks things in house and is destructive
_____ child demands much attention
_____ child does poorly in school

_____ child not liked by others
_____ child rarely smiles or gives affection
_____ child has awkward movements

_____ child needs special diets
_____ child has seizures (epilepsy)
_____ child needs one or more medicine(s) each day

_____ child is in wheelchair
_____ child cannot talk or use simple language
_____ child cannot feed self or use spoon or cup
_____ child hits or abuses self

_____ child hits others
_____ child has temper tantrums
_____ child often yells and screams
_____ child will not follow directions

_____ child is hyperactive
_____ child often sad or pouting
_____ child unusually fearful of others
_____ child often cries or whines

_____ child often touches strangers
_____ child needs to go to doctor frequently
_____ child needs constant supervision (cannot be left alone)

_____ child regurgitates (throws up) food
_____ child drools
_____ child doesn't respond to attention

If you can think of other behaviors or problems that you have reason to believe would be very difficult for you to handle, please describe them here. _____

_____

_____

_____

_____

Which of the following comes closest to describing your personal experience with mentally retarded or handicapped individuals? Check all that apply or describe your experience.

_____ I have had no personal experience with handicapped persons.
_____ My (brother) (sister) was handicapped.
_____ A close friend was handicapped.
_____ I am the parent of a handicapped child.

_____ Although I have known persons who were handicapped I have not had any real personal experience.
_____ I have cared for children (not my own) or adults who were handicapped.
_____ Other. Please give other information that describes your personal experience with persons who have physical or mental handicaps._____

_____

_____

If you were a foster parent, how do you think you would feel about the child's natural parents visiting the child in your home?

_____ I would be opposed to such visits.
_____ I would favor such visits.
_____ Other (explain)_____

_____

If you were a foster parent, how do you think you would feel about a social worker and/or home trainer visiting on a regular basis to see how things were going or to provide training or guidance?

_____ As often as once a year would be O.K.
_____ As often as twice a year would be O.K.
_____ As often as once a month would be O.K.
_____ As often as once a week would be O.K.
_____ Other (please explain)_____

_____

Have you had other children stay overnight with you without their parents? (check one)
_____ no _____ yes

If yes, what was the longest period of time any one child stayed with you? (check one)

_____ one, two or three days and nights
_____ more than three days or up to one week
_____ more than one week or up to one month
_____ more than one month
_____ other (explain)_____

As compared to where you live, where do your parents live? (check one)

_____ in same house   _____ in same state
_____ in same neighborhood   _____ outside of state
_____ in same town/city   _____ other (explain)_____

In miles, how far are your parents from you? _____ miles

How much contact do you have with your parents?

_____ daily   _____ once a year
_____ at least weekly   _____ less than once a year
_____ one to three times a month   _____ other (explain)_____
_____ two to four times a year

_____

Husbands and wives do not always agree on who should do which tasks around the house (e.g., cleaning, repair, shopping, etc.). In your case, how would you describe the degree of agreement on who does what around your home? (check one)

_____ usually agree   _____ disagree more often than
_____ agree more often than   agree
     disagree   _____ usually disagree

Husbands and wives, mothers and fathers, may not always agree on who should carry most responsibility for care of children. Given your present situation, which of the following comes closest to your personal views? (check one)

_____ mother 90% responsibility, father 10% responsibility
_____ mother 75% responsibility, father 25% responsibility
_____ mother 50% responsibility, father 50% responsibility
_____ mother 25% responsibility, father 75% responsibility
_____ mother 10% responsibility, father 90% responsibility

Now, assuming that you were to become foster parents to a handicapped child, thereby acquiring more work and responsibility, which of the following would be your view on the division of responsibility between foster mother and foster father?

_____ mother 90% responsibility, father 10% responsibility
_____ mother 75% responsibility, father 25% responsibility
_____ mother 50% responsibility, father 50% responsibility
_____ mother 25% responsibility, father 75% responsibility
_____ mother 10% responsibility, father 90% responsibility

Which of the following comes closest to describing how you were disciplined as a child? Check <u>all</u> of those that describe your experience.

_____talk things over   _____"chewed out" verbally
_____loss of privileges   _____frequent and severe
_____occasional physical punishment   physical punishment
_____other (describe)_____

_____

How would you describe your childhood? (check one)

_____very happy   _____sometimes troubled
_____usually happy   _____very difficult and troubled

How would you rate <u>your parent's</u> marriage? (check one)

_____very happy   _____sometimes troubled
_____usually happy   _____very difficult and troubled

Taking all things together, how would you describe <u>your marriage</u>? (check one)

_____very happy   _____not as happy as the average
_____happier than the average   _____very unhappy

We all get upset at times. We probably all handle stress in different ways. For example, some of us keep things to ourselves, some of us "blow up." Below are some ways people behave when they are under stress or under pressure. Which comes closest to describing how you usually handle stress.

_____get out of house or away from source of stress

_____pray or engage in spiritual reading

_____talk to friends or neighbors

_____yell and scream for a while

_____take it out on others or punish others

_____talk to mother, father, brother or sister

_____have a few drinks and relax

_____go off by myself and be alone for a while

_____talk to minister or clergyman

_____talk to family doctor or other professional person

_____other (specify) _____

Being a foster parent to a developmentally disabled child can be hard work and quite demanding. Often parents need help to do a good job. Which, if any, of the following types of help or assistance do you think you would need in order to do a good job of foster parenting. Check all that apply.

_____no help would be needed
_____just somebody to talk to once in a while
_____relief or time off (respite care)

_____more help with housework
_____skilled professional guidance and advice
_____special training in how to care for child

_____sharing of responsibility and work with my husband/wife
_____moral support from other foster parents
_____close supervision by a professional

_____other services such as school programs, medical services
_____toys and other special equipment
_____other (If you can think of other types of help you would need or want, please describe here.)_____

_____

_____

Given your thoughts at present, about how long do you think you would like to be a foster parent to a handicapped child? Check one.

_____about 6 months   _____2 to 4 years
_____about 1 year   _____4 to 8 years
_____about 2 years   _____as long as child needs a home

Functional Knowledge and Skill Categories

(Florida Human Service Task Bank*)

KNOWLEDGE OF SOCIOLOGICAL THEORY AND CONCEPTS

Knowledge of concepts of role, class, culture, disengagement.

Knowledge of concepts of family and kinship systems.

Knowledge of concepts of social systems, social institutions and social control.

Knowledge of concepts of organizational behavior (how the agency works).

Knowledge of concepts of social learning and social interaction.

Knowledge of concepts of group dynamics and group process.

Knowledge of concepts of special group behaviors, e.g. professions, communities, minorities, the disadvantaged.

Knowledge of the implications of lack of provision of services for consumers.

KNOWLEDGE OF THE HUMAN SERVICE FIELD

Knowledge of the history and scope of the field and theories underlying various programs (prevention, rehabilitation, income maintenance).

Knowledge of a range of specific agencies—their legal, fiscal and administrative structures, their client groups, eligibility requirements, systems of serving, scope of activities and settings.

Knowledge of the roles and functions of specialized community resource persons (clergymen, school counselors, marriage counselors, nurses, doctors and lawyers).

Knowledge of emerging social welfare trends (pending changes, new organizational and delivery models).

Knowledge of community (town, county, city) structure and process (industry, business, politics, government, public administration, health and welfare agencies).

Knowledge of social indicators of community process and problems.

Knowledge of the major professions (social work, law, teaching, psychology, psychiatry, public health, rehabilitation, etc.).

---

* By permission of the State University System of Florida, 107 West Gaines Street, Tallahassee, Florida.

KNOWLEDGE OF PERSONALITY THEORY AND FUNCTIONS

Knowledge of concepts of personality growth and development from infancy to maturity to old age.

Knowledge of the common personality theories, i.e. the unconscious, common psychoanalytic concepts, ego psychology, learning theory, etc.

Knowledge of common personality patterns and behaviors (passivity, aggressiveness, compulsiveness, authoritarianism).

KNOWLEDGE OF ABNORMAL PSYCHOLOGY

Knowledge of the behavior descriptions, developmental patterns and basic psychodynamics of the major psychoses, neuroses, personality disorders and psychosomatic disorders.

Knowledge of the psychopathological conditions affecting children, adolescents, young and middle life adults and the aged.

Knowledge of the behaviors, etiology and dynamics of special problems such as mental retardation, sex problems, and alcohol and drug abuse.

KNOWLEDGE OF THE CONCEPTUAL BASIS FOR VARIOUS MODELS OF INTERVENTION

Knowledge of the concepts and theoretical basis of treatment, prevention, rehabilitation, support, limited disability, and social competence.

Knowledge of the status of functioning versus pathology.

Knowledge of the concepts of positive social functioning, anticipatory guidance, and intervention.

KNOWLEDGE OF METHODS OF INTERVENTION

Knowledge of physical methods such as medications (tranquilizers, anticonvulsants) or hospital care.

Knowledge of the principles of counseling and case work.

Knowledge of group treatment methods.

Knowledge of educational methods (teaching, coaching, behavior modification, etc.).

Knowledge of behavioral models, therapeutic use of self, group process, group organization and directed social groups.

Knowledge of community intervention, consultation, community planning, public education, legislative and public administrative process.

KNOWLEDGE OF DATA GATHERING TECHNIQUES AND EVALUATION PROCEDURES

Knowledge of the purposes of data and records (archival, legal, communications, program planning and evaluation, social history, including issues of confidentiality).

Knowledge of special studies (uses and implications).

Knowledge of simple questionnaires and community surveys and how to design and use them.

Knowledge of impact versus process data and relating data to goals and objectives.

Knowledge of data monitoring and processing techniques (uses of indices, card files, simple statistical concepts, etc.).

Knowledge of how to analyze and interpret information and data.

KNOWLEDGE OF SELF

Knowledge of one's own abilities, personality, values, needs and motivations (the ability to assume an objective posture).

Knowledge and acceptance of one's limitations, hang-ups, reaction patterns.

KNOWLEDGE OF HUMAN DEVELOPMENT AND FUNCTIONING

Knowledge of normal physiology, endocrinology and drives.

Knowledge of human sexual development and behavior.

KNOWLEDGE OF CONTEMPORARY EVENTS, ISSUES AND PROBLEMS RELEVANT TO SOCIAL WELFARE

Knowledge of state, local, and federal laws and actions specific to social welfare.

Knowledge of regulations, court decisions and administrative issues and actions related to the human service field.

Knowledge of relevant educational and professional issues.

Knowledge of social action movements.

KNOWLEDGE OF LEARNING THEORY AND INSTRUCTIONAL METHODS

Knowledge of components of learning (knowledge, skills, values).

Knowledge of learning theory, reinforcement and motivation.

Knowledge of experiential learning methods.

Knowledge of available learning resources (local community colleges, technical schools, extension services).

KNOWLEDGE OF PUBLIC INFORMATION AND THE MEDIA

Knowledge of what is of public interest, elements of news, human interest approaches.

Knowledge of how the major media work (newspapers, radio, television, contact points and persons).

SKILL IN INTERVIEWING NORMAL AND DISABLED PERSONS

Skill in talking comfortably, productively and effectively with a wide range of advantaged and disadvantaged persons.

Skill in listening, obtaining information, understanding the feeling tones of what people say.

Skill in giving and interpreting information and appropriately responding to the feeling, tones and reactions of people.

Skill in sensing the impact of one's self on others and responding appropriately.

Skill in determining areas in which one cannot relate.

SKILL IN OBSERVING AND RECORDING

Skill in observing behavior, and social and physical characteristics of people and settings.

Skill in using ordinary forms to record observations and other information.

Skill in recording observations and interview data in a simple, descriptive style.

Skill in recording subjective evaluations of an interview, activity or document.

SKILLS IN INTERPERSONAL RELATIONS

Skill in establishing a supportive, helping relationship with a consumer.

Skill in establishing rapport and trust (credibility).

Skill in helping a person interpret his expectations realistically.

Skill in dealing with other professionals in various role relationships.

Skill in relating to other levels of workers in consulting relationship.

SKILL IN WORKING WITH GROUPS

Skill in organizing, developing and leading groups.

Skill in group counseling (giving information, exploring alternatives, teaching) to effect behavioral change.

Skill in group work.

Skill in group therapy and family counseling.

SKILL IN BEHAVIOR CHANGING AND PROMOTING INDIVIDUAL GROWTH

Skill in coaching for new behavior patterns (persuading, practicing, supporting).

Skill in counseling persons to behavior adjustment patterns (helping to explore alternatives, asking questions, etc.).

Skill in applying treatment modalities (casework, psychotherapy, behavior modification, etc.).

Skill in judging ability of individuals to cope for themselves and supporting them to do so.

Skill in helping persons to overcome stigmas and resistances.

SKILL IN INSTRUCTIONAL METHODS

Skill in teaching living skills and knowledge to individuals (budgeting, home management, grooming, etc.).

Skill in teaching small groups. (This includes use of reinforcement, common visual aids, simulations and other instructional skills.)

Skill in teaching other staff persons.

Skill in providing anticipatory guidance to persons to help them avoid or minimize stresses and disability.

SKILL IN THE EXERCISE OF AUTHORITY

Skill in being honest and firm and yet supportive when exercising control functions.

SKILL IN CONSULTATION

Skill in consulting with colleagues about individuals and problems (establishing role of consultant, clarifying the problem, helping the consultee to arrive at solutions).

Skill in informal consultation (helping workers and agencies become aware of and deal with problems).

Skill in using consultation and technical assistance.

SKILL IN COMMUNITY PROCESS

Skill in establishing and using coalitions and transitory federations of community persons and groups.

Skill in participating as a member of a board or committee, using rules of order.

Skill in activating community resources on behalf of persons or programs, manipulating policies and procedures, identifying key leaders and control groups.

Skill in personal negotiation and protocol with persons and agencies.

SKILL IN SOCIAL WELFARE PROBLEM SOLVING

Skill in using a critical approach in evaluating the problems of a family or individual, setting an action plan after considering alternatives, implementing action and evaluating the results.

Skill in critically evaluating the problems of a group, agency or community, weighing alternatives and consequences, setting a plan, implementing action and evaluating the results.

SKILL IN GATHERING AND USING DATA

Skill in determining what data is needed, gathering service data, analyzing, abstracting and using such data.

Skill in gathering statistical service data, organizing it into records or tables, analyzing it and abstracting it as needed for program planning and evaluation.

Skill in organizing information into logical and clear reports for both written and oral presentation. (This includes both reports of clinical information about individuals and information about programs or community problems.)

Skill in varying reports appropriately for professionals or lay persons.

Skill in writing program proposals and grant requests.

SKILL IN UTILIZING COMMUNITY RESOURCES

Skill in working with agency representatives to mobilize their services on behalf of consumers.

Skill in bargaining and negotiating (redefining problems, persuading, knowing and quoting laws, rules, regulations, keeping the person from giving a firm "no," identifying and using self interest of groups and individuals).

Skill in mobilizing community resources to serve groups and classes of persons, e.g. the aged, the retarded.

Skill in mobilizing community opinion and support.

SKILL IN ADVOCACY

Skill in obtaining exceptions to rules, policies, practices for individuals (pleading, persuading, redefining the problem, being responsibly aggressive, and threatening if necessary).

Skill in bringing about changes in policies and procedures to obtain services for persons and client groups who would otherwise be excluded.

Skill in using legal processes.

Skill in political and public administrative process (effecting policy, writing to and talking to political leaders, developing and modifying rules and regulations, testifying in committees and hearings).

Skill in productive confrontation.

SKILL IN FIRST LEVEL PHYSICAL DIAGNOSIS

Skill in recognizing and evaluating the signs and symptoms of common illness (heart disease, diabetes, cancer, epilepsy, arthritis, drug abuse, delirium tremens, etc.).

Skill in making appropriate referrals or counseling individuals and families when signs or symptoms present themselves. (This involves avoiding inappropriate and unnecessary referrals.)

SKILLS IN DAILY LIVING

Skill in ordinary social adaptive functions, e.g. grooming, sense of time, sense of responsibility. (This implies that the worker should have the competence to provide a role model for individuals.)

Skill in some of the more common special living functions (personal budgeting, home management, diet management, etc.).

SKILL IN ADMINISTRATION

Skill in determining goals and objectives.

Skill in creating and modifying organizations.

Skill in budget and resource management.

Skill in working with consumers in service planning and program development.

SKILL IN MANAGEMENT

Skill in directing people.

Skill in supervising and developing staff (not just monitoring).

Skill in evaluating and enhancing performance.

Skill in organizational communications.

Skill in leadership (creative and divergent thinking, implementing action, anticipating the future).

Skill in staffing and personnel management.

Skill in coordinating work.

Skill in performing routine clerical duties.

Skill in leaving on-the-job functions.

SKILL IN STATISTICAL RESEARCH AND EVALUATION

Skill in deciding what data are needed and appropriate data gathering techniques.

Skill in data gathering, reduction, analysis and interpretation. [Pp. 51-58]

Foster Home Study: Summary of Selected Information

Type of Home

This study concerns the specialized foster home (e.g., foster child with a developmental disability and/or physical handicap).

Codes

The following codes or abbreviations may be used in the report:

DOB = date of birth
NA = not applicable
MIS = information is missing
      or was not obtained
FF = foster father
FM = foster mother
NC = natural child
AC = adopted child

FC = foster child
SC = step child
HH = hired help living in
     household
GF = grandfather
GM = grandmother
OR = other relative

Information on Study Process

Date home study began_____

Date study completed_____

Number and nature of contacts with foster parents used to gather
data for report_____

Number and nature of contacts with references or other collateral
sources of information_____
_____

Worker completing home study_____

Describe how FF/FM learned of need for foster homes_____
_____

326

Identifying Data

Full name of FF _____
Full name of FM _____
Home address (st./rt.) _____
        (city) _____ (zip) _____ (home phone) _____
Directions to home _____
_____

FF place of work _____   FM place of work _____
FF work phone _____   FM work phone _____
Name of FF employer _____   Name of FM employer _____
FF age in years _____   FM age in years _____
FF DOB _____   FM DOB _____
FF place of birth _____   FM place of birth _____
FF Social Security No. _____   FM Social Security No. _____
FF citizenship _____   FM citizenship _____

Applicant's Motivation/
Views of Foster Care

FF motivation for wanting to be   FM motivation for wanting to be
a foster parent _____   a foster parent _____
_____   _____
_____   _____
_____   _____
_____   _____

Describe degree to which decision to become foster home is a joint
decision by both FF and FM _____
_____
_____
_____
_____

Foster child characteristics   Foster child characteristics
that would be unacceptable   that would be unacceptable
to FF _____   to FM _____
_____   _____
_____   _____
_____   _____

Foster child characteristics   Foster child characteristics
desired by FF _____   desired by FM _____
_____   _____
_____   _____
_____   _____

Describe explanation given to foster parents regarding foster care, payment, standards, supervision, etc._____

_____

_____

_____

Describe attitudes/views of FF and FM regarding interaction with and visits by FC's natural parents/relatives_____

_____

_____

_____

Household and Family Composition

Below name all individuals (except FF and FM) now living in the household. Also, give birthdate or age and assign a descriptive code to each or explain.

Name	DOB	Age in Years	Code or Explain Relationship to FF and FM
(1)			
(2)			
(3)			
(4)			
(5)			
(6)			
(7)			
(8)			
(9)			

Below list children reared by FM or FF who are no longer living in household or are deceased.

Name	DOB	Age in Years	Code or Explain Relationship to FF and FM
(1)			
(2)			
(3)			
(4)			
(5)			
(6)			

Description of FF and FM

Marital history of FF
_____never married
_____now in first
    marriage
_____other, explain_____

_____

_____

Marital history of FM
_____never married
_____now in first
    marriage
_____other, explain_____

_____

_____

Education of FF_____   Education of FM_____

_____   _____
_____   _____

Ethnicity/race of FF_____   Ethnicity/race of FM_____

Current occupation of FF_____   Current occupation of FM_____

_____   _____

Name and address of current   Name and address of current
employer or explain_____   employer or explain_____

_____   _____
_____   _____

Employment history of FF_____   Employment history of FM_____

_____   _____
_____   _____
_____   _____

Religion of FF and comments on   Religion of FM and comments on
his religious beliefs and   her religious beliefs and
relationship to motivation/   relationship to motivation/
capacity for foster parenting   capacity for foster parenting

_____   _____
_____   _____
_____   _____

Health of FF. Describe how   Health of FM. Describe how
physical condition, handicaps   physical condition, handicaps
or medical problems would   or medical problems would
affect foster parenting_____   affect foster parenting_____

_____   _____
_____   _____
_____   _____

Name of physicians who care   Name of physicians who care
for FF_____   for FM_____

_____   _____
_____   _____

Hobbies, interests, recreation   Hobbies, interests, recreation
of FF_____   of FM_____

_____   _____
_____   _____
_____   _____

Description of FF with regard to personality or habitual modes of behavior in relation to capacity for foster parenting_____

_____
_____
_____

Description of FM with regard to personality or habitual modes of behavior in relation to capacity for foster parenting_____

_____
_____
_____

Significant background or life experience of FF as it relates to capacity for parenting of child, especially one with special needs_____

_____
_____
_____
_____

Significant background or life experience of FM as it relates to capacity for parenting of child, especially one with special needs_____

_____
_____
_____
_____

Willingness of FF to receive agency supervision/training____

_____
_____

Willingness of FM to receive agency supervision/training____

_____
_____

Willingness/capacity of FF to engage in systematic training of FC_____

_____
_____

Willingness/capacity of FM to engage in systematic training of FC_____

_____
_____

Experience of FF with handicapped children/adults (include special training received)____

_____
_____

Experience of FM with handicapped children/adults (include special training received)____

_____
_____

Experience of FF with normal children_____

_____
_____

Experience of FM with normal children_____

_____
_____

Capacity of FF to handle stress and demands of handicapped FC

_____
_____

Capacity of FM to handle stress and demands of handicapped FC

_____
_____

Family Environment

Describe apparent strength of marriage, parent-child and family
relationships as they relate to capacity to cope with demands of
handicapped FC_____
_____
_____
_____

Describe any special experiences, abilities, training, interests,
problems or characteristics of other children in family or others
living in household that may affect--positively or negatively--a
foster child placed in this home._____
_____
_____
_____
_____

Describe positive and negative attitudes and reactions of other
children (NC, FC, etc.) toward possibility of a FC coming into
home._____
_____
_____

Describe positive and negative attitudes and reactions of others
in household (GF, GM, OR, HH, etc.) toward possibility of a FC
coming into home._____
_____
_____
_____

Description of family income and financial resources._____
_____
_____

Describe or present any additional information/observations
regarding the FM, FF, other children, marital or family dynamics
that may affect the parenting, care and training of a foster child.
_____
_____
_____
_____
_____
_____
_____
_____

Community Environment

Describe transportation resources available to FC._____

_____

In miles/minutes, distance from foster home to:
      special ed. program____   name of school_____
      grade school_____   name of school_____
      high school_____   name of school_____
      general hospital_____   name of hospital_____

Describe professional resources of community available to assist
FC and foster parents (e.g., respite care, home training, case
management, physicians, etc.)_____

_____
_____
_____

Description of neighborhood/community in which prospective foster
parents live, especially those features creating opportunities for
or presenting problems to handicapped FC._____

_____
_____
_____

Physical Features of House

Describe basic physical characteristics of house (number of rooms,
structure, etc.), especially features that might be an
architectural barrier (narrow doors, stairways)._____

_____
_____
_____

Other physical features in or near home (e.g., neighborhood) that
may present either a danger or a learning opportunity to a handicapped child (e.g., open ditches, exposed electrical wiring, open
water, chemicals, machinery, slippery floors, playgrounds, animals,
pets, etc.)_____

_____
_____

Describe sleeping arrangement for FC._____

_____

Below is a checklist that can be used to describe the physical characteristics of the house and immediate physical environment in which the foster child will be living. Check (√) yes or no on each characteristic. Each no answer may warrant an explanation.

	yes	no	explain/ comment
"safe" stairway (if any)			
"child proof" storage for medicines			
"child proof" storage for household chemicals			
safe play area in house			
safe play area out of doors			
safe fireplace/heating system			
indoor toilet			
telephone			
fire extinguishers			
smoke detector			
free of fire hazards			
sanitary water supply			
separate bed for FC			
adequate lighting			
proper ventilation			
sanitary bath and toilet facilities			
adequate food storage			
adequate/safe play materials--toys			
first aid supplies			
storage for FC clothing			
storage for FC toilet articles			

References

Identify references used and summarize their observations regarding applicants' motivation/capacity. Also their observations regarding neighborhood/community acceptance by and opportunities for handicapped child should be noted. _____
_____
_____
_____
_____
_____
_____
_____

Evaluation

Worker's overall evaluation of applicant's motivation and capacities to parent a foster child and to work cooperatively with agency personnel and other professionals. Also, provide information on type of foster child the family could parent._____

_____
_____
_____
_____
_____
_____
_____
_____
_____

Recommendation

Provide specific recommendation for acceptance or rejection of this family as a foster home. If rejection, give specific reasons.

_____
_____
_____
_____
_____

References

Abbott, Grace. *The Child and the State* (Vol. II). Chicago: University of Chicago Press, 1938.

Aldridge, Martha; Cautley, Patricia; and Lichstein, Diane. *Guidelines for Placement Workers*. Madison, Wisconsin: Center for Social Service, University of Wisconsin Extension, 1974.

American Academy of Child Psychiatry. *Supportive Care, Custody, Placement and Adoption of American Indian Children*. Washington, D. C.: American Academy of Child Psychiatry, 1977.

American Public Welfare Association. *Standards for Foster Family Services Systems*. Washington, D. C.: American Public Welfare Association, March, 1975.

Arkava, Morton. *Behavior Modification: A Procedural Guide for Social Workers*. Missoula: University of Montana, 1974.

———. *Foster Care for Developmentally Disabled Children: A Functional Analysis*. Boise, Idaho: Bureau of Social Services, State Department of Health and Welfare, Aug., 1977.

Arzin, Nathan, and Foxx, Richard. *Toilet Training in Less than a Day*. New York: Simon and Schuster, 1974.

Association on American Indian Affairs, Inc. *Indian Family Defense*, No. 2, Summer, 1974. New York: Association on American Indian Affairs, Inc.

Axinn, Jane, and Levin, Herman. *Social Welfare: A History of the American Response to Need*. New York: Harper and Row, 1975.

Axline, Virginia. *Play Therapy*. Boston: Houghton Mifflin Co., 1947.

Bahr, Howard; Chadwick, Bruce; and Day, Robert (Eds.). *Native Americans Today: Sociological Perspectives*. New York: Harper and Row, 1972.

Baldwin, Victor; Fredricks, H. D.; and Brodsky, Gerry. *Isn't It Time He Outgrew This or A Training Program for Parents of Retarded Children*. Springfield, Illinois: Charles C Thomas, Publisher, 1973.

Bast, David, and Crass, Kenneth. *Telling the Public Welfare Story: A Casebook of Five Wisconsin Public Information Programs*. Madison, Wisconsin: Center for Social Service, University of Wisconsin-Extension, 1977.

Becker, Wesley. *Parents Are Teachers: A Child Management Program*. Champaign, Illinois: Research Press, 1971.

Becker, Wesley, and Becker, Janis. *Successful Parenthood*. Chicago: Follett Publishing Co., 1974.

Bell, Cynthia. "Legal Consultation for Child Welfare Workers." *Public Welfare* (Summer 1975), 33(3):33-40.

Bell, Cynthia, and Mlyniec, Wallace. "Preparing for a Neglect Proceeding: A Guide for the Social Worker." *Public Welfare* (Fall 1974), 26-37.

Bennett, Charlene, and Nofen, Carol. "The Use of Contracting with Neglectful or Abusing Families." Project PACER, 1975. (Mimeo)

Bertsche, Anne, and Horejsi, Charles. "Coordination of Client Services: An Instructional Module for the Social Work Educator," paper presented at the 1978 Annual Program Meeting of the Council on Social Work Education, New Orleans, Louisiana, February 26-March 1, 1978.

Birch, Herbert; Chess, Stella; and Thomas, Alexander. *Your Child Is a Person.* New York: Simon and Shuster, 1971.

Bliss, Edwin. *Getting Things Done: The ABC's of Time Management.* New York: Charles Scribner and Sons, 1976.

Bonlender, Mary. *Someone Needs Someone Special Like You: Adolescent Foster Care Recruitment Program.* St. Cloud, Minnesota: Sherburne County Social Services, 1977.

Bowlby, John. *Separation Anxiety: A Critical Review of the Literature.* New York: Child Welfare League of America, 1962.

Brieland, Donald, and Lemmon, John. *Social Work and the Law.* St. Paul, Minnesota: West Publishing Co., 1977.

Brown, Gordon. "What Was Done—And What Was Found." In Gordon Brown (Ed.), *The Multi-Problem Dilemma.* Metuchen, New Jersey: The Scarecrow Press, 1968.

Bryce, Marvin, and Ryan, Michael. "Intensive In-Home Treatment: An Alternative to Out-of-Home Placement," paper presented at the Fifth Biennial National Association of Social Workers Professional Symposium, San Diego, California, November 19-22, 1977.

Buckley, Walter. *Sociology and Modern Systems Theory.* Englewood Cliffs, New Jersey: Prentice-Hall, Inc., 1967.

Cautley, Patricia, and Aldridge, Martha. "Predicting Success for New Foster Parents." *Social Work,* January, 1975, *20*(1):48-53.

Cautley, Patricia, and Lichstein, Diane. *The Selection of Foster Parents: Manual for Homefinders.* Madison: University of Wisconsin Extension, 1974.

Center for Social Research and Development. *Indian Child Welfare: A State-of-the-Field Study.* Denver, Colorado: Denver Research Institute, University of Denver, July, 1976.

Center for Social Research and Development. *Legal and Jurisdictional Problems in the Delivery of S.R.S. Child Welfare Services on Indian Reservations.* Denver, Colorado: Denver Research Institute, University of Denver, October, 1975.

Chestang, Leon, and Heymann, Irmgard. "Preparing Older Children for Adoption." *Public Welfare* (Winter 1976), 35-40.

Children's Rights Report (Vol. 1, No. 6). New York: Juvenile Rights Project of the American Civil Liberties Union Foundation, March, 1977.

Child Welfare League of America. "CWLA Intake Interview Guide." New York: Child Welfare League of America, August, 1972; also in Phillips,

Michael; Haring, Barbara; and Shyne, Ann. *A Model for Intake Decisions in Child Welfare*. New York: Child Welfare League of America, 1972.

——. *Standards for Child Protective Service* (Rev. ed.). New York: Child Welfare League of America, 1973.

——. 1975 Directory of Member Agencies. New York: Child Welfare League of America, 1975(a).

——. *Standards for Foster Family Service* (Rev. ed.). New York: Child Welfare League of America, 1975(b).

The City of New York. *Policy Statement on Adoption*. New York: Human Resources Administration, Department of Social Services, Special Services for Children, February 28, 1978.

Claburn, W. Eugene; Magura, Stephen; and Resnick, William. "Periodic Review of Foster Care: A Brief National Assessment." *Child Welfare*, June 1976, *LV*(6):395-404.

Cohen, Nathan. *Social Work in the American Tradition*. New York: Holt, Rinehart and Winston, 1958.

Coll, Blanche. *Perspectives in Public Welfare: A History*. Washington, D. C.: U. S. Government Printing Office, 1969.

Collins, Alice. *The Lonely and Afraid: Counseling the Hard to Reach*. Indianapolis: Western Publishing Company, 1969.

Compton, Beulah, and Galaway, Burt. *Social Work Processes*. Homewood, Illinois: *The Dorsey Press*, 1975.

Corsini, Raymond, and Painter, Genevieve. *The Practical Parent: ABC's of Child Discipline*. New York: Harper and Row, 1975.

Creer, Thomas, and Christian, Walter. *Chronically Ill and Handicapped Children*. Champaign, Illinois: Research Press, 1976.

Cross, Crispin (Ed.). *Interviewing and Communication in Social Work*. London: Routledge and Kegan Paul, 1974.

Culley, James; Healy, Denis; Settles, Barbara; and VanName, Judith. "Public Payments for Foster Care." *Social Work*, May, 1977, *22*(3):219-223.

Cummins, David. "The Assessment Procedure." In Morton Arkava and E. Clifford Brennen (Eds.), *Competency-Based Education for Social Work*. New York: Council on Social Work Education, 1976.

Darbonne, Allen. "Crisis: A Review of Theory, Practice and Research." In Joel Fischer (Ed.), *Interpersonal Helping: Emerging Approaches to Social Work Practice*. Springfield, Illinois: Charles C Thomas, 1973.

Della-Piana, Gabriel. *How to Talk with Children (and Other People)*. New York: John Wiley and Sons, Ltd., 1973.

Derek, Jehu; Hardiker, Pauline; Yelloly, Margaret; and Shaw, Martin. *Behavior Modification in Social Work*. New York: John Wiley and Sons, Ltd., 1972.

DeRisi, William, and Butz, George. *Writing Behavioral Contracts*. Champaign, Illinois: Research Press, 1975.

Didier, Maureen. "What Separation Means to a Foster Child." In Bernodette Ambrose (Ed.), *Child Abuse and Neglect: Social Services Reader II*. Albany, New York: School of Social Welfare, State University of New York at Albany, 1977.

Dinkmeyer, Don, and McKay, Gary. *Parents' Handbook*. Circle Pines, Minnesota: American Guidance Service, Inc., 1976.

Dodson, Fitzhugh. *How to Parent*. New York: Signet Books, 1971.

Downs, Glen, and Volkman, John. *A Concise Legal Study of Foster Care in the United States*. Portland, Oregon: Regional Research Institute for Human Services, Portland State University, 1977.

Dreikurs, Rudolph. *Children: The Challenge*. New York: Hawthorn Books, Inc., 1964.

Dreikurs, Rudolph; Gould, Shirley; and Corsini, Raymond. *Family Council*. Chicago: Henry Regnery Co., 1974.

Edwards, E. Daniel, and Edwards, Margie. "American Indians." In John Turner (Ed.), *Encyclopedia of Social Work* (Vol. II). New York: National Association of Social Workers, 1977, 946-952.

Emlen, Arthur. "What Does It Take to Implement Permanency Planning." *Case Record: Permanent Planning Project Bulletin*, August, 1977, *1*(3):1.

Emlen, Arthur; Lahti, Janet; Downs, Glen; McKay, Alec; and Downs, Susan. *Overcoming Barriers to Planning for Children in Foster Care*. Portland, Oregon: Regional Research Institute for Human Services, Portland State University, 1977.

Fanshel, David. *Far from the Reservation—The Transracial Adoption of American Indian Children*. Metuchen, New Jersey: The Scarecrow Press, Inc., 1972.

————. "Parent Visiting of Children in Foster Care: Key to Discharge." *Social Service Review*, December, 1975, *49*:493-514.

Fanshel, David, and Grundy, John. *First Analysis from a Management Information Service in New York City*. New York: Child Welfare Information Services, Inc., 1975.

Fanshel, David, and Shinn, Eugene. *Children in Foster Care: A Longitudinal Investigation*. New York: Columbia University Press, 1978.

Farris, Charles, and Farris, Lorene. "Indian Children. The Struggle for Survival." *Social Work*, September, 1976, *21*(5):386-389.

Feldman, Frances, and Scherz, Frances. *Family Social Welfare: Helping Troubled Families*. New York: Atherton Books, 1967.

Felker, Evelyn. *Foster Parenting Young Children: Guidelines from a Foster Parent*. New York: Child Welfare League of America, 1974.

Ferleger, Beatrice, and Cotter, Mary Jane (Eds.). *Children, Families and Foster Care: New Insights from Research in New York City*. New York: Community Council of Greater New York, December, 1976.

Festinger, Trudy. "The Impact of the New York Court Review of Children in Foster Care: A Follow-up Report." *Child Welfare,* September-October, 1976, *LV*(8):515-544.

Findling, Joseph. *Legal Aspects of Fostering and Preparing for the Court Hearing.* Ypsilanti, Michigan: Foster Parent Training Project, Eastern Michigan University, 1977.

Fischer, Joel. *Effective Casework Practice: An Eclectic Approach.* New York: McGraw-Hill Book Co., 1978.

Fischer, Joel (Ed.). *Interpersonal Helping: Emerging Approaches for Social Work Practice.* Springfield, Illinois: Charles C Thomas, Publisher, 1973.

Fischer, Joel, and Gochros, Harvey. *Planned Behavior Change: Behavior Modification in Social Work.* New York: Free Press, 1975.

Fleischmann, David (Ed.). *The Parents' Handbook: A Guide for Parents of Children in Foster Care.* New York: Department of Social Services, City of New York, January, 1977.

Gambrill, Eileen. *Behavior Modification: Handbook of Assessment, Intervention and Evaluation.* San Francisco: Jossey-Bass, Inc., 1977.

Garrett, Beatrice. "Foster Care: America's Lost Children." *Public Welfare* (Summer, 1977), *35*(3):4-8.

Geiser, Robert L. *The Illusion of Caring: Children in Foster Care.* Boston: Beacon Press, 1973.

Geismar, Ludwig. *Preventive Intervention in Social Work.* Metuchen, New Jersey: The Scarecrow Press, 1969.

———. *Family and Community Functioning: A Manual of Measurement for Social Work Practice and Policy.* Metuchen, New Jersey: The Scarecrow Press, 1971.

———. *Early Supports for Family Life: A Social Work Experiment.* Metuchen, New Jersey: The Scarecrow Press, 1972(a).

———. "Thirteen Evaluative Studies." In Edward Mullen, James Dumpson and Associates (Eds.), *Evaluation of Social Intervention.* San Francisco: Jossey-Bass, Inc., 1972(b).

Ginott, Haim. *Between Parent and Child.* New York: Macmillan, 1965.

———. *Between Parent and Teenager.* New York: Macmillan, 1969.

Glasser, Paul, and Glasser, Lois. *Families in Crisis.* New York: Harper and Row, 1970.

Golan, Naomi. "Crisis Theory." In Francis Turner (Ed.), *Social Work Treatment.* New York: The Free Press, 1974.

Goldfried, Marvin, and Davidson, Gerald. *Clinical Behavior Therapy.* New York: Holt, Rinehart and Winston, 1976.

Goldstein, Arnold. *Structured Learning Therapy: Toward a Psychotherapy for the Poor.* New York: Academic Press, 1973.

Goldstein, Howard. *Social Work Practice: A Unitary Approach.* Columbia: University of South Carolina Press, 1973.

Goldstein, Joseph; Freud, Anna; and Solnit, Albert. *Beyond the Best Interests of the Child.* New York: The Free Press, 1973.

Goodluck, Charlotte Tsoi. "Indian Adoption Program: An Ethnic Approach to Child Welfare," paper presented at the 54th Annual Meeting of the American Orthopsychiatric Association, New York, New York, April 14, 1977.

Good Tracks, Jimm G. "Native American Non-interference." *Social Work,* November, 1973, *18*(6):30-34.

Gordon, Thomas. *Parent Effectiveness Training.* New York: Peter H. Wyden, Inc., 1970.

Gordon, William E. "Basic Constructs for an Integrative and Generative Conception of Social Work." In Gordon Hearn (Ed.), *The General Systems Approach: Contributions Toward an Holistic Conception of Social Work.* New York: Council on Social Work Education, 1969.

Gottman, John, and Leiblum, Sandra. *How to Do Psychotherapy: A Manual for Beginners.* New York: Holt, Rinehart and Winston, 1974.

Greeley, Andrew. "White Ethnics." In John Turner (Ed.), *Encyclopedia of Social Work* (Vol. II). New York: National Association of Social Workers, 1977, 979-984.

Gruber, Alan. *Children in Foster Care.* New York: Human Sciences Press, 1977.

Haley, Jay. *Problem Solving Therapy.* San Francisco: Jossey-Bass Inc., 1976.

Harris, Linda Hall. *Support Skills for Direct Service Workers: Managing Your Job.* Minneapolis: Minnesota Resource Center for Social Work Education, 1976.

Hartman, Ann. "The Genogram: The Family System Through Time." Ann Arbor: University of Michigan School of Social Work, December, 1976. (Unpublished class handout)

Hearn, Gordon. "The Progress Toward an Holistic Conception of Social work." In Gordon Hearn (Ed.), *The General Systems Approach: Contributions Toward an Holistic Conception of Social Work.* New York: Council on Social Work Education, 1969.

Heimler, Eugene. *Heimler Scale of Social Functioning.* Calgary: University of Calgary, School of Social Welfare, Centre of Social Functioning, 1967.

Hooker, Carol. "Learned Helplessness." *Social Work,* May, 1976, *21*(3): 194-198.

Horejsi, Charles, and Gallacher, Kathleen. "Guidelines for Screening Foster Homes for Developmentally Disabled Children." Missoula, Montana: University of Montana, 1977. (Mimeo)

Horner, William, and Morris, Lynne. "Social Terms for Social Assessment," paper presented at the Big Sky Summer Symposium, Big Sky, Montana, August, 1977.

Jarrett, Janeil. "Handbook for Natural Parents of Children in Foster Care." Athens, Georgia: Department of Human Services, 1977(a). (Mimeo)

————. "Some Do's and Don'ts for Foster Parents." Atlanta, Georgia: Department of Human Resources, 1977(b). (Mimeo)

Johnston, Ed. *Parent Counsellor Education Resource Material.* Calgary: Alberta Parent Counsellor's Program, Alberta Social Services and Community Health, Child Welfare Branch, 1976.

Joint Commission on Accreditation of Hospitals. *Standards for Community Agencies.* Chicago: Joint Commission on Accreditation of Hospitals, 1973.

Jones, Mary Ann; Neuman, Renee; and Shyne, Ann. *A Second Chance for Families—Evaluation of a Program to Reduce Foster Care.* New York: Child Welfare League of America, 1976.

Kadushin, Alfred. *The Social Work Interview.* New York: Columbia University Press, 1972.

————. *Child Welfare Services* (2nd ed.). New York: Macmillan, 1974(a).

————. "Beyond the Best Interests of the Child: An Essay Review." *Social Service Review,* December, 1974, *48*(4):508-513(b).

————. *Supervision in Social Work.* New York: Columbia University Press, 1976.

————. "Child Welfare: Adoption and Foster Care." In John Turner (Ed.), *Encyclopedia of Social Work* (Vol. I). New York: National Association of Social Workers, 1977, 114-125.

Kahn, Alfred. 'Child Welfare." In John Turner (Ed.), *Encyclopedia of Social Work* (Vol. I). New York: National Association of Social Workers, 1977, 100-113.

Kanfer, Frederick, and Goldstein, Arnold (Eds.). *Helping People Change.* New York: Pergamon Press, 1975.

Kaplan, David; Smith, Aaron; Grobstein, Rose; and Fischman, Stanley. "Family Mediation of Stress." *Social Work,* July, 1973, *18*(4):60-69.

Katz, Stanford. "The Changing Legal Status of Foster Parents." *Children Today,* November-December 1976, *5*(6):11-13.

Keniston, Kenneth, and The Carnegie Council on Children. *All Our Children: The American Family Under Pressure.* New York: Harcourt Brace Jovanovich, 1977.

Kline, Draza, and Overstreet, Helen-Mary Forbush. *Foster Care of Children: Nurture and Treatment.* New York: Columbia University Press, 1972.

Krumboltz, John, and Krumboltz, Helen. *Changing Children's Behavior.* Englewood Cliffs, New Jersey: Prentice-Hall, 1972.

Kübler-Ross, Elisabeth. *On Death and Dying.* New York: Macmillan, 1969.

Lavine, Abe. "Foster Care: "America's Lost Children." *Public Welfare* (Summer 1977), *35*(3):4-8.

Law and Social Work: Statements Prepared by the National Conference of Lawyers and Social Workers. Washington, D. C.: National Association of Social Workers, 1973.

Lazarus, Arnold. *Behavior Therapy and Beyond.* New York: McGraw-Hill Book Co., 1971.

————. *Clinical Behavior Therapy*. New York: Brunner/Mazel, 1972.

Lewis, Ronald, and Ho, Man Keung. "Social Work with Native Americans." *Social Work*, September, 1975, *20*(5):379-382.

Liebo, Stephen. *The Social Worker as Expert Witness in the Courtroom*. Minneapolis: Minnesota Resource Center for Social Work Education, 1971.

Littner, Ner. "Traumatic Effects of Separation and Placement." In *Casework Papers*. New York: Family Service Association of America, 1956.

————. *The Strains and Stresses on the Child Welfare Worker*. New York: Child Welfare League of America, 1957.

Locklear, Herbert. "American Indian Myths." *Social Work*, May, 1972, *17*:72-80.

Loewenberg, F. M. *Fundamentals of Social Intervention*. New York: Columbia University Press, 1977.

Longres, John. "Puerto Ricans." In John Turner (Ed.), *Encyclopedia of Social Work* (Vol. II). New York: National Association of Social Workers, 1977, 973-979.

Lukton, Rosemary. "Crisis Theory: Review and Critique." *Social Service Review*, September, 1974, *48*(3):384-402.

Lundberg, Emma O. *Unto the Least of These: Social Services for Children*. New York: Appleton-Century-Crofts, 1947.

Maas, Henry. "Children in Long Term Care." *Child Welfare*, June, 1969, *XLVIII*(6):321-333.

Maas, Henry, and Engler, Richard. *Children in Need of Parents*. New York: Columbia University Press, 1959.

Magler, Robert, and Pipe, Peter. *Analyzing Performance Problems*. Belmont, California: Lear Siegler/Fearon Publishers, 1973.

Mahoney, Michael. *Cognition and Behavior Modification*. Cambridge, Massachusetts: Ballinger Publishing Co., 1974.

Malcolm, Janet. "A Reporter at Large: The One Way Mirror." *The New Yorker*, May 15, 1978.

Maluccio, Anthony, and Marlow, Wilma. "The Case for the Contract." *Social Work*, January, 1974, *19*(1):28-37.

Martin, Lucinda, and Keltner, Ronald. "Report on the Eastern Navajo Agency Foster Care Program, Crown Point, New Mexico." In *National Action for Foster Children: A Survey of Activities Based on Reports Submitted by States and Communities*. Washington, D. C.: U. S. Department of Health, Education and Welfare, Office of Child Development, 1975.

Maslach, Christina. "Burned Out." *Human Behavior*, September, 1976, 16-22.

Matek, Ord. "Some Guidelines in Choosing a Placement Facility for the Disturbed Child," paper presented at the Annual Conference of the Ontario Welfare Council, May 18, 1966.

Mayer, Morris; Richman, Leon; and Balcerzak, Edwin. *Group Care of*

Children: Crossroads and Transitions. New York: Child Welfare League of America, 1977.

McGuire, Florence, and Reistroffer, Mary. *Thank Goodness Foster Parents Are Hooked on Helping.* Butler, Wisconsin: Chelsea Associates, Inc., 1975.

Meier, Elizabeth. "Current Circumstances of Former Foster Children." *Child Welfare,* April, 1965, 44:196-206.

Miller, James G. "Living Systems Basic Concepts." *Behavioral Science,* July, 1965, 10(1):193-237.

Miller, James. *Living Systems.* New York: McGraw-Hill Book Co., 1977.

Mindell, Carl, and Gurwitt, Alan. "The Placement of American Indian Children—The Need for Change." Washington, D. C.: American Academy of Child Psychiatry, April 13, 1977. (Mimeo)

Minuchin, Salvador, Montalvo, Braulio; Guerney, Bernard; Rosman, Bernice; and Schumer, Florence. *Families of the Slums.* New York: Basic Books, 1967.

Mnookin, Robert. "Foster Care: In Whose Best Interest." *Harvard Educational Review,* November, 1973, 43(4):599-638.

———. "Foster Care Program." *Children's Rights Report,* March, 1977, 1(6):6-9.

Murase, Kenji. "Asian Americans." In John Turner (Ed.), *Encyclopedia of Social Work* (Vol. II). New York: National Association of Social Workers, 1977, 953-960.

National Association of Attorneys General, Committee on the Office of Attorney General. *Legal Issues in Foster Care.* Raleigh, North Carolina: National Association of Attorneys General, February, 1976.

National Foster Parents Association. "Code of Ethics for Foster Parents." St. Louis, Missouri: National Foster Parents Association, Code Adopted in 1975.

O'Connell, Marie. *Helping the Child to Use Foster Family Care.* New York: Child Welfare League of America, 1953.

Oppenheimer, Jeanette. "Use of Crisis Intervention in Casework with the Cancer Patient and His Family." *Social Work,* April, 1967, 12(2):44-52.

Overton, Alice; Tinker, Katherine; and Associates. *Casework Notebook.* St. Paul, Minnesota: Family Centered Project, 1957.

Parad, Howard. "Crisis Intervention." In John Turner (Ed.), *Encyclopedia of Social Work* (Vol. I). New York: National Association of Social Workers, 1977, 228-236.

Parad, Howard; Selby, Lola; and Quinlan, James. "Crisis Intervention with Families and Groups." In Robert Roberts and Helen Northen (Eds.), *Theories of Social Work with Groups.* New York: Columbia University Press, 1976.

Pare, A., and Torczyner, J. "The Interests of Children and the Interests of the State: Rethinking the Conflict Between Child Welfare Policy and

Foster Care Practice." *Journal of Sociology and Social Welfare,* November, 1977, *IV*(8):1224-1245.

Pasewark, Richard, and Albers, Dale. "Crisis Intervention: Theory in Search of a Program." *Social Work,* March, 1972, *17*(2):70-77.

Patterson, Gerald. *Families: Applications of Social Learning to Family Life.* Champaign, Illinois: Research Press, 1971.

Patterson, Gerald, and Gullion, M. Elizabeth. *Living with Children* (Rev. ed.). Champaign, Illinois: Research Press, 1978.

Perlman, Helen. *Persona: Social Role and Personality.* Chicago: University of Chicago Press, 1968.

Pflanzer, Steven. "Caseload Management in Local Departments of Social Services." In Bernadette Ambrose (Ed.), *Child Abuse and Neglect: Social Service Reader II.* Albany, New York: School of Social Welfare, State University of New York at Albany, 1977.

Phillips, Michael; Haring, Barbara; and Shyne, Ann. *A Model for Intake Decisions in Child Welfare.* New York: Child Welfare League of America, 1972.

Pike, Victor. "Permanent Planning for Foster Children: The Oregon Project" *Children Today,* November-December, 1976, 22-41.

Pike, Victor; Downs, Susan; Emlen, Arthur; Downs, Glen; and Case, Denise. *Permanent Planning for Children in Foster Care: A Handbook for Social Workers.* DHEW Publication No. OHDS 77-30124. Washington, D. C.: U. S. Government Printing Office, 1977.

Pincus, Allen, and Minahan, Anne. *Social Work Practice: Model and Method.* Itasca, Illinois: F. E. Peacock, 1973.

Polansky, Norman; DeSaix, Christine; and Sharlin, Shlomo. *Child Neglect: Understanding and Reaching the Parent.* New York: Child Welfare League of America, 1972.

Porter, Robert. "Crisis Intervention and Social Work Models." In Joel Fischer (Ed.), *Interpersonal Helping.* Springfield, Illinois: Charles C Thomas, Publisher, 1973.

Primeaux, Martha. "Caring for the American Indian Patient." *American Journal of Nursing,* January, 1977, 77(1):91-96.

Pumphrey, Ralph, and Pumphrey, Muriel. *The Heritage of American Social Work.* New York: Columbia University Press, 1961.

Rapoport, Lydia. "Crisis Intervention as a Mode of Brief Treatment." In Robert Roberts and Robert Nee (Eds.), *Theories of Social Casework.* Chicago: University of Chicago Press, 1970.

Red Horse, John. "Culture as a Variable in Human Services." In *PSRI Report: Child Abuse and Neglect* (Vol. 2, No. 7). Piscataway, New Jersey: Protective Services Resources Institute, Rutgers Medical School, August-September, 1977.

Redl, Fritz. *When We Deal with Children.* New York: Macmillan, 1966.

Regional Institute of Social Welfare Research, Inc. *The Case Management*

Model: Concept and Process Definition (Vol. I); *The Case Management Model Implementation Requirements* (Vol. II); *The Case Management Model Trainers Guide* (Vol. III). Athens, Georgia: Regional Institute of Social Welfare Research, Inc., 1977.

Regional Research Institute for Human Services. *Barriers to Planning for Children in Foster Care* (Summary of Vol. I). Portland, Oregon: Portland State University, February, 1976.

Reid, William. "Foster Care: America's Lost Children." *Public Welfare* (Summer, 1977), *35*(3):4-8.

Reid, William, and Epstein, Laura. *Task Centered Casework.* New York: Columbia University Press, 1972.

Reid, William, and Epstein, Laura (Eds.). *Task Centered Practice.* New York: Columbia University Press, 1977.

Reistroffer, Mary. *What You Always Wanted to Discuss about Foster Care but Didn't Have the Time or the Chance to Bring Up.* New York: Child Welfare League of America, 1971.

———. *What's So Special about Teenagers.* New York: Child Welfare League of America, 1972.

———. *Foster Family Care: A Collection of Papers and Abstracts.* Madison: Center for Social Services, University of Wisconsin-Extension, 1974(a).

———. *Foster Parents and Social Workers on the Job Together.* New York: Child Welfare League of America, 1974(b).

Rhodes, Sonya. "Contract Negotiation in the Initial Stages of Casework Service." *Social Service Review,* March, 1977, *51*(1):125-140.

Rich, John. *Interviewing Children and Adolescents.* London: Macmillan and Co., 1968.

Rich, Margaret. *A Belief in People: A History of Family Social Work.* New York: Family Service Association of America, 1956.

Riessman, Frank; Cohen, Jerome; Pearl, Arthur (Eds.). *Mental Health of the Poor.* New York: The Free Press, 1964.

Romanyshyn, John. *Social Welfare: Charity to Justice.* New York: Council on Social Work Education and Random House, 1971.

Rose, Sheldon. *Group Therapy: A Behavioral Approach.* Englewood Cliffs, New Jersey: Prentice-Hall, 1977.

Rothman, David. *The Discovery of the Asylum.* New York: Little Brown, 1971.

Rutter, Barbara. *A Way of Caring: The Parents Guide to Foster Care.* New York: Child Welfare League of America, 1978.

Salmon, Wilma. "A Service Program in a State Public Welfare Agency." In William Reid and Laura Epstein (Eds.), *Task Centered Practice.* New York: Columbia University Press, 1977.

Sarason, Irwin; Linder, Karen; and Crnic, Keith. *A Guide for Foster Parents.* New York: Human Sciences Press, 1976.

Satir, Virginia. *People making.* Palo Alto, California: Science and Behavior Books, Inc., 1972.

Sauber, Mignon, and Jenkins, Shirley. *Paths to Child Placement.* New York: Community Council of Greater New York, 1966.

Schmidt, Jerry. *Help Yourself—A Guide to Self-Change.* Champaign, Illinois: Research Press, 1976.

Schoenberg, Carl. "Introduction." *Child Welfare, October,* 1973, *LII*(8): 481.

Schubert, Margaret. *Interviewing in Social Work Practice: An Introduction.* New York: Council on Social Work Education, 1971.

Schwartz, Arthur, and Goldiamond, Israel. *Social Casework: A Behavioral Approach.* New York: Columbia University Press, 1975.

Selbo, Janis, and Lynaugh, Ann. *Legal Training for Child Welfare Workers.* Madison, Wisconsin: Center for Social Service, University of Wisconsin-Extension, 1975.

Settles, Barbara; Culley, James; and VanName, Judith. *How to Measure the Cost of Foster Family Care.* DHEW Publication No. OHDS 77-30126. Washington, D. C.: U. S. Government Printing Office, 1977.

Shapiro, Deborah. *Agencies and Foster Children.* New York: Columbia University Press, 1976.

Sharp, Roland, and Wetzel, Ralph. *Behavior Modification in the Natural Environment.* New York: Academic Press, 1969.

Shulman, Lawrence. *A Study of the Helping Process.* Vancouver: University of British Columbia, 1977.

———. Personal correspondence, March, 1978.

Simon, Julian. "The Effect of Foster-Care Payment Levels on the Number of Foster Children Given Homes." *Social Service Review,* September, 1975, *49*(3):405-411.

Siporin, Max. *Introduction to Social Work Practice.* New York: Macmillan, 1975.

Skolnick, Arlene. "The Myth of the Vulnerable Child." *Psychology Today,* February, 1978, *II*(9):56-65.

Slaughter, Ellen. *Indian Child Welfare: A Review of the Literature.* Denver, Colorado: Center for Social Research and Development, Denver Research Institute, University of Denver, January, 1976.

Slingerland, W. H. *Child-Placing in Families.* New York: Russell Sage Foundation, 1919.

Sotomayor, Marta. "Chicanos." In John Turner (Ed.), *Encyclopedia of Social Work* (Vol. II). New York: National Association of Social Workers, 1977, 966-972.

State University System of Florida, Office of the Vice Chancellor for Academic Affairs. *Florida Human Service Task Bank.* Tallahassee, Florida: State University System of Florida, October, 1975.

Stein, Theodore, and Gambrill, Eileen. *Decision Making in Foster Care:*

A Training Manual. Berkeley, California: University Extension Publications, University of California, 1976.

———. "Facilitating Decision Making in Foster Care: The Alameda Project." *Social Service Review,* September, 1977, *51*(3):502-513.

Stein, Theodore; Gambrill, Eileen; and Wiltse, Kermit. "Foster Care: The Use of Contracts." *Public Welfare* (Fall, 1974), *32*(4):20-25.

———. "Contracts and Outcome in Foster Care." *Social Work,* March, 1977, *22*(2):148-149.

Stone, Helen, and Hunzeker, Jeanne. *Creating a Foster Parent-Agency Handbook.* New York: Child Welfare League of America, 1974.

Street, Lloyd. "Minorities." In John Turner (Ed.), *Encyclopedia of Social Work* (Vol. II). New York: National Association of Social Workers, 1977, 931-946.

Stuart, Richard. *Trick or Treatment: How and When Psychotherapy Fails.* Champaign, Illinois: Research Press, 1970.

———. "Behavior Modification: A Technology of Social Change." In Francis Turner (Ed.), *Social Work Treatment: Interlocking Theoretical Approaches.* New York: The Free Press, 1974.

Sundel, Martin, and Sundel, Sandra. *Behavior Modification in the Human Services.* New York: John Wiley and Sons, 1975.

The Temporary State Commission on Child Welfare. *Barriers to the Freeing of Children for Adoption, Final Report to the New York State Department of Social Services.* New York: The Temporary State Commission on Child Welfare, 1976.

Thomas, Carolyn. "The Resolution of Object Loss Following Foster Home Placement." *Smith College Studies in Social Work,* June, 1967, *37*(3).

Thomas, Edwin (Ed.). *Behavior Modification Procedure: A Sourcebook.* Chicago: Aldine Publishing Co., 1974.

Thoresen, Carl, and Mahoney, Michael. *Behavioral Self Control.* New York: Holt, Rinehart and Winston, 1974.

Tidwell, Billy. "Blacks." In John Turner (Ed.), *Encyclopedia of Social Work* (Vol. II). New York: National Association of Social Workers, 1977, 960-966.

Touliatos, John, and Lindholm, Byron. *Potential for Foster Parenthood Scale: Manual.* St. Louis, Missouri: National Foster Parents Association, Inc., 1978.

Unger, Christopher; Dwarshuis, Gladys; and Johnson, Elizabeth. *Chaos, Madness and Unpredictability.* Chelsea, Michigan: Spaulding for Children, 1977.

Unger, Steven (Ed.). *The Destruction of American Indian Families.* New York: Association on American Indian Affairs, 1977.

U. S. Department of Health, Education and Welfare. Children's Bureau. *Report of the Advisory Council on Child Welfare Services.* Washington, D. C.: U. S. Government Printing Office, 1960.

U .S. Department of Health, Education and Welfare, Office of Human Development. *Action for Foster Children: Community Self Evaluation Chart*. Washington, D. C.: U. S. Government Printing Office, 1974.

———. *Child Welfare in 25 States—An Overview*. DHEW Publication No. OHD 76-30090. Washington, D. C.: U. S. Government Printing Office, 1976.

U. S. Department of Health, Education and Welfare, Office of Human Development Services. Administration on Children, Youth and Families. Children's Bureau. *Comprehensive Emergency Services*. DHEW Publication No. OHDS 77-30008. Washington, D. C.: U. S. Government Printing Office, 1977.

———. *Indian Child Welfare: A State of the Field Study*. DHEW Publication No. OHD 77-30096. Washington, D. C.: U. S. Government Printing Office, 1977.

U. S. Department of Health, Education and Welfare, Social Security Administration. *Public Assistance Statistics: March, 1977*. Washington, D. C.: U. S. Government Printing Office, 1977.

U. S. Department of Health, Education and Welfare. National Center on Child Abuse and Neglect. *Interdisciplinary Glossary on Child Abuse and Neglect: Legal, Medical, Social Work Terms*. DHEW Publication No. OHDS 78-30137. Washington, D. C.: U. S. Government Printing Office, February 1, 1978.

United Way of Milwaukee. *Referral Criteria for Specialized Placement Resources*. Milwaukee, Wisconsin: Reprinted by Center for Social Service, University of Wisconsin-Extension, 1974.

Utah Division of Family Services, Task Force on Alternative Methods of Treatment for Families at Risk. *Task Force Committee Report*. Salt Lake City: Utah Division of Family Services, 1975.

Vasaly, Shirley. *Foster Care in Five States*. DHEW Publication No. OHD 76-30097. Washington, D. C.: U. S. Department of Health, Education and Welfare, Office of Human Development, Office of Child Development, U. S. Government Printing Office, 1976.

Von Bertalanffy, Ludwig. *Robots, Men and Minds*. New York: George Braziller, 1967.

———. *General Systems Theory*. New York: George Braziller, 1968.

Wald, Michael. "State Intervention on Behalf of Neglected Children: Standards for Removal of Children from Their Homes, Monitoring the Status of Children in Foster Care and Termination of Parental Rights." *Stanford Law Review*, April, 1976, *28*(4):623-706.

Walker, William. "Persistence of Mourning in the Foster Child as Related to the Foster Mother's Level of Maturity." *Smith College Studies in Social Work*, June, 1971, *41*(3).

Washington State Department of Social and Health Services. *Final Report to the Legislature: The Adoption Support Demonstration Act of 1971*.

Olympia, Washington: Washington State Department of Social and Health Services, January, 1975.

Watson, David, and Tharp, Roland. *Self-Directed Behavior: Self Modification for Personal Adjustment.* Belmont, California: Brooks/Cole Publishing Company, 1972.

Whittaker, James. *Social Treatment.* Chicago: Aldine Publishing Co., 1974.

Wiehe, Vernon. "The Foster Home Study: Evaluation or Preparation," paper presented at the National Association of Social Workers Fifth Biennial Professional Symposium, San Diego, California, November 19-22, 1977.

Wilensky, Harold, and Lebeaux, Charles. *Industrial Society and Social Welfare.* New York: Russell Sage Foundation, 1958.

Wilkes, J. R. "The Impact of Fostering on the Foster Family." *Child Welfare,* June, 1974, *LIII*(6):373-379.

Williams, Jon. "Crisis Intervention Among the Bereaved: A Mental Health Consultation Program for Clergy." In Gerald Specter and William Claiborn (Eds.), *Crisis Intervention* (Vol. II). New York: Behavioral Publications, 1973.

Wolfensberger, Wolf. *The Principle of Normalization in Human Services.* Toronto: National Institute on Mental Retardation, 1972.

Young, Leontine. *Life Among the Giants, A Child's Eye View of the Grown Up World.* New York: McGraw-Hill Book Co., 1971.

Zietz, Dorothy. *Child Welfare: Principles and Methods.* New York: John Wiley and Sons, 1959.

Zwerdling, Ella. *The ABC's of Casework with Children: A Social Work Teacher's Notebook.* New York: Child Welfare League of America, 1974.

Index